Reading Faulkner

READING
FAULKNER

Introductions to the
First Thirteen Novels

Richard
Marius

Compiled and Edited by
Nancy Grisham Anderson

THE UNIVERSITY OF TENNESSEE PRESS • KNOXVILLE

Copyright © 2006 by The University of Tennessee Press / Knoxville.
All Rights Reserved. Manufactured in the United States of America.
Cloth: First printing, 2006.
Paper: First printing, 2007.

Frontispiece: Photo courtesy of The Bern and Franke Keating Collection, Archives & Special
Collections, J. D. Williams Library.

University of Mississippi dust jackets for Faulkner's novels are reproduced
courtesy of Special Collections, University of Virginia Library.

> *Soldiers' Pay.* New York: Boni & Liveright, 1926.
>
> *Mosquitoes.* New York: Boni & Liveright, 1927.
>
> *Sartoris.* New York: Harcourt, Brace, 1929. (Later published under its restored original title, *Flags in the Dust*)
>
> *The Sound and the Fury.* New York: Jonathan Cape and Harrison Smith, 1929.
>
> *As I Lay Dying.* New York: Jonathan Cape and Harrison Smith, 1930.
>
> *Sanctuary.* New York: Jonathan Cape and Harrison Smith, 1931.
>
> *Light in August.* New York: Harrison Smith and Robert Haas, 1932.
>
> *Pylon.* New York: Harrison Smith and Robert Haas, 1935.
>
> *Absalom, Absalom!* New York: Random House, 1936.
>
> *The Unvanquished.* New York: Random House, 1938.
>
> *The Wild Palms.* New York: Random House, 1939. (Later published under its restored original title, *If I Forget Thee, Jerusalem*)
>
> *The Hamlet.* New York: Random House, 1940.
>
> *Go Down, Moses.* New York: Random House, 1942.

This book is printed on acid-free paper.

Library of Congress Cataloging-in-Publication Data

Marius, Richard.
  Reading Faulkner: introductions to the first thirteen novels / Richard Marius; compiled
and edited by Nancy Grisham Anderson.— 1st ed.
      p. cm.
Lectures originally written for a course on Faulkner at Harvard by Richard Marius.
Includes bibliographical references (p.) and index.

ISBN 10 (cloth): 1-57233-449-5 (acid-free paper)
ISBN 13 (cloth): 978-1-57233-449-6
ISBN 10 (paper): 1-57233-603-X
ISBN 13 (paper): 978-1-57233-603-2

  1. Faulkner, William, 1897–1962—Criticism and interpretation.
  I. Anderson, Nancy G., 1940–
II. Title.

PS3511.A86Z94693 2006

Dedicated to
Lanier Smythe
and
Rick Anderson

Contents

Preface

English 174F. William Faulkner from *Soldiers' Pay* to *Go Down, Moses*
Catalog Number: 5922
Richard C. Marius
Half course (fall term). Tu., Th., at 1. EXAM GROUP: 15
Examines Faulkner's most creative period from his first novel to his
mature wrestling with problems of race, fate, and tragedy. The novels
will be read in the order he wrote them with some consideration of
the biographical, social, and political context of each of them.

So reads the description of a course in the 1996–97 Courses of Instruc-
tion for Harvard College, Radcliffe College, and [Harvard University] Graduate School of Arts and Sciences. The course, to be taught by Richard C.
Marius, was offered as one of the term's undergraduate seminars, described
as: "These introductions to specialized study of literature are restricted to
undergraduates and have enrollments limited to 15. Preference is given to
English concentrators."

Richard Marius had resigned in the spring of 1996 as director of Harvard's Expository Writing Program, a position he had held for eighteen years,
and was returning to teaching full-time. For several years he had been teaching a seminar in Shakespeare's History Plays, a logical development from
his graduate work in Renaissance and Reformation history, and he had proposed a course on classical and Shakespearean tragedy for the fall term of
1996. Instead, the English department asked him to teach a Faulkner course.
Marius mused that the request was a result of his southern accent rather
than his knowledge. After all, he was a southerner.

Richard Marius's childhood in East Tennessee, in the small town of
Martel—later known as Dixie Lee Junction—was anything but typical for
a southerner of his age in that rural setting. His father, Henri S. Marius,
born in Smyrna, Turkey, had been a student in Ghent, Belgium, when World
War I broke out. He immediately enlisted in the local infantry. In the first
six weeks of the war, he sustained a serious head wound and spent the
next three years in a British Army hospital in London. Some study in chem-
istry and engineering and a coincidence or two brought him to Lenoir City,

Tennessee, where he became a chemist and later a superintendent at the Southern Railway foundry. Richard's mother, Eunice Henck, granddaughter of a Union soldier and daughter of a Methodist evangelist, was a native Tennessean working as a newspaperwoman in Knoxville after similar jobs in Alabama, Texas, and Missouri. Marius met Henck at a boardinghouse in Lenoir City when she came to town to cover a story. They married in 1918 and moved to Burma, where Henri Marius worked as a chemist with the silver mining industry. After the collapse of the silver market, they returned to Knoxville. The birth of their first son with Down syndrome prompted the Mariuses to move to the rural isolation of Martel for the sake of their child and to be closer to Marius's job, once again with the railroad foundry in Lenoir City. (Richard Marius used this family background as the skeleton outline and inspiration for his novel *After the War*, his third fictional work set in Bourbonville, Tennessee.)

Mrs. Marius's love of words and writing had an obvious effect on the young Richard. Worried about the isolation they had chosen because of their oldest son, Mrs. Marius read classic literature—Dickens, Twain, Kipling, Poe—to her daughter and three sons, and she read the Bible to them all the way through, at least once a year. In his autobiographical essay "The Middle of the Journey," Marius fondly recalls the sound of her "strong voice rising to the sublime cadences of the Old Testament by the fireplace on wintry nights when both the flames in the grate and the divine words worked to thrust back the cold dark that crept in from the woods outside." While attending Lenoir City High School, Richard began writing for the *Lenoir City News* and became a news editor in 1952, a job he continued to hold during his undergraduate studies in journalism at the University of Tennessee–Knoxville. In 1954, he received his BA degree from UTK, graduating *summa cum laude.*

Mrs. Marius had another profound influence on the life of her second son. When the first son was born to Henri and Eunice Marius, his mother promised the life of her next son to God to atone for the sins that had resulted in her first son's affliction, and Richard was the second son. Throughout his childhood and youth, Richard Marius followed the path ordained by his mother's promise to God, dutifully following his mother to, first, the Methodist church and then the Martel Baptist Church after a Methodist seminary student told Mrs. Marius that even Jesus made mistakes. In his freshman year at UT, however, a reading assignment in his composition course irrevocably changed the course of his life: W. T. Stace's "Man Against Darkness," in Marius's words, "devastated" or "destroyed " his faith. Stace writes of a world that is "purposeless, senseless, meaningless." In the essay he says that "The world is just what it is, and that is the end of all inquiry. There is no reason for its being what it is. Everything might just as well have been quite different, and there would have been no reason for that either." Stace's cosmic view echoes throughout Marius's four novels and his biographies of Martin Luther and Sir Thomas More, and it can also be frequently detected in his commentary on William Faulkner's novels.

After graduation from the university, Richard Marius continued in his efforts to fulfill his mother's promise by pursuing a divinity degree. He entered, first, the Baptist seminary in New Orleans and, after one year, transferred to the Southern Baptist Seminary in Louisville, Kentucky, from which he received his bachelor of divinity. After the two years of seminary study and one year on a Rotary Club scholarship at the University of Strasbourg in France, Marius was not convinced that he could enter the ministry. Instead, he delayed the commitment by entering Yale University to study the ancient Near East. He claimed that the language requirements for that major forced a change to Renaissance and Reformation history. He received an MA in 1959 and a PhD in 1962, with a dissertation on Sir Thomas More. During his graduate years at Yale, he also began serving as an editor of the Yale edition of the complete works of More and continued to contribute his scholarship and editorial work to this massive undertaking into the 1990s.

After receiving his doctorate, he taught history for two years at Gettysburg College, in his spare time studying the nearby battlefield. In 1964 he returned to the University of Tennessee as a member of the history faculty. Here he began to incorporate writing into his history courses as a crucial learning tool and gradually was recognized as a persuasive voice in the writing-across-the-curriculum program. During his years at UT he also wrote and published a biography of Martin Luther and his first novel, *The Coming of Rain*, in which his fictional world of Bourbonville, in Bourbon County, Tennessee, first appeared.

In 1978, because of his advocacy of writing as part of all teaching and his reputation as a writer of fiction and nonfiction, Marius accepted the appointment of director of expository writing at Harvard University. Over the years he also established himself as a novelist, a biographer, an editor, a book reviewer, a playwright (in the mid-1990s, he adapted *The Coming of Rain* for the stage, and it premiered at the Alabama Shakespeare Festival in 1998), and a speaker on subjects ranging from Thomas More and Shakespeare to civil rights and writing. His commitment to writing in all classrooms also brought him back to UT for nearly three weeks each summer, from 1986 through 1996, to direct the Tennessee Academy for Teachers of Writing. Meanwhile, at Harvard, he taught a wide range of subjects, including the teaching of writing, Shakespeare, Italian Reformation history, and finally, in 1996 and 1997, William Faulkner.

Richard Marius was a southerner by background and by undergraduate education. Yet he always bristled when someone classified him as a "southern writer," preferring to be called "a novelist of the border." All four of his novels, three published during his lifetime and one posthumously, use the "border" area of east Tennessee, with Lenoir City and Loudon County transformed into his fictional Bourbonville and Bourbon County. This saga provides, through the four novels, a history of his fictional place spanning from the 1830s and 1840s to the end of the twentieth century, where people from generation to generation are "wrestling with problems of race, fate, and tragedy," just as Marius describes Faulkner's novels in the course description. Even though the second novel, *Bound for the Promised Land*, tells stories of the westward movement in the 1850s, his protagonist is from Bourbonville and longs for the peace and routine of his rural Tennessee home as the journey toward San Francisco becomes more difficult. On some level, conscious or unconscious, Marius must have felt some affinity for Faulkner's efforts to transform his "postage stamp of native soil" in northern Mississippi into his fictional Yoknapatawpha County. In an interview with Carroll Viera, published in *Carolina English Teacher* in 1994–95, before he began formal preparations for teaching the course on Faulkner's novels, Marius said, "Living intimately with a town—seeing its conflicts and its virtues and its hypocrisies—has given me the sense that there's enough to keep writing about in Loudon County (alias Bourbon County in my novels) as long as I live." Even the phrasing echoes Faulkner's claim that he had "discovered that [his] own little postage stamp of native soil was worth writing about and that [he] would never live long enough to exhaust it." Whether a southern novelist or "a novelist of the border," as a writer of novels set in an identifiable locale, Marius had an appreciation of Faulkner's fiction and an understanding of his struggles to write those works of fiction set in a specific place identified with the author's own life.

Ironically, except for the early reading of "A Rose for Emily," a memory recalled in his introductory lecture to the Faulkner course, Richard Marius did not read William Faulkner until his graduate years at Yale. Judging from the dates and notes he wrote in the copies of Faulkner's novels in his personal library—from his copy of *Pylon* bought in Greenville, Mississippi, on 24 June 1971 through the most recent authoritative and annotated editions—he read and reread these works from the early 1970s through the late 1990s. Each new edition contains his markings, notes, underlinings, and questions, revealing his ongoing efforts to think and rethink the texts with each new reading. Kriss Basil, one of the two teaching fellows for the 1996 course, believes that "For Richard, the material was alive, and he was engaged in a kind of dialectic with it. [. . .] the novels were a challenge to be struggled with rather than documents to summarize. [. . .] Richard left the impression that the ideas encountered in reading are not dead-letters. They are current and provocative in the reading experience."

Marius was not content just to read the novels. Three long shelves in his study at home contain, in addition to different editions of the novels, numerous biographical and critical books on Faulkner's life and fiction (see primary and secondary bibliographies). He also kept black-and-white marbled composition books with handwritten notes, comments, and ideas and quotations and bibliographic entries from the novels and critical sources.

For the course offered in the fall of 1996, Marius spent the previous summer writing out the lectures in ink in two black-bound, eight-and-a-half-by-eleven-inch blank volumes, of approximately one hundred pages each. He wrote on the right-hand pages, leaving the left side for additions and revisions as he continued to prepare for classes. Occasionally, typed quotations are taped to the pages. For the Faulkner passages, he always carefully cited page numbers, with the specific edition often noted.[1] He was also meticulous in crediting the biographers and critics whose ideas he incorporated into his lectures. Apparently for the second offering of the course, in the fall of 1997, Marius went back to the original drafts in the bound volumes and did additional editing and, in some cases, typed new drafts of the same lectures. The lectures assume an audience of individuals who have read the novels and who want to know more about the author, his writing career, and the richness and complexity of the works.

This publication is a collection of the manuscript lectures including the revisions and additions, unless there is a later typescript of the lecture.[2] Taken together, Marius's lectures form an extraordinary volume. Its breadth of scholarship and insight from perspectives of both the academician and the artist, its appeal and accessibility, and the coherence of vision and personality that informs it all make it the most useful general introduction to Faulkner's fiction since those of Cleanth Brooks. The lectures

1. Quotations and paraphrases from primary and secondary Faulkner sources have been checked against the editions in Marius's library and are all cited. In addition, he frequently cited other novelists, poets, and dramatists. When a number of different editions of the same work appear on the shelves of his library, as in the case with such writers as T. S. Eliot, John Keats, Richard Lovelace, William Shakespeare, Sophocles, and others, these quotations have been checked for accuracy but have not been cited to a specific edition.

2. The lectures have been transcribed as written, or typed, with changes in the case of omitted words, repeated words, or errors. A few minor changes in punctuation or phrasing have been made for the sake of a reading audience instead of a listening audience.

seem almost to have been written with secondary and undergraduate teachers and general readers in mind, in addition to his Harvard students.

The course "William Faulkner—Novels from *Soldiers' Pay* to *Go Down, Moses*" appeared in the 1996–97 course catalogue with fifteen students as maximum capacity. The class was "surprisingly over-enrolled" in the fall of 1996, with seventy-one names on the final grade sheet. In addition to reading thirteen novels, the students were required to write two papers (three thousand to five thousand words or ten to twelve pages) and to identify and interpret selected paragraphs quoted from the novels for the take-home final examination. They were also directed to critical works about Faulkner, with a lengthy, secondary bibliography attached to the syllabus in 1997. The class met twice a week for Richard Marius's lectures, organized to cover the thirteen novels chronologically. In addition, two teaching fellows each led two discussions a week.

Despite demanding reading and writing requirements, students praised the course. According to the report published in the 1997–98 Harvard University Course Evaluation Guide (known as CUE), students raved about the "superb instructor," his "wonderful personality," and his "entertaining presentations." In fact, several members of the class noted that the professor was a "compelling reason" to take the class on Faulkner. The popularity resulted in the course's being offered again in the fall of 1997, with similar enrollment.

Such popularity for a course must have resulted from more than Richard Marius's thorough readings of Faulkner's novels, the breadth of knowledge he brought to the course, and his southern background. As a novelist struggling to create his own fictional world of Bourbonville, in Bourbon County in east Tennessee, he empathized with Faulkner's struggles as a writer. He knew firsthand the challenges of creating a plot and a sense of place, developing characters, and getting the words on paper. He never hesitated to express these personal feelings—the passion and empathy—in his lectures. Even the wording on his syllabus foreshadows the intensity of the course: "*embrace* enough of the novels to demonstrate thorough knowledge of several novels so that I can believe you have been immersed in Faulkner." The 1997 syllabus has the added notice that "[. . .] I warn you, I love *Pylon*." The power of his feelings culminated in the final lecture of the course, the lecture on *Go Down, Moses*. As described by Kriss Basil:

> he became quite emotional towards the end of the lecture. The
> pathos of the lecture rose up as it might in a sermon. Richard
> seemed to forget that the class was there and to be engaged with

the literature quite effectively. It was a remarkable scene. It is rare in my experience for academics to show the intensity of their feelings for the material, and it is my sense that the students were deeply impressed with Marius's involvement in the reading. Needless to say, when he concluded he received a resounding round of applause.

Perhaps most important for the success of the course on "Novels of William Faulkner from *Soldiers' Pay* to *Go Down, Moses,*" was one simple fact: in the words of Kriss Basil, "Richard loved the material." Marius informed that passion for Faulkner's novels with his own rich Renaissance education and interests and his empathy for a fellow writer.

At the end of the 1998 academic year, Richard Marius retired to devote full time to his own writing. His first goal was to complete *An Affair of Honor*, the fourth novel in the Bourbonville saga, a goal he accomplished in September 1999. In early November 1999, he died of pancreatic cancer at his home in Belmont, Massachusetts, survived by his wife, Lanier Smythe; three sons—Richard, Fred, and John; and younger brother, John.

A Note on Biographical Sources

I have gathered the information in this biographical introduction from the following sources.

During a friendship spanning nearly twenty years, Richard and I had many occasions to discuss writing, teaching writing, and books—by him and by others. As background for the essay on Richard for the *Dictionary of Literary Biography Yearbook 1985*, I did extensive reading in primary and secondary sources and have tried to keep up with both categories since the publication of that reference volume. From 1987 through 1996, I served as a member of the faculty for the Tennessee Governor's Academy for Teachers of Writing and attended Richard's institute on writing Tennessee history in 1990. After Richard's death in 1999, his widow, Lanier Smythe, gave me access to his personal library and papers (with some restrictions) prior to deposit in Special Collections at the University of Tennessee. On the first of three research trips to Boston, I found the Faulkner lectures and quickly recognized their potential for a reading audience.

Nancy Grisham Anderson
Auburn University Montgomery
January 2005

Acknowledgments

A book such as this one could not be published without the help of several people. Even at the risk of omitting someone, I must express my appreciation to a few people who made special contributions to my research.

Ann Close, Richard Marius's editor at Alfred A. Knopf, Inc., to whom he entrusted his literary estate.

Mary Hicks and Monica Tindol, whose friendship and laughter and computer expertise maintained my sanity on at least a weekly basis.

Donald G. Nobles, whose friendship and informed, constructive readings improved the preface.

Fariba Deravi, who is a strong advocate of faculty research at Auburn University Montgomery and does all she can to assist us in our work.

Ralph and Connie Norman, whose friendship and advice provided valued encouragement.

Matthew J. Bruccoli, a friend who has provided encouragement and numerous opportunities over the years.

Judith G. Grisham, a long-time friend who also assisted with research at Harvard.

Katherine Menges, of Random House.

Kriss Basil, a teaching fellow for Marius's 1996 Faulkner course at Harvard.

The Kimbrough Faculty Sabbatical Endowment Fund, compliments of Ouita and John Kimbrough, established to underwrite costs related to faculty research activities at Auburn University Montgomery.

The research that resulted in this book was partially supported by grants from Auburn University Montgomery Research Grant-in-Aid Program.

Chronology

29 July 1933   Richard Curry Marius, born in Martel, Tennessee, second son and third child of Henri Marius and Eunice Henck Marius

1948   Becomes writer for *Lenoir City News* and, in 1952, is promoted to news editor

1951   Graduates from Lenoir City High School

1951–54   Attends University of Tennessee–Knoxville, living at home and hitchhiking to the university while also working for the newspaper

June 1954   Graduates from UTK *summa cum laude* with a degree in journalism

1954–55   Attends Baptist seminary in New Orleans

1955–56   Attends Southern Baptist Seminary, Louisville, Kentucky

1956–57   Attends University of Strasbourg, France, on a Rotary Club scholarship studying medieval and renaissance history

1957–58   Returns to Louisville seminary and receives BD

1957–62   Attends Yale University, studying Renaissance and Reformation history and writing a dissertation on Sir Thomas More; also begins serving as an editor of the Thomas More papers, work he continued into the 1990s

     1959—MA

     1962—PhD

1962–64   Becomes member of history faculty at Gettysburg College, Gettysburg, Pennsylvania

1964–78   Serves as history professor at University of Tennessee–Knoxville, becoming an activist against

	the Ku Klux Klan and the Vietnam War and for civil rights and freedom of speech (on and off campus)
1969	Publishes *The Coming of Rain*, his first novel, set in Bourbonville, Tennessee; 1969 Best First Novel by Friends of American Writers; alternate selection of the Book of the Month Club
1974	Publishes *Luther: A Biography*
1976	Publishes his second novel, *Bound for the Promised Land*
1978–98	Joins the faculty of Harvard University
	1978–94—director of expository writing
	1994–98—senior lecturer
1984	Publishes his first textbook on writing, *A Writer's Companion*
1984	Publishes *Thomas More: A Biography*; 1985 National Book Award finalist; alternate selection of the Book of the Month Club
1985	Publishes, with coauthor Harvey S. Weiner, *The McGraw-Hill College Handbook*
1985	Publishes *A Short Guide to Writing about History*
1986–96	Directs the Tennessee Governor's Academy for Teachers of Writing
1992	Publishes his third novel, *After the War*
1994	Edits and publishes *The Columbia Book of Civil War Poetry from Whitman to Walcott*
1996–98	Adapts *The Coming of Rain* into a play, which premieres as a repertory show at the Alabama Shakespeare Festival in 1998
1999	Publishes *Martin Luther: The Christian between God and Death*
5 November 1999	Dies at home in Belmont, Massachusetts
2001	*An Affair of Honor*, fourth novel, released posthumously

"A ROSE
FOR EMILY"

Time and again I am asked by people, anxious and even embarrassed, "Why should I read William Faulkner?" or, "What book of Faulkner's should I read first?" a question that carries with it the dreadful implication that the person who asks it has not read Faulkner at all. Both these questions come to me with much the same spirit that someone might ask for a recommendation of a dentist who might do a quick and not too painful root canal.

Faulkner may well be our greatest American writer. That kind of judgment is, of course, fragile at best and certainly depends on the elusive taste of readers. Critics at least consider him one of the greatest writers of our century—but even here we find dissent. Clifton Fadiman never liked him, and his review of *Absalom, Absalom!* is often quoted as one of the most devastating reviews of a "great" book ever written (Blotner 377).[1] John Barth admits freely that he has never taken to what he calls the "immemorial wagon wheels" of Faulkner's prose. During most of Faulkner's life he lived on the edge of poverty. People did not buy great numbers of his books. Until he won the Nobel Prize in 1950, he was scarcely known even to most professors of English as anything more than a regional writer of some interest. The French picked him up early. But why should anyone pay any attention to the modern tastes of the French who also profess to see profound importance in Dean Martin and Jerry Lewis comedies from the 1950s? If I am not

---

1. In his 1936 review of *Absalom, Absalom!* published in the *New Yorker*, Fadiman used wording like: "few comprehensible sentences," "consistently boring novel by a reputable writer," "confusing the reader," "the final blowup of what was once a remarkable, if minor talent."

mistaken, none of Faulkner's greatest novels made the best-seller lists before he won his Nobel Prize, and he had to lower himself by going to Hollywood to grind out screenplays for the movies—a task he hated and one that from time to time pitched him into the alcoholic binges with more frequency and violence than he had previously experienced—although I should say that he was an alcoholic almost from his teenaged years and that he died in an alcoholic hospital in Byhalia, Mississippi, on July 6, 1962.

But we are speaking of a different issue—not so much Faulkner and money but Faulkner and popularity. He remains to many educated people elusive, difficult, painful, even incomprehensible. Not even in the "classics" section of the bookstores in the Atlanta airport do I see copies of Faulkner, although the one book by his contemporary Margaret Mitchell—*Gone With the Wind*, published the same year as *Absalom, Absalom!* (1936)—is always available.

I sympathize with the bewildered multitudes. How does the following passage from *The Sound and the Fury* make sense to the reader who revels in Tom Clancy or Ayn Rand?

> It was a while before the last stroke ceased vibrating. It stayed in the air, more felt than heard, for a long time. Like all the bells that ever rang still ringing in the long dying light-rays and Jesus and Saint Francis talking about his sister. Because if it were just to hell; if that were all of it. Finished. If things just finished themselves. Nobody else there but her and me. If we could just have done something so dreadful that they would have fled hell except us. *I have committed incest I said Father it was I it was not Dalton Ames.* And when he put Dalton Ames. Dalton Ames. Dalton Ames. When he put the pistol in my hand I didn't. That's why I didn't. He would be there and she would and I would. Dalton Ames. Dalton Ames. Dalton Ames. If we could have just done something so dreadful and Father said That's sad too people cannot do anything that dreadful they cannot do anything very dreadful at all they cannot even remember tomorrow what seemed dreadful today and I said, You can shirk all things and he said, Ah can you. (49)

When you consider that this passage is almost unpunctuated and that we are forty-nine pages (by the Norton first edition) into the book and have not been introduced to Dalton Ames, that indeed we have no idea who he is, we may forgive the conclusion of the reader who finds himself submerged in unmeaning.

Here is one of our greatest difficulties with Faulkner. He is an outlaw to the narrative form of the novel and the short story as these genres developed in the eighteenth and nineteenth centuries, a narrative form that still rules the popular fiction of our time and that also rules the movies. This is the form that begins with a clear problem confronting usually one character, a tension that envelops the character from the circumstance we meet usually on the first page. The novel, the short story, or the movie develops the form of the tensions, usually increasing it to a climax when all the different threads of the plot come together. The tension is resolved. The murderer is discovered. Darcy and Elizabeth get married. Robert Jordan is left with his machine gun and a broken leg to cover the retreat of the others. The great white whale crashes into the *Pequod* and Ishmael alone is left.

In conventional narrative, the storyteller—the writer, the director of the film—is in charge all the way, and we the readers or the spectators sit back, expecting to have everything explained to us, suspending disbelief, and as though relaxing in a warm bath, we easily transpose ourselves into another world.

Now we *know* that life is not like that. Life as it unrolls for us is plotless, and only in retrospect can we make a story out of it, and we can make the story only by leaving out most details. The art of storytelling is always an art of deletion. The storyteller is like the classical sculptor who is presented with a block of marble and who must then find the statue in the marble and cut it out. But the storyteller is presented with a block of experience and cuts into it to find the story, separating the story and casting away all that does not contribute to the story. The consequence is that any narrative becomes a deceit, something arranged by the writer to lead the reader to be satisfied with the plot that the writer has made of life—when all the while in that world where we *really* live, we know that life is not like this. Life is chaos happening day after day. The story we tell about life—even the story of our own lives, our autobiography—is something made, a fiction, from the Latin word *fictio*—to fashion, to create. Or it is a poem from the Greek *poiew*—to make, to form.

Throughout most of his fiction Faulkner has a deep distrust with simple narrative where everything is neatly put together. He is in the family of writers that include James Joyce—or at least the Joyce of *Ulysses*—and Virginia Woolf. The novels come to us as a block of experience, and it is up to us to make sense of them in just the way that it is up to us to make sense of the body of experience that is our own life. No wonder that Faulkner is hard for many readers, for he deliberately throws unidentified flying objects in our way and expects us to make the most of them. He and Ernest Hemingway had a difficult relation and never managed to be friends, although each admired the other. Faulkner remarked once that Hemingway had no courage, an accusation, or merely a comment, that cut Hemingway to the bone. Faulkner was not speaking of Hemingway's physical courage. He was speaking of Hemingway's unwillingness to experiment—and to experiment in writing is inevitably to make things hard on the reader since writing is a medium that from time immemorial has been designed as the best sort of *communication* next to *viva voce* communication by human beings speaking face to face.

We shall think more on these matters as we go along. For the moment I shall conclude this part of my lecture today by saying that you will have difficulty understanding Faulkner, that some parts of his work defy consensus of interpretation, and that you will probably ask me a lot of questions during the term to which I can reply honestly only with an asseveration: "Damned if I know." The only comfort in all that is that Faulkner—like Joyce—intended for us to have the difficulties.

Yet with the difficulties are tremendous rewards. And here I can only do the supremely southern thing in offering to explain what those rewards are. I can tell a story. It is the story of my own experience with Faulkner, and I hope it will be a means of helping you become your own reader of Faulkner. For certainly that is my own major desire for this course, that you will become good and thoughtful readers of Faulkner, and other literary texts as well, so that for the rest of your life, literature will remain part of your very identity. I always have believed Flaubert's comment that one can be truly educated by knowing five books well. But I also like to think that his wisdom can be extended to the further observation that to know any book by heart and any author well is to know how to read any other book, and I believe that if one can get acquainted intimately with Faulkner, one is on the way to feeling confidence about reading anyone.

Let me tell you my story about Faulkner.

I encountered him first in his great short story "A Rose for Emily." It appeared in a big anthology called *Great Tales of Terror and the Supernatural* published by Modern Library.[2] "A Rose for Emily" appeared in the first section—the great tales of terror. I was a teenager and was already addicted to Kipling and Poe and was also in love with ghost stories. I read "A Rose for Emily" sitting out in the woods behind our house on a large oak stump left when loggers had cut away the largest trees—the sort of thing Faulkner often wrote about. It was a bright summer day, and I had already read sev-

---

2. As a teenager, Marius could have read either the 1944 or 1947 edition of this book (this anthology was reprinted as recently as 1994). Since neither one of the early editions was on his bookshelves, "A Rose for Emily" is cited to his copy of the *Collected Stories*.

eral of the tales of the supernatural, feeling the pleasant chill that a good ghost story can evoke. Then I read "A Rose for Emily"—not a ghost story at all but rather a story of a woman with a domineering father who grows old and dies in the small Mississippi town of Jefferson. It is written in a style that compared to the rest of Faulkner is straightforward, clear, without long, wrap-around sentences and without startling oxymorons or unusual words. So the reader I was went along without misgiving, wondering I suppose why I was reading a story about a woman becoming a stubborn recluse, and perhaps I was a little impatient because in what I read I found no evidence of terror—until I reached the thunderous final sentences:

> Then we noticed that in the second pillow was the indentation of
> a head. One of us lifted something from it, and leaning forward, that
> faint and invisible dust dry and acrid in the nostrils, we saw a long
> strand of iron-gray hair. (*Collected Stories* 130)

I don't believe that any sentence I had read until that time in my life had such an impact. I read again to be sure that I was understanding the meaning of what I thought I was reading. Very gradually I convinced myself that there could be no other meaning, and I felt the most prodigious and disagreeable thrill of horror that I had ever felt in my life. That horror was so strong in the teen-aged boy I was that it made me suppose that I did not want to read Faulkner ever again. For a young teenager he seemed dirty and grotesque in the most disagreeable way that I could imagine.

Since that time I have concluded that to read "A Rose for Emily" as I did, to feel a sunny summer woods suddenly turn dark and threatening with menace, and to feel such revulsion as perhaps only a very young reader inexperienced with much literature can feel—perhaps this combination of intellect and emotion was the best introduction to "A Rose for Emily" and to Faulkner that anyone can have.

Here are techniques and themes that will abound in all Faulkner's career. For example, Faulkner loves to withhold information. He teases us, confuses us, makes us wonder why he is telling us this detail or that, introduces characters simply by giving us their names, and only slowly tells us what they mean to his story. The traditional form of narration was to build a narrative step by step, identifying characters as they come on so that the nineteenth-century novelist locates the character firmly in the story and even describes his or her appearance in detail. But here we have characters briefly touched upon and identified not so much by their appearance but by their actions, and Miss Emily Grierson's actions seem on first reading to be random and disconnected—so disconnected in fact that the only tie we see between them is her stubbornness and her strangeness. Yet at the end with these two sentences that I read for you, everything comes together. This strange and horrific story seems at first like a loose ball of yarn left on the page, so twisted up that it cannot be unwound. But then with these last sentences the story is pulled as taut as a piano wire in its element, and every random incident is seen to be essential to the story. We do not know *why* it is essential until the end, but at that moment the cumulative weight of the story falls on us.

Faulkner's style is a challenge always to our memory and concentration. The traditional style in Western languages is keyed continually to helping our short-term memory retain the information from first to last that will let readers keep in mind the building purpose of what the writer is trying to accomplish. We learn all sorts of stylistic tricks to help the short-term memory. Keep sentences simple and direct. Don't use too many adjectives. Be sure the various parts of any exposition are joined together by careful transitions. Faulkner seems at times to delight in affronting them all. So it is with "A Rose for Emily": we don't know why we are reading these details until the very last, and then they all come together like a thunderclap.

In this course we will read novels where Faulkner will drop details along the way vital to his story, and yet we are likely to read over them with such haste that we fail to see them, to see their importance. When he wrote "A Rose for Emily," Faulkner was also writing one of his great novels, *As I Lay Dying*, intricate and confusing. We will encounter the character Darl, who is crazy, and in the end Darl is packed off to an institution that to Faulkner is the earthly equivalent of hell—the Mississippi Hospital, the "asylum," as these places are usually called, for the insane.

What's wrong with Darl? We get an important clue late in the book from one phrase uttered by one of his brothers. Apart from that one phrase we find, so far as I can see, no hint of the source of Darl's insanity in the rest of the book. So it is with much of Faulkner's work—the advancement of both character and incident in prodding and withdrawal.

Note too that at the end of the story Faulkner does not give us a direct statement. Tom Clancy would say something like this: "We rushed into the room and found the mummified corpse of a man in bed, and next to it on a pillow we found a strand of Miss Emily's hair, hair that was iron-gray as it was when she was old, and you know what that proved? It proved that that poor, lonely old woman had been sleeping with that corpse for decades, ever since she killed him with rat poison all those years before."

No. Faulkner writes, "One of us lifted something from it, and leaning forward, that faint and invisible dust dry and acrid in the nostrils, we saw a long strand of iron-gray hair." He leaves it to us to say, "What? What's that?" And when we incredulously look again at the sentence, the meaning rushes up within us. Faulkner does not make a direct statement. He leaves us to tell ourselves what has happened, and whenever we tell ourselves, the event falls on us with far more impact than it would if Faulkner told us.

That indirection comes to a head in *Absalom, Absalom!* where we are left puzzling over these great questions: What really happened? How do we separate what really happened from the speculations about what happened, speculations hurled about by people with contradictory recollections and contradictory motives, and contradictory points of view? We struggle to penetrate the mass of tale to get to truth. And yet tale, story, and truth finally get so mixed up together that we cannot separate them.

Again, is this indirection, this demand that we join the author in telling the story, is this not more true to life than the narration that tells all the story for us? A story is almost inevitably about the past. Yes, I suppose you can have a story told in the present tense that unfolds in a continuing present. But even if we watch a movie developing in a present, we know that it is really *past*—something directors and actors have already done. Stories are efforts to make sense of the past, and in a narration, the storyteller usually commands the meaning and the facts and tells them to suit his or her motives.

But what really happened? Faulkner often draws us into this conundrum. He tells us what Miss Emily did up to a point. But we must tell the rest of the story ourselves, and then we must wrestle with why she did it and what the story means.

But if he is indirect, the images in Faulkner's fiction are so powerful that we must respond to them. All right. Maybe the powerful symbolic function of these images comes from the simple fact that they are so grotesque! They are bizarre. Faulkner is filled with bizarre images, bizarre people doing strange things. He is no Tolstoy or Proust working over the soul of cultivated men and women with ironic perception of all the contrary pretensions and true motives of civilized life. You can't imagine Proust or Tolstoy putting a reclusive old woman in bed with a corpse at night while during the day she teaches the demure young women of a Mississippi town how to paint china cups, saucers, and plates, the sort of harmless talent expected of innocent young women expected to grow up to be harmless and innocent old ladies, as decorative to their husbands as the painted china is to the house where it may be displayed in chaste and circumspect order on the shelves of cupboards or closets. No, Miss Emily is grotesque, a product of that strange human zoo in Mississippi, where Faulkner seems to look at the spectrum of the grotesque, perhaps at one end extending to the genial grotesqueries of Dickens where an old woman like Miss Betsy Trotwood seems sweetly eccentric, while Faulkner treats the other end of that grotesque spectrum and finds Miss Emily Grierson, who sleeps every night for decades with the desiccated corpse of a man she has quietly, almost genteelly murdered. We look at that image, and we cry out, "What does it *mean*?" It can't be just an image, can it? Must it not be a symbol? But if so, a symbol of what?

We can make all sorts of guesses, and people have done just that—guess. Can Miss Emily be a symbol of the South itself asleep with the dead, claiming the high standing of maidenhood, virginity, the ideal of chivalry but in fact behind the facade of romance being nothing but a barren and murderous old woman finally pitiful in her fate? That's an explanation I've seen of her in a couple of dozen undergraduate papers. Did Faulkner have anything like that in mind? I doubt it. Does it matter if he didn't? Do his intentions rule and command his work? No. It is a commonplace since Freud's view of the subconscious that all of us operate from drives and motives not fully comprehensible to ourselves so that our own intentions and explanations about any utterance are subject to further interpretation. I am suspicious of elaborate Freudian interpretation. Too often it seems to me like much ado about nothing. I suppose I am suspicious about any system that purports to explain in a deterministic way why people are what or who they are. Freudianism too often feels to me like astrology or Biblical prophecy.

The issue is complicated with Faulkner because we know he picked up some of the enthusiasm for Freud that percolated through the United States in the 1920s. Now in fact Faulkner denied that Freud had influenced him—although he mentions both Freud and Havelock Ellis in *Mosquitoes*. He said once in an interview that during that time in his early life he spent in New Orleans, everybody was talking about Freud but that he himself never read him. He said, "What little of psychology I know the characters I have invented and playing poker taught me. Freud I'm not familiar with" (qtd. in Irwin 5). But as John T. Irwin has suggested, the conversations about Freud would have been enough to influence some of Faulkner's own ideas. So we will have to come back now and then to Freudian interpretations without in any way making them the centerpiece of our own interpretations.

Most plausible to me is the belief that Faulkner's intent is to present Miss Emily Grierson as a character in herself without symbolic intent. His fiction is filled with grotesques, perhaps because life is filled with grotesques. Walk through Harvard Square in the late afternoon or on the Boston Common at almost any hour of the day, and you see grotesques. The artistic imaginations may seize on them purely out of a desire to explore human possibility to the limits. People can be like this. If they are like this, what is the role of the artist in relation to themselves?

This view does not stop us from finding symbolic meaning in the character. But it keeps from following a character in literature off into a sort of gnosticism where the characters don't represent themselves so much as they represent a knowledge hidden to all but the cognoscenti, to all but the gnostics.

Faulkner delighted in creating characters, and sometimes he played with mythological schemes. We shall have occasion from time to time to speak of allusions to Frazer's *The Golden Bough*, and Faulkner's novels *Mosquitoes* and *Pylon* have explicit references to the watery mysticism and mythology of T. S. Eliot. William Faulkner named Rowan Oak for the rowan tree, which James Frazer says in *The Golden Bough* is a Scottish tree, symbol of peace and security, and a tree that guards a house from witches.

Yet finally the characters stand for themselves—Ab Snopes, Quentin Compson, Thomas Sutpen, and Miss Emily Grierson. A novelist stands or falls finally not on plot or on symbolism or on mythology. A novelist finally must rest his or her reputation on the characters that he or she creates on the page. The characters must spring to life as we read, or else the novelist is dead.

Now I think we have to take up another issue about a writer and the characters he or she creates. In the most common style of the novel, the author clearly likes some characters and just as clearly dislikes others, and the reader drawn along by the vise of the writer's narrative usually is compelled to follow the writer's implacable lead. Near the beginning of *Pride and Prejudice*, Jane and Elizabeth Bennet are discussing the first dance of the book where the young, handsome, very charming and rich Mr. Bingley has danced twice with Jane, the older of the two. Says Jane:

> "I was very much flattered by his asking me to dance a second time. I did not expect such a compliment."
>
> "Did not you? *I* did for you. But that is one great difference between us. Compliments always take *you* by surprise, and *me* never. What could be more natural than his asking you again? He could not help seeing that you were about five times as pretty as every other woman in the room. No thanks to his gallantry for that. Well, he certainly is very agreeable, and I give you leave to like him. You have liked many a stupider person."
>
> "Dear Lizzie!"
>
> "Oh! you are a great deal too apt, you know, to like people in general. You never see a fault in anybody. All the world are good and

9

agreeable in your eyes. I never heard you speak ill of a human being
in my life." (238)

Lizzie makes the remark about Jane. But what do you think Jane Austen thinks about Jane? And what does Stephen King think of Danny Torrance, the little kid with the crazy father in his novel *The Shining*, and what does Ernest Hemingway think of Robert Jordan in *For Whom the Bell Tolls*? These characters are all heroes or heroines in one way or another. We want things to come out right for them because the author wants things to come out right. The authors are involved with them.

Faulkner is very often different. He stands back from his characters. He puts a distance between himself and them most of the time. He takes the same Shakespearean detachment that we find in some of the great tragedies. Does Shakespeare *love* Hamlet or Othello or Lear or Macbeth? I am not sure that he does. He is the spectator in the theatre looking on with a certain distance as these characters go to their respective dooms, and although he will describe their falls step by agonizing step, he will not lift a hand to help them.

I should point out here one of the primary qualities of much southern literature. The writer merely by being a writer, being educated well enough to take up the profession of letters, becomes alienated from the society that otherwise holds him in its tight communal grasp. Both sides of this equation are essential. Until the past three decades, the South was a small-town society with the small towns as oases of commerce dependent on the farms lying around them. Both rural and small-town societies from time immemorial exercise sharp or heavy authority on the individual, enforcing conformity, tolerating eccentricity only when it seems harmless. A Miss Emily Grierson does not appear to be dangerous. Southerners regularly ask strangers where they are from, who their kinfolks are, whom they know, and finally where they go to church as a means of assuring themselves that the stranger is not dangerous.

All this reassurance and control took place in a region that was woefully illiterate, that had no use for books, that found books effete at worst, epicene at best, a region with wretched schools and an educational level even with those schools that was the lowest in the country. In 1900, 10 to 15 percent of the whites in the South could not read or write (Ayers 418), and that figure cannot measure the rarity of any groups of readers. Females read more than males, but whenever anyone male or female was educated enough to be a writer, that person became *ipso facto* radically different from his or her surroundings. One consequence has been that the southern writers have by and large written about people radically different from themselves. Faulkner is a prime example. Ernest Hemingway wrote about people, especially men, much like the image he cultivated for himself. John Updike, Philip Roth, Margaret Atwood write about an imagined world, often thinly disguised autobiography, where protagonists are much like the writer. But Faulkner was alienated in life from Mississippi—even while he recognized that he could be nothing other than a Mississippian. And I think it is almost impossible to look at a Faulkner character and say, "This is the image of the author; this is how Faulkner imagined himself." And one may argue for Faulkner, as perhaps one may argue for Shakespeare, that the alienation from the people of his time allowed him to slip into the skins of all the characters he created to give them a life of their own without an obvious bias by an author unable to see their side at all.

So Faulkner stands in a detachment from his characters so that whether they are tragic or comic or neuter, Faulkner presents them as though at a distance.

> When Miss Emily Grierson died, our whole town went to the funeral: the men through a sort of respectful affection for a fallen monument, the women mostly out of curiosity to see the inside of her house which no one save an old man-servant—a combined gardener and cook—had seen in at least ten years. (119)

Why does Faulkner use the first person plural in this story? He speaks of "our whole town." And, throughout, the narrator never speaks as "I." It is always "we." The detached tone at the start is held throughout. Nobody goes sadly to Miss Emily's house. To the men she is symbolic. To the women she is the mysterious possessor of a house to which they have been denied admission for ten years and thus denied the pleasures of superior comparison that we instinctively feel is their main motive. Miss Emily is an artifact, seen at a distance by a mysterious "we" or "us," and the real power of the story is that, as we perceive her macabre history, she becomes a person, and we pity her as the town has never been able to do.

At a moment we perceive that Miss Emily has played a huge joke on the town. A town that supposed she was a helpless and absurd eccentric discovers in one supremely macabre moment that she is a woman capable of powerful and profound feelings and able to perform an act—sleeping with a corpse—that none of them could do, and that surely she was not a virgin when she decided to murder Homer Barron and that surely, too, he had not told her that he would leave her; she knew him well enough to predict his act and to plan to kill him before he could desert so that she takes her place in the mythical pantheon that includes Clytemnestra, who killed her husband,

Agamemnon. And in particular, she has played a macabre practical joke on the two cousins from Alabama who appear thirty years after they had come to defend the family honor against Homer Barron's incursion. Now they appear to hold her funeral, and we may suppose that they appeared feeling proud of themselves for having saved the family's reputation. What a surprise waits for them.

We may see all these things or rather we may surmise them, but Faulkner himself never feels compelled to be on the side of the angels. He is not explicit in telling us that this person is good or that this person is bad. We are left to draw such conclusions for ourselves, and usually when we are confronted with characters, our judgments are ambiguous just as these judgments are ambiguous in real life. Seldom does Faulkner seem compelled to see to it that the good people triumph while the bad people are brought to doom and justice. The novel *Intruder in the Dust* is an exception. It is not one of his best although, as far as I know, it is the only one of Faulkner's novels to be made into a good movie.

None of this means that Faulkner does not give us moral wrestling. On the contrary. By the time we arrive at *Go Down, Moses*, we are confronted with the titanic moral dilemma of race in a turbulent swirl of conflict and emotion. Yet the resolution of such a dilemma remains cloudy, ambiguous, the moral lessons wrapped in puzzles and enigmas.

I want to make mention of another feature of Faulkner's work evident in "A Rose for Emily." This is his treatment of time. The story moves through time in the almost heedless way that time moves through our own consciousness, the way memory sweeps uncontrolled once stirred by some stimulus that is itself unpredictable.

The most famous literary monument to the capricious relation between external stimulus and mental response is found early in Marcel Proust's great reconstruction of the past in *A la recherche du temps perdu*—a work Faulkner knew, though not one I think that influenced him much, though of that I am not as sure as I would like to be. The madeleine cake dipped into the tea brings back a whole world of the village of Combray, where Proust spent so much of his childhood.

Faulkner begins "A Rose for Emily" with Miss Emily's funeral. It jumps back to a moment some time before Colonel Sartoris died when her taxes were remitted. The story leaps forward again to debate in a later time, after Colonel Sartoris died, about the legality of the dispensation he had given her. Then back we go to thirty years before when we have the problem of the smell, and when that part of the story is over we go back to Miss Emily's girlhood and youth when her dictatorial father did not consider any man worthy of her—and, we infer—evidently told her that no man was trustworthy. We come forward to his death when we have been told that Miss Emily is not above thirty years old. We move forward again to the coming of the Yankee, Homer Barron, into her life, and we move to a year later when she buys the rat poison, and then we go back again to the year earlier when she began to be seen with Homer Barron riding around in the yellow-wheeled buggy that he rented from the livery stable. Back we go to the year after their first courtship. The cousins come from Alabama to remonstrate with her, we assume. Homer disappears. A week passes. The cousins depart. In three days Homer is back—enters the house one evening and is never seen again. An indeterminate time passes. Miss Emily grows old and fat, and we rush forward to her death at age seventy-four when her hair is still the iron-gray color it has been for several years. Back we go again to the time when she is about forty and then she grows old again, and she dies, and her Negro servant lets the town in and vanishes. We have the brief description of the southern funeral and finally the macabre discovery of the corpse in bed, mummified in the nightshirt she bought for him thirty years before.

All this wrenching of time rolls on in the space of about twelve printed pages in the *Collected Stories*. Faulkner has whirled time around his head, and we take it all naturally because that is the way we experience time. One incident in the story causes the mysterious narrators to remember something else. Who are these narrators? How old are they? These are questions Faulkner does not answer for us. But whoever this strange voice is, it presents the collection of fragments that he or she or they put together in a story exactly as we will put together fragments of widely disparate parts of our lives to tell any story we decide to tell. Past and present collide again and again in Faulkner's work in the random, ceaseless energy of memory and time that creates our consciousness.

Faulkner himself in this truly great tale gives us a brilliantly evocative expression of the idea of time that runs through all his work.

Here is his long sentence:

> They held the funeral on the second day, with the town coming to look at Miss Emily beneath a mass of bought flowers, with the crayon face of her father musing profoundly above the bier and the ladies sibilant and macabre; and the very old men—some in their brushed Confederate uniforms—on the porch and the lawn, talking of Miss Emily as if she had been a contemporary of theirs, believing that they had danced with her and courted her perhaps, confusing time with its mathematical progression, as the old do, to whom all the past is not

a diminishing road but, instead, a huge meadow which no winter ever quite touches, divided from them now by the narrow bottle-neck of the most recent decade of years. (*Collected Stories* 129)

Here is one of Faulkner's most important concepts—time as consciousness. And, in fact, he describes here a consciousness that every one of us experiences—and not merely these old Confederate soldiers who believe that Miss Emily is one of their contemporaries. For most of us time beyond the most recent decade becomes a confusion of shapes. The best of us have trouble after a while remembering in what year this or that event happens, and if we give that issue a little thought we are brought to acknowledge just how fragile and amorphous a construct time is.

The narrator of "A Rose for Emily" seems to stand out of time, viewing all these events from a distance that, as I have already touched upon, leaves him or her or them almost as a disembodied voice of the whole community that transcends the life of the individual within the community, in particular the character of Miss Emily. I would like to suggest that this transcendence of time in the narrator is a sort of corollary to the detached voice that Faulkner often assumes in his fiction. The author does not go down from Olympus to fight his characters' battles. He watches with an Olympian detachment as they work out their destinies.

I want to say something else about Faulkner and time and then move on. In the passage I have read from "A Rose for Emily," he writes of time seen through the "bottle-neck" of the past decade. Remember that the bottleneck also has an opening, the point where the bottle begins—consciousness existing in this moment, a moment ceaselessly flowing that we cannot grasp. I believe this sense of the instability of the moment is one of the grand impulses of serious modern literature.

The fundamental character of consciousness is that it is momentary, mysteriously elusive, so that although our memories give us the illusion of an extended present, the actual present is a point without dimension so that the very act of pronouncing a word means that by the time we get to the last syllable, the first syllable is already in the past. St. Augustine with his fatal combination of Greek and Hebrew conceptions of God wrestled fruitlessly with this problem in the *Confessions.* God is represented in the Bible as speaking. In particular St. Augustine recalled God speaking at the Baptism of Jesus: "This is my beloved son in whom I am well pleased." But how can God speak, asks the worried saint, when the very act of speaking reduces the speaker to the confines of time? God should be timeless according to Platonic thought. Yet the enunciation of syllables immerses us in time because only extension in time can allow our auditory sense and our minds to absorb the meaning of the words. Without time, speech would be impossible.

I am not interested here in St. Augustine's efforts to solve the problem. I am suggesting only that with the advent of the twentieth century the problem itself came rushing back to prominence and expressed itself vividly in the so-called stream-of-consciousness writing by various authors including most prominently James Joyce.

We are likely to think of stream-of-consciousness writing as words rushing out helter-skelter, and young writers who do it badly are likely to imagine that stream-of-consciousness is an excuse for chaos. But perhaps as far as Faulkner is concerned, we should jettison the "stream" and settle instead on the problem of consciousness, which is a problem of sorting out coherence, meaning, cause and effect, purpose from the multitude of sensations that impinge on us at every waking moment and even in our dreams, sorting out the real, making a distinction between the ever-present impress of memory and the dissolving and momentary reality of the present consciousness.

Faulkner's work is filled with the difficulties of reconciling memory, imagination, and reality. In "A Rose for Emily" we get the narrative voice that takes the consciousness, the perceptions, of Miss Emily's life and manufactures them into a story, only to discover at the end that the narrative voice has been ridiculously wrong.

In *Soldiers' Pay* very early on we meet the character Januarius Jones, who like the god Janus, lord of doors, is found first leaning on a gate and contemplating the spire of a small church, the spire seen against a background of clouds. The clouds seem motionless; the spire seems to be moving, falling. The rector who finds him there is puzzled, and Januarius explains:

> "I referred in a fit of unpardonable detachment to your spire. It was ever my childish delight to stand beneath a spire while clouds are moving overhead. The illusion of slow falling is perfect. Have you ever experienced this, sir?" (56–57)

To some degree, Januarius Jones seems for a moment to embody one of Faulkner's persistent themes that the moment of consciousness cut off from context can lead to illusion, the contradiction between perception and reality. Immanuel Kant pondered the relation of dreams to waking and concluded that the difference between the two was the difference between continuity and disruption, that our dreams take us into different worlds every night but that our waking moments take us into the same world every day. But that neat, rational scheme of things tends to break down when we get to a character like Miss Emily Grierson, who may dream every night that she is in bed with a man who loves her and wakens every morning to discover that she is in bed with a corpse and seems to be able to ignore that so-called "reality" with magnificent aplomb. The interplay between consciousness, illusion, and reality is one of Faulkner's most insistent themes, and through various characters a kind of tragic burden crushes those whose illusions, fantasies, dreams, nightmares take over their conscious world and drive it to destruction.

One of the ironic problems of the relation of consciousness to memory is that this moment of consciousness, this fleeting instant that we name "present time," can never be repeated. The great nineteenth-century Danish philosopher Søren Kierkegaard wrote an annoying little book called in English *Repetitions*. He set up various efforts to duplicate exactly various experiences, but every time he did so, he discovered that no two experiences can be the same. I believe this insight is now perhaps a commonplace—the unique quality of every moment in time. But *memory* is by its nature repetitive. We remember the same things again and again. Memory seems to rule time, and for some of Faulkner's characters—notably Quentin Compson in *The Sound and the Fury* and *Absalom, Absalom!*—memory becomes time or at least it seems to make time go in circles, and as John T. Irwin has argued, this repetitiveness of memory makes it seem to some characters that nothing new is possible. Irwin points out that, in *Absalom, Absalom!*

> when Shreve [Quentin's Harvard roommate] begins to sound like Quentin's father, Quentin thinks, *"Am I going to have to hear it all again. . . . I am going to have to hear it all over again I am already hearing it all over again I am listening to it all over again I shall have to never listen to anything else but this again forever so apparently not only a man never outlives his father but not even his friends and acquaintances do."* (in Irwin 110)

But perhaps the most striking manifestation of Faulkner's consciousness, his preoccupation with consciousness, lies in his style—rich, rife, often confusing. His boyhood friend and mentor Phil Stone—seemingly jealous of his protege when Faulkner became famous—complained that Faulkner used too many words he didn't know the meaning of.

I think we have a stylistic working out here of an effort by Faulkner to dissect the infinitesimal moment of consciousness by pushing words to the limits of meaning. But sometimes the effect to me at least can be dense and beautiful. This from *Flags in the Dust*:

> The moon had gotten up beyond the dark eastern wall of the hills and it lay without emphasis upon the valley, mounting like a child's balloon through the oaks and locusts along the drive. Bayard Sartoris sat with his feet on the veranda rail, in the moonlight. His cigar glowed at spaced intervals, and a shrill monotone of crickets rose from the immediate grass, and further away, from among the trees, a fairy-like piping of young frogs like endless silver small bubbles rising, and a thin sourceless odor of locust drifted up intangible as fading tobacco-wraiths, and from the rear of the house, up the dark hall, Elnora's voice floated up in meaningless minor suspense. (42)

Now, what does it mean to say the moon lay "without emphasis" or that the grass is "immediate" or that the sound of the frogs rises "like endless small bubbles," or that a "sourceless odor of locust drifted up intangible as fading tobacco-wraiths" or that Elnora's voice "floated up in meaningless minor suspense"?

For some of us the precise meanings don't matter. The words stand for themselves with vague significance to something else, and what they seem to do is to capture a moment of peaceful consciousness in the mind of old Bayard Sartoris as he sits on his verandah on a warm summer night and draws into one point all these sensory impressions of a world that at the moment seems solid and enduring but that in fact is as fleeting as consciousness itself.

This is a fairly manageable passage—"accessible," I think the word is now. It is not as complex and difficult as other Faulkner texts that we will explore. It shows us a fully developed Faulknerian style that we will see later, a style here lovingly developed in his third novel.

It is a poetic style in a mode that tries to capture everything that can possibly be captured by words about a moment of consciousness. It's worth pointing out here that Faulkner aspired first to be a poet, published a fair quantity of poetry—none of it highly regarded by critics—and that he was influenced by poets such as Algernon Charles Swinburne in England, T. S. Eliot, and later on Conrad Aiken. Except for Eliot, these poets are largely forgotten.

I suppose what all these poets shared was a reaction against the excessive rationalism and optimism that constituted a sort of "official" dogma of Victorian life. Here was a faith expressed in the public press and in political pronouncements that progress was inevitable and that technology and organization offered no end of cumulative benefits leading to a golden age. These poets rejected optimism and the obsessive faith in rationality that in poetry made itself felt in precise meter, rhyme, and a certain worn predictability.

All that Faulkner was to absorb. The influences that touched him were sometimes called "decadent" because in opposition to the "official" dogmas of optimism, reason, and progress, these poets saw pain, evil, and the horror of meaninglessness. This "decadent" attitude naturally put all moral values in question, for in a meaningless world, nothing is absolute.

Faulkner was born into a time when circumstances of history seemed to guarantee the triumph of the decadents, and he grew up in a social background that furthered a critical attitude towards the romantic fantasies of some Victorians where all the troubles of life had a happy ending. He was born on September 25, 1897, in New Albany, Mississippi, the son of a weak and unsuccessful father who nevertheless came from a proud old Mississippi family. They spelled the name *Falkner*, probably a derivation of the word "falconer," someone who trains and uses falcons to hunt other birds. He speaks in *Soldiers' Pay* of falcons making love, locked together, and plummeting from the heights.

Faulkner had a hard time making an impression in early life. He was small and skinny. Joseph Blotner, who knew him late in Faulkner's life at the University of Virginia, says that William Faulkner was 5' 5". A friend of mine who taught at the University of Mississippi for years and knew Faulkner there says that he was 5' 8". The woman he fell in love with first, Helen Baird, was told by a friend that she collected screwballs. She said of Faulkner, "He was one of my screwballs." And she said, explaining why she rejected him, "he reminded me of a fuzzy little animal" (Blotner 150–51).

He knocked around in a purposeless way. In 1918 he went to Canada to join the Royal Canadian Air Corps. But before he could fly, the First World War ended, and he was mustered out of service. Later on he developed a mythology about himself that included hair-raising tales of aerial combat against the Germans and misadventures such as crashing his plane on landings. He came back to Oxford dressed up in a British officer's uniform that he had no official right to wear, but he had it tailored somewhere in Canada, and he wore it. He also walked with a limp and used a cane, and the story spread that he had been wounded in combat. Late in his life, when he was lecturing at the University of Virginia, he could sit with Professor Frederick L. Gwynn, who had flown in combat in World War II, and tell imaginative tales of his own combat flying experience in World War I.

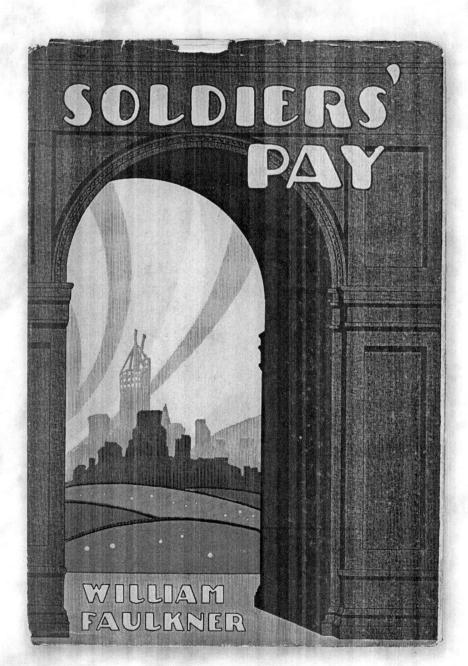

SOLDIERS' PAY

WILLIAM FAULKNER

SOLDIERS' PAY

It's worth saying a couple of things here to introduce William Faulkner's first novel, *Soldiers' Pay*, which he published in February 1926—the same year that Ernest Hemingway published *The Sun Also Rises*, his first novel. Hemingway's book was wildly successful; Faulkner's was not.

World War I was the greatest calamity to fall on Western Civilization since the Black Death of the late Middle Ages in Europe. It was undertaken on all sides with an enormous faith in progress and in Social Darwinism— the offshoots of the "official" Victorian optimism (which was by no means shared by all poets and writers of Victorian times). Darwinism is inherently pessimistic. Darwin himself did not believe in God and did not believe in any ultimate purpose to the life of the individual, the nation, or the human race.

But people like Herbert Spencer and Heinrich von Treitschke and to some extent Henri Bergson taught that the survival of the fittest meant the survival of the greatest. War was for many of these thinkers the way that the fit were distinguished from the unfit. Here is part of a lecture that Professor Heinrich von Treitschke gave to his students at the University of Berlin, published in 1897, the year after his death:

> The grandeur of war lies in the utter annihilation of puny man
> in the great conception of the state, and it brings out the full magnifi-
> cence of the sacrifice of fellow-countrymen for one another. In war
> the chaff is winnowed from the wheat.
>
> [. . .]
>
> It is war which fosters the political idealism which the materialist
> rejects. What a disaster for civilization it would be if mankind blotted
> its heroes from memory. The heroes of a nation are the figures which
> rejoice and inspire the spirit of its youth, and the writers whose words
> ring like trumpet blasts become the idols of our boyhood and our early
> manhood. He who feels no answering thrill is unworthy to bear arms
> for his country. To appeal from this judgment to Christianity would be

sheer perversity, for does not the Bible distinctly say that the ruler
shall rule by the sword, and again that greater love hath no man than
to lay down his life for his friend? (I, 66–67)

All this fine talk seemed in retrospect to be not merely ridiculous but insane before the bloody reality of combat in World War I when heavy artillery and the .30 calibre machine guns swept battlefields and stacked corpses up like windrows of grain. We still don't know how many people died in World War I. The French with a total population of about forty million lost about one million soldiers, and to visit even a small French village in a remote rural area and to see the names in ranks on the inevitable monument to the dead in the war of 1914–1918 is to get just a hint of the horror of that conflict. When we consider that in all our wars put together from the time of the American Revolution we have lost about one million men and that our bloodiest war was the Civil War, we only begin to perceive the magnitude of Europe's loss in the War of 1914–1918. Since our own age is not notably optimistic, we have an even harder time comprehending the psychological collapse of Europe in the post-war period. The age of the hero seemed dead, for what was heroism worth against the technology of modern war that leaves men no choice except to burrow down into a muddy trench and pray that an artillery shell does not land on top of you and blow your body to smithereens?

The men in Faulkner are seduced by outmoded canons of chivalry rendered obsolete and foolishly romantic by the technology of destruction in World War I. The war has made all values worthless. Now a new and unmapped world brings new values into being, and the men are unable to give up the old and yet unable also to find their way in a new world, which is no man's land.

I've often reflected on the grim fact that World War I was the first war in history when the bodies of soldiers were almost routinely dismembered or utterly destroyed in combat. I have visited many of the battlefields on the western front on foot and by bicycle. At Verdun, where nearly a million French and German soldiers perished in the battle of 1916, bones of the dead are still being picked up on the battlefield, and at Thiepan in Northern France, where the British engaged the Germans in the battle of the Somme—also in 1916—a gothic monument lists the names of seventy-three thousand British soldiers missing in action. That is, these men went into battle and simply vanished from the earth.

The United States suffered nothing comparable to those losses—about fifty thousand dead in the six months we were actively engaged in combat. Yet it was enough to bring in a reaction here, too. That reaction was particularly felt among writers who found no value in making war a heroic, triumphant business. Gertrude Stein is supposed to have told Ernest Hemingway, "You are a lost generation." Hemingway considered calling *The Sun Also Rises* "The Lost Generation." As it was, the title Hemingway chose came from the most solemn and tragic of books in the Bible, where the chorus resounds, "Vanity of vanities, saith the Preacher, vanity of vanities; all *is* vanity."[1] And we may understand things better if we say "emptiness" instead of vanity.

Soldiers' Pay, the title Faulkner finally chose for his own first novel, is part of the mystique of the "lost generation." He called it "Mayday" at first— the word that ships at sea send when they are sinking and need help fast. *Soldiers' Pay*, as a title, reflects that the soldiers' pay is never sufficient to compensate the soldier for what he has suffered.

The novel revolves around the figure of Donald Mahon, son of an Episcopal rector in Georgia. We meet Mahon on a train as he is in the company of a gang of rowdy soldiers going home or to indeterminate destinations. Mahon has been dreadfully wounded in a plane crash of some sort. We meet Mahon through the eyes of Cadet Lowe, who has never been in combat. "He saw a belt and wings, he rose and met a young face with a dreadful scar across his brow. My God, he thought, turning sick" (25).

But the book is not really about Mahon. It revolves around him. Faulkner never writes a novel where there is one protagonist, one hero on whom the novel focuses throughout. He uses multiple points of view in this novel, writing in the third person, shifting from the minds of his characters in an omniscient way. These multiple points of view will be a feature of most of his fiction, and sometimes as in *The Sound and the Fury* and *As I Lay Dying* he does multiple points of view in the first person, a technique that *ipso facto* eliminates the omniscient narrator.

I want to make a suggestion here that I will come back to, that Faulkner in experimenting with multiple points of view is engaging in something like the striving of the cubist painters a little earlier, the effort to place all the dimensions of reality on a single plane, here the plane of our consciousness. I am reminded of the provocative passage in Robert M. Pirsig's *Zen and the Art of Motorcycle Maintenance* where he speaks of the motorcycle we see and the *a priori* motorcycle, the motorcycle we assume is completely

---

1. Ecclesiastes 1.2. "*One* generation passeth away, and *another* generation cometh; but the earth abideth forever. The sun also ariseth, and the sun goeth down, and hasteth to his place where he arose." Ecclesiastes 1.4–5.

there although we can see only a part of it from any one point of view. The cubists were striving to free vision from the limitation of a single point of view, and in some measure Faulkner is striving to do the same thing, making much more dramatic shifts than omniscient third-person narrators of the nineteenth century—Dickens comes to mind—were likely to do.

The various soldiers in *Soldiers' Pay* are returning from the utterly indescribable horror and chaos of war to a world that to the people who live in it seems utterly normal, denizens of a routine society where everything is so homogenized that even people seem as mass produced as the automobiles that so many Americans are eager to buy. The soldier found that normal world strange and himself an alien in it. On the train rolling down towards Cincinnati, the soldiers sit around Donald Mahon, who sleeps while they drink and look out the window. "New York was Ohio, and Ohio became a series of identical cheap houses with the same man entering gate after gate, smoking and spitting" (38). We have some reflection here, I think, of T. S. Eliot's "Love Song of J. Alfred Prufrock":

> Shall I say, I have gone at dusk through narrow streets
> And watched the smoke that rises from the pipes
> Of lonely men in shirt-sleeves, leaning out of windows? (lines 70–72)

A passage from *The Waste Land* describes Mahon, "The Burial of the Dead":

> "You gave me hyacinths first a year ago;
> They called me the hyacinth girl."
> — Yet when we came back, late, from the hyacinth garden,
> Your arms full, and your hair wet, I could not
> Speak, and my eyes failed, I was neither
> Living nor dead, and I knew nothing,
> Looking into the heart of light, the silence. (lines 35–41)

Probably there is another allusion to Eliot where Margaret Powers is speaking with Gilligan and tells him that the rector has shown her Donald's things, including "a girl's undie and a hyacinth bulb he carried with him in France" (107), also recalling *The Waste Land*. Hyacinthus was so beautiful that he was beloved by Apollo. But when the two were throwing the discus, the wind struck it and threw it into Hyacinthus's head, killing him. Apollo took his blood and made it into a fragrant flower.

We find a sort of emptiness amid absurdity. War has made all the conventional values absurd and has not replaced them with anything. The novel begins with the soldiers drinking bad whiskey on a train going home, getting drunk, the drunkenness a symbol of the rejection of the nice rationality torn all to hell by the war.

Most shocking to Mississippians who abhorred the book was the casual sexuality reflected throughout. And yet some of the sexuality has a dead, unfeeling side to it. It is the satisfaction of animal desire and nothing more. People don't have feelings of romantic love. Januarius Jones is described as goat-like, a satyr figure out of classical mythology except that he is also fat. Faulkner makes explicit references to sexual intercourse: "Afternoon lay in a coma in the street, like a woman recently loved. Quiet and warm: Nothing now that the lover has gone away" (151). And yet romantic love is shown to be without enduring depth or value. The book turns somewhat improbably on the decision of the soldier Joe Gilligan, an enlisted man, to accompany Donald Mahon home to a small town in Georgia where Donald's father, Dr. Mahon, rector of the church, awaits him. Awaiting him, too, is Donald Mahon's fiancee, Cecily. In the typical romantic novel, the fiancee is supposed to rush into the arms of her wounded hero, and the music is supposed to swell to a crescendo of consummation. But what happens when Donald Mahon comes home? He is helped up onto the porch of the rector's home, and there Cecily Saunders, the fiancee, is waiting for him. The rector helps his son out of the cab that has brought them from the train. The rector has seen his son, seen the scar, knows that Donald is losing his memory. Donald Mahon's loss of memory delivers him over to the momentary consciousness that flees as we think about it. He is helpless, and he does not know it, does not know himself. He goes blind in the end, the result of a war that came about because people had memory. Wars like World War I come about because people remember the past and either fear revenge or desire it. Januarius Jones is in the house with Cecily:

> He looked again at the party coming through the gate, the rector looming above them all. There was something changed about the divine: age seemed to have suddenly overtaken him, unresisted, coming upon him like a highwayman. He's sure sick, Jones told himself. The woman, that Mrs. Something-or-other, left the party and hastened ahead. She mounted the steps to Cecily.
>
> "Come darling," she said taking the girl's arm, "come inside. He is not well and the light hurts his eyes. Come in and meet him there, hadn't you rather?"
>
> "No, no: here. I have waited so long for him."
>
> The other woman was kind but obdurate. And she led the girl into the house. Cecily reluctant, with reverted head cried; "Uncle Joe! his face! is he sick?"

> The divine's face was gray and slack as dirty snow. At the steps
> he stumbled slightly and Jones sprang forward, taking his arm.
> "Thanks, buddy," said the third man, in a private's uniform, whose
> hand was beneath Mahon's elbow. They mounted the steps and
> crossing the porch passed under the fanlight, into the dark hall.
>   "Take your cap, Loot," murmured the enlisted man. The other
> removed it and handed it to him. They heard swift tapping feet
> crossing a room and the study door opened letting a flood of light
> fall upon them and Cecily cried:
>   "Donald! Donald! She says your face is hur—oooooh!" she
> ended, screaming as she saw him.
>   The light passing through her fine hair gave her a halo and
> lent her frail dress a fainting nimbus about her crumpling body like
> a stricken poplar. Mrs. Powers moving quickly caught her, but not
> before her head had struck the door jamb. (93–94)

In all of this is a rich trove of association, all associations betokening I think a sense of loss. Cecily in particular here becomes an image of the fallen female saint. Faulkner gives her a halo of light, the nimbus of a frail dress, the saintly female figure who in so many World War I posters provided comfort for the man in danger or in death. You can see a splendid representation of the World War I woman in the murals by John Singer Sargent that adorn the walls on the monumental stairway inside Widener Library [Harvard University]. The *Blue Guide to Cambridge and Boston* calls them "probably the very worst works of public art ever done by a major American painter" (Freely 386). But here is the female figure blessing the soldiers and taking the dead in her arms. Faulkner has, I think, this poster figure in mind, reproduced in a hundred or thousand different forms in World War I art, and by the time he wrote *Soldiers' Pay*, it was as discredited among Americans as the rest of the war. Cecily sees Donald Mahon's wound, and she faints.

I might say here that Faulkner's assault on romantic love may be in part a reflection of his own predicament. The woman he loved as a youth, Estelle Oldham, had not married him, probably because he had no money, no decent job, and no prospects. She married a man named Cornell Franklin, who had everything. Later she divorced him and married Faulkner. She said much later on that she thought Cecily was a portrait of her, and it hurt her feelings. Certainly throughout this novel women are not drawn in much depth. As Richard Gray says of Faulkner and his characters, they are like Joe Gilligan, who cannot say what he wants:

> Like the other men in the book, he cannot say what he wants: he can
> only see that want reflected or projected, in a woman. In this, he is
> like his creator: for whom the female characters of *Soldiers' Pay* are,
> eventually, no more and no less than vessels of male desire and the
> text that incorporates them is, in turn, no more than a sublimation of
> similar feelings—a revelation of, and possible compensation for, loss.
> (Gray 117)

I think what Gray means to tell us here is that these men long for a world
of things that they cannot express in words because these yearnings are
huge and vague and aching in their very impossibility of being defined. So
the male characters transfer these desires to women, and yet we are left
with the melancholy possibility that even if these longings for a woman are
consummated in sexual intercourse, the fundamental longing will not be
assuaged, and it is just in this thought that Faulkner is finally opposed to
romance.

This becomes perhaps the greatest theme of the novel—the melancholy
sense of loss. These characters all lose something. Donald Mahon loses
his memory. He is one of the first of the many Faulkner characters who
come to us in the immediacy of consciousness, without memory or presup-
positions to interpret for him the meaning of his perceptions. He is, like
Eliot's hyacinth girl, neither living nor dead. And slowly before he dies, he
goes blind.

Everyone looks at Donald Mahon and sees his or her own loss.

Cadet Julian Lowe wakes up with a hangover in a hotel room where
Donald Mahon is sleeping, and he is filled with envy:

> He tasted his sour mouth, knowing his troubled stomach. To have
> been him! he moaned, just to be him. Let him take this sound body of
> mine! Let him take it, to have got wings on my breast, to have wings;
> and to have got his scar, too, I would take death to-morrow. (45)

It is the young man's yearning for proof of manhood, proof of worth—something Faulkner himself was denied.

And then there is the figure of the rector. He is like the priest in Camus's
La Peste, who insists that God exists though the chaos and suffering of the
world might make ordinary people doubt. The rector has a naive quality. He
is not tragic, I suppose, because he is too ordinary, having neither grandeur
nor the ability to feel and desire that might give him a tragic dimension. He
wants everything to be "normal." He is happy for Cecily Saunders to marry
Donald no matter how grotesque the marriage may be because he cannot

make himself believe that Donald is going to die. In fact, the rector convinces himself that Donald is going to be perfectly well in a year's time. He represents religion throughout as the normal, the ordinary, and he lives a comfortable life where he gardens and eats satisfying meals and drinks whiskey and lives a life without incident until his son comes home to die and to bring with him the reality of the world beyond the garden, a fallen world where death and meaninglessness haunt the people who live in that world as innocent victims. The rector's garden is a kind of Eden. But in the person of the rector's son, the world of Cain and Abel enters the garden, bringing death with it.

At the end of the book with Donald dead, Gilligan and the rector walking at night come to a black church where the singing of pure voices without musical instruments lifts a hymn, as Faulkner says, "like a flight of gold and heavenly birds" (319). The blacks are outcasts, on the edge of society, and somehow they have retained their faith when all the whites have discovered the absurdity of life. They sing on,

> taking the white man's words as readily as it [their passion] took his remote God and made a personal Father of Him.
>   Feed Thy sheep, O Jesus. All the longing of mankind for a Oneness with Something, somewhere. Feed Thy sheep, O Jesus. . . . The rector and Gilligan stood side by side in the dusty road. The road went on under the moon, vaguely dissolving with perspective. Worn-out red-gutted fields were now alternate splashes of soft black and silver; trees had each a silver nimbus, save those moonward from them, which were sharp as bronze. (319)

I think it is possible to give a religious interpretation to this passage that may seem positive to traditional Christianity. The men listening to the rise and fall of these voices of poor black people in the night may signify a hope that, in the midst of death, it is still possible to cling to some remnant of a father God who loves us no matter how bleak the circumstances may be.

But I take a different point of view. Much religious expression may be considered what we wish were true even when something strong within us says that it is not. At the southern funerals that I have attended all my life, the minister of a Baptist or a Presbyterian or Methodist church or one of the lesser groups is likely to declare that the person we have come to bury is not dead, and the hymns that testify to hope in the resurrection are most likely to elicit tears from the grieving congregation. It is a strange but I think natural experience, a paradox, that the very affirmation of a religious expression may make us all the more aware of the bleakness of reality. Gilligan and the rector have both lost something. The rector has lost his godlike son, and Gilligan has not so much lost Margaret Powers as he has lost the idea that a lasting love is possible. The two of them stand listening to a poor black congregation singing beautifully in the dark amid fields that are "red-gutted" and "worn-out," a reality that is silvered by moonlight so that it seems magical and filled with peace. But it is a moment that is doomed to the flow of time that takes all the illusions away. So Faulkner ends the book:

> They stood together in the dust, the rector in his shapeless black, and Gilligan in his new hard serge, listening, seeing the shabby church become beautiful with mellow longing, passionate and sad. Then the singing died, fading away along the mooned land inevitable with to-morrow and sweat, with sex and death and damnation; and they turned townward under the moon, feeling the dust in their shoes. (319)

This is a somber ending to a somber book, somehow uplifting because it presents people with a capacity to endure and an ability to recognize their place as thinking and feeling reeds in a world that finally crushes us. It is a truly tragic catharsis, a cleansing. Oh, so this is what we are; this is the nature of our existence. Well, so it is. Part of our magnificence as human beings is our ability to recognize who we are and what we are in a finite world where everything is in motion, and all is carried away. *Soldiers' Pay* is a novel of loss, and the nobility of the characters who are noble—Gilligan and the rector in particular—is that they can recognize that we do lose in the end.

Yet the tragic figure does not surrender without a fight. In some way, the rector has fought against death by his steadfast refusal to admit that Donald is going to die until Donald does die. He is not Ahab or Job or Oedipus. But he does not submit without striving against the inevitable.

MOSQUITOES

A NOVEL BY
WILLIAM FAULKNER
AUTHOR OF SOLDIERS' PAY

MOSQUITOES

I would like to suggest that in the wake of World War I, great masses of people sought something to fill the horrible vacuum left by the collapse of old ideologies in the massacre and meaninglessness of the war. Some turned to communism, some to forms of Statism like Fascism and Naziism, all of them tending to divide the "masses" from the upper middle-classes and that part of the intelligentsia still devoted to the Western liberal traditions. To such people, leaders like Mussolini and Hitler seemed absurd, the target of jokes and satire. T. S. Eliot in this group turned to Christianity, and others turned inward in various ways. Faulkner turned to his art, to imaginative genius, to creation in a bold and experimental way that put him into a relationship with his own material that is idiosyncratic and selfconscious. Faulkner stands inside his novels looking at his own work. And in large measure *Mosquitoes* is a novel in which the writer looks at the world and at art and tries to find a place for himself.

Mosquitoes is generally considered Faulkner's worst novel, and because we have so much to do in this course, I'm not going to spend much time on it. It is a novel where not much happens. A group of people are run aground in a yacht on Lake Pontchartrain outside of New Orleans, and they talk a lot. The Semitic man, Julius, in *Mosquitoes*, makes a comment that seems to apply to the ideologies of the world.

> "After all, it doesn't make any difference what you believe. Man is
> not only nourished by convictions, he is nourished by any conviction.
> Whatever you believe, you'll always annoy some one, but you yourself

will follow and bleed and die for it in the face of law, hell, or high
water. And those who die for causes will perish for any cause, the
more tawdry it is, the quicker they flock to it. And be quite happy at
it, too. It's a provision of providence to keep their time occupied." He
sucked at his cigar, but it was dead.

"Do you know who is the happiest man in the world today?
Mussolini, of course. And do you know who are next? The poor devils
he will get killed with his Caesar illusion. Don't pity them, however:
were it not Mussolini and his illusion, it would be someone else and
his cause. I believe it is some grand cosmic scheme for fertilizing
the earth. And it could be so much worse," he added. "Who knows?
They might all migrate to America and fall into the hands of Henry
Ford." (131)

The Semitic man is the witness, the observer, the truth teller, and conse-
quently the author's voice. In the course of their talk they mention Freud
and Havelock Ellis, both of these names associated with various risqué
theories about sex at the time Faulkner was writing the novel—which he
published in April 1927. The group talks a lot about art, and Faulkner
gives us a character Dawson Fairchild, somewhat modeled on Sherwood
Anderson. Anderson had written *Winesburg, Ohio*, and he had befriended
Faulkner and given him good advice—Go back to Mississippi and write
about that little patch of ground. Anderson was in the train of American
writers who wrote about life here and did not have to take up the expatri-
ate role to be whole. Dawson Fairchild is described by one of the characters thus:

> His writing seems fumbling, not because life is unclear to him, but
> because of his innate humorless belief that though it bewilders him
> at times, life at bottom is sound and admirable and fine. (242)

Faulkner was to be cruel to Anderson. But the cruelty may have been the
necessary break from a constraining mentor.

But Faulkner seems throughout trying to examine himself, trying to
work out where he stands in the world of art. And he is making a recognition, as Richard Gray has suggested, that Faulkner takes the book to bed
rather than the woman he really wants. As David Minter has suggested,
Faulkner tended throughout his life to associate great writers with failure
to reach the unattainable (62).

In a part always noted by critics, Faulkner appears in his own novel,
though at a distance. A young woman named Patricia, the niece, tells of

being in New Orleans at the French Market and meeting "A little kind of black man," black because he was sunburned:

> "He was a white man, except he was awful sunburned and kind of shabby dressed—no necktie and no hat. Say, he said some funny things to me. He said I had the best digestion he ever saw, and he said if the straps of my dress was to break I'd devastate the country. He said he was a liar by profession, and he made good money at it, enough to own a Ford as soon as he got it paid out. I think he was crazy. Not dangerous: just crazy." (144–45)

After some effort to remember the name, the niece finally comes up with it. The crazy liar was named Faulkner. It's easy enough to see young Faulkner asking himself if he ever would be remembered and if perhaps he might be a crazy man for his efforts to make a living by writing.

Very briefly I'd like to point out how important drowning as a means of death comes up in the novel. I suspect this is an influence from *The Golden Bough* conveyed through T. S. Eliot. But we will come back to Faulkner's strange fascination with the life and death present in water.

SARTORIS

WILLIAM FAULKNER

FLAGS IN THE DUST

Flags in the Dust, as we have it, is a composite work. Faulkner did not—according to his own testimony—take part in cutting it. Ben Wasson did the work. But we do not have the transcript Ben worked from, and the galley proofs Faulkner worked from have also disappeared.

One important thing to say about *Flags in the Dust* is that it is a novel of actions. No longer do we have the world-weary people who, as in *Mosquitoes*, are stalled on a grounded yacht where they are reduced to impotence and the endless talk that impotence engenders. *Flags in the Dust* was published in 1929, after it had been turned down by Faulkner's first publisher, Boni and Liveright. Harcourt Brace accepted it on condition that it be cut by about one-third. Ben worked on the cutting at his tiny apartment in New York while Faulkner came up—with a set of golf clubs—from Mississippi to meet his new publishers and to work on *The Sound and the Fury.* Ben said that Faulkner made no effort to supervise the cutting. Some critics have doubted the story. I believe it because the writer's preoccupation is always the next book, and Faulkner was already engaged on *The Sound and the Fury,* which required great concentration and many revisions.

Faulkner had called the book *Flags in the Dust,* a title that conveys the sense of loss and fall that is part of most of Faulkner's work. The book appeared in its truncated form as *Sartoris,* the title following the story line as Ben shaped it around the Sartoris family and its seeming death wish. When the book was finally reissued in 1973 with the cuts in the manuscript restored, it received the title Faulkner had intended for it, *Flags in the Dust,* and it gave us then two Faulkner books with "dust" in the title, the other being *Intruder in the Dust*. Dust here is a metaphor for death, drawn from the biblical text where, when Adam and Eve are cursed by the God who created them, God declares:

> In the sweat of thy face shalt thou eat bread, till thou return unto the ground; for out of it wast thou taken: for dust thou art and unto dust shalt thou return. (Genesis 3:19)

So when we come to the title *Flags in the Dust* our minds are turned to a suggestion of former triumph brought down to death. The notion of "dust" as a metaphor of death gives to the subject a sort of biblical nobility and intensifies the Greek sense of tragedy that permeates so much of Faulkner—characters brought to doom because they are impulsive and headstrong and not suited to live in a world of normal people.

But *Flags in the Dust* is much more than a tragedy. It has the tragic element. Young Bayard Sartoris comes home from World War I. He has been a fighter pilot, part of the last rays of the setting sun of chivalry in a war that was a theatre of such carnage that nobility seemed to have been utterly dissolved, vanished in the grinding maw of technological destruction where a heavy calibre artillery shell landing on a trench killed people like insects and gave them no chance to be heroic. I have been to Verdun, where German shells fell on a French trench at a moment when French soldiers were standing with their rifles ready and they were prepared to go over the top, as the saying went for soldiers called on again and again to get up out of the trenches and to charge the German machine guns. And just at that moment, as I saw, a shell or shells fell on them and caved in the trench and buried all the French *poilus* alive where they stood, and after the battle someone noted that a line of rifles with the bayonettes sticking out of the ground remained, and it was discovered that the soldiers who held them were still standing there, holding their rifles with skeletal fingers, eternally at the ready for a charge they never made. No chance for heroism or valor or chivalry in a war like that. Faulkner eventually went to Verdun, saw the trench of the bayonettes—as you can still see it today—and put that horror into his novel *A Fable*. But in 1927 and 1928, when he was writing *Flags in the Dust*, he was thinking of the war in the air where some semblance of valor and chivalry was still possible.

Faulkner named Bayard after the hero of chivalry, the French knight Pierre du Terrail Bayard, called *Le chevalier sans peur et sans reproche*, the great French hero of the Italian wars, noted for his gestures of chivalry. Bayard's twin brother, John, has died in a foolish, solitary lunge for German fighters who outnumber him and who have superior equipment, and Bayard must then come home with survivor's guilt to face his old grandfather, the elder Bayard, whose memories run back to the Civil War and his father, Colonel John Sartoris.

War is now seen as a theatre, not as a crusade for a cause, and the slaughter of the First World War takes even the theatre away. Old man Falls talks relentlessly and repetitiously about the Civil War. Old Bayard asks him:

> "Will," he said, "what the devil were you folks fighting about, anyhow?"
> "Bayard," old man Falls answered, "damned if I ever did know." (252)

The fact that John and Bayard were twins must increase young Bayard's guilt. James Frazer in *The Golden Bough* notes that some American Indians thought twins had magical powers and could bring rain. Twins were called "children of the sky," and their graves were supposed to be kept wet so that rain would come to make the crops grow (76–77). What better way can Faulkner make his twins children of the sky than to make them airmen and to suggest by their seeming love of death a sacrifice?

But does the sacrifice accomplish anything? This is problematic. The mythological justification for such sacrifice is that, by its example, a superior race of men grew up in the South. That is the sense of the opening of the book, when old man Falls roars out the story of how Colonel Sartoris outwitted Yankees who had come to arrest him and take him prisoner. Old man Falls tells the story as a southerner will, part of reliving an event, living it over and over again to war against the fateful propensity of time to allow things to happen only once before sweeping them away forever. Faulkner often uses repetition in his style to illustrate the same quality of our existence in time, and here is old man Falls participating in the strange ritual of telling a story in which old Bayard, then twenty-three years old, played a major role. The result for us is a thrilling tale of a man who treated life and death as jokes to be bravely laughed at, feeling—we think—that he would be immortal because this story would always be told. The dying Hamlet says to Horatio:

> If thou didst ever hold me in thy heart,
> Absent thee from felicity a while,
> And in this harsh world draw thy breath in pain
> To tell my story. (V.ii.358–61)

You feel that John Sartoris knew that someone like *old* man Falls would do exactly what he does as he shouts at deaf old Bayard, recalling the Yankees running and shooting at Colonel Sartoris and hollering at him to stop:

> "And thar you was a-standin', holdin' the hoss and that 'ere
> Yankee patrol yellin' up behind, until Cunnel got his boots on. And
> then he tole you to tell yo' aunt he wouldn't be home fer supper." (5)

That's a certain kind of man, spirited, brave, bold, and free of the most terrible fear, the fear of death, able to joke, with a Yankee patrol in full gallop after him, trying to kill him.

If we don't get the lesson, we get the story of another Bayard, a collateral member of the family, the Carolina Bayard who rode with the dashing cavalry commander Jeb Stuart. Says Faulkner the narrator:

> The war was also a godsend to Jeb Stuart, and shortly there-
> after, against the dark and bloody obscurity of the northern Virginia
> campaigns, Jeb Stuart at thirty and Bayard Sartoris at twenty-three
> stood briefly like two flaming stars garlanded with Fame's burgeoning
> laurel and the myrtle and roses of Death, incalculable and sudden as
> meteors in General Pope's troubled military sky, thrusting upon him
> like an unwilling garment that notoriety which his skill as a soldier
> could never have won him. (15)

And then we get the story of the anchovies, how the Carolina Bayard Sartoris is shot down in General Pope's camp after Stuart has led a daring and successful raid for coffee. A few minutes after a fantastic escape, a captured Federal major taunts Jeb Stuart:

> "No gentleman has any business in this war," the major retorted.
> "There is no place for him here. He is an anachronism, like ancho-
> vies. General Stuart did not capture our anchovies," he added taunt-
> ingly. "Perhaps he will send Lee for them in person?" (21)

And at that the Carolina Bayard Sartoris rides alone back to the plundered Federal camp to liberate the canned anchovies, "and a cook who was hidden under the mess stuck his arm out and shot Bayard in the back with a derringer" (22).

In these apparent digressions into tales of the Civil War, we have a mirror to the stories of young John, already dead when *Flags in the Dust* opens, and Bayard, whose doom is foreshadowed from the beginning. War has for centuries offered to brave and bold young men a chance for glory. But now war is not decided by a few men dueling in great, swift movements over open fields. War is now an affair of mass armies locked together in bloody wars of attrition where the outcome is decided by superior firepower rather than by superior men. The Civil War was that kind of war, a harbinger of all the wars that would come afterward—except that Europeans did not recognize it for what it was. "This is not bravery," the captured Federal major says; "it is the rashness of a heedless and headstrong boy" (21). Old Bayard, we learn, reads himself to sleep at night by reading the novels of Alexandre Dumas one after another and starting through again. Dumas, who wrote *The Three Musketeers* and *The Count of Monte Cristo*, was the great romantic about chivalry and the Middle Ages, and we may assume that Faulkner read him, too.

Is all this tragedy? The comment of the Federal major is arresting. Can we have tragedy if the tragic figure is brought to earth because his flaw is that he is immature, "a headstrong and heedless boy"? Can we respond to the death of young Bayard Sartoris as we respond to the death of King Lear, who perishes as a fond, foolish old man because he makes the human mistake of believing that flattery is the same as love and that honesty means hatred?

My own answer to that question is NO. Narcissa Benbow, who marries young Bayard, sees Bayard's flaw, the "smoldering, abrupt violence" in both young Bayard and his doomed brother, John. "He and his brother had both had this, but Bayard's was a cold, arrogant sort of leashed violence, while in John it was a warmer thing, spontaneous and merry and wild" (76). As Richard Gray has suggested, Bayard ends not by being tragic, but by being like young Hotspur in Shakespeare's *Henry IV, Part 1*, whose rashness brings him into battle against great odds and ultimately to death so that finally Hal makes him "food for worms" (130).

The word "Sartoris" is related to the Latin or Old French word "Sart," someone who hoes and weeds, someone who prepares the ground for crops, who keeps the earth cultivated. I suppose that Faulkner intended the name to reflect the southern myth that true aristocrats take care of the land. But Faulkner explodes the myth even as he brings it into his book. For the old Colonel has left farming after war to build a railroad, and old Bayard can contemplate the lighted cars moving across the track in the distance. So the nostalgia of romance and the hard wonder of technology are both present in lonely old Bayard's mind—as they are in Faulkner's. The train moving across the dark, going to a destination out of sight after emerging from an equally unseen place, is in some respects a symbol of the problems the Sartoris clan confronts. The past is in their minds, invisible, departed, and yet ruling them as the steel rails of the railroad fix the train and all its passengers on a destiny that they cannot change.

Old Bayard and young Bayard are equally caught up in the past. Colonel Sartoris stands in old Bayard's memory as an example that the old man— old and young at once when we meet him in this novel—can never equal.

When old Bayard joins young Bayard in careening around the unpaved roads of the county, the old man who is addicted to danger, a man who has become a banker, that most prosaic and unaristocratic of professions, at last gets his chance for speed and danger, with the horsepower of an engine rather than the horses of Colonel Sartoris's or Jeb Stuart's cavalry, and so he meets death when young Bayard, seeking death for himself, wrecks the car.

Young Bayard cannot escape the death of his brother, John, another past event that cannot be changed. It revolves in his mind, tormenting him. Irrationally, we may think he tried to stop John in John's last mad foray against the German Fokkers. But John loosed a burst of machine gun fire at him. So Bayard's reaction amounts to an obsession and a death wish.

Flags in the Dust is called a flawed novel, and Horace Liveright, who had published Faulkner's first two novels, turned it down—saying it was too loose, that it had neither plot nor structure. But we can see now that Liveright was opposed to the very qualities that led to Faulkner's greatest work. As I said in my first lecture, Faulkner has an ultimate distrust of some of the qualities of narrative that make it most entrancing, the aspect of narrative that cuts the story line away from everything else. Faulkner's fundamental view is that life is a diffuse experience ultimately disconnected in that one thing after another happens by chance and fatality but that as life goes along we have an unquenchable desire to tame the chaos of experience by framing narratives that give a nice order and form to that which, except for its happening along a continuum of time, has no order at all.

Flags in the Dust is of essential importance for Faulkner because it starts him along the chronicles of Yoknapatawpha County. It is the Genesis of his Bible. And yet it is important structurally to note about this novel that it takes place in a tight little community where inevitably the stories lived and told by one group of people, one family like the Sartoris family, impinge on all the other stories in town and inevitably influence how the stories are told.

Horace Benbow also returns from the war in *Flags in the Dust*, but what a difference he is from Bayard! His sister Narcissa marries young Bayard. So in a legal sense, Bayard and Horace become brothers too. But while Bayard was a pilot engaged in individual duels of aerial combat, Horace was serving in a non-combatant role as an officer in the YMCA. His sister Narcissa—she is the Greek chorus of the book—calls him "Horry." He comes home with souvenirs and the materials necessary to do glass blowing. Faulkner makes him a character of "taut and delicate futility" and gives him a somewhat incestuous relation with Narcissa. They kiss each other on the mouth. Their relations are more like lovers than brother and sister. He talks endlessly, and Narcissa listens patiently with some amusement but also with real affection. Young Bayard and old Bayard Sartoris are silent men, so silent that we hear them speak only in occasional bursts. But Horace talks all the time. It is almost as if Faulkner were going back to the root meaning of the English word "conversation," which is sexual intercourse. Horace leads the conversation, and Narcissa receives it so that Horace seems to be having a kind of verbal sex with his sister.

Yet she seems sometimes to doubt his manhood, to consider him not one of them. As they are driving home from the railroad station, Narcissa speaks about the antics of Bayard Sartoris in the car and says angrily, "I hate all men" (176). But she obviously loves Horace. So the inference to be drawn is that Horace is not a man. He seems to be the eternal boy, for although she is seven years younger than he is, she acts as his mother, but as they sit together in the evenings and talk, she becomes something else.

The theme of incest is constant and recurring in Faulkner's novels. It reaches its most intense level in *The Sound and the Fury*, and it is at the heart of the construction of the past by Quentin Compson and his friend Shreve in *Absalom, Absalom!* It turns up in *Go Down, Moses*, and it is hinted at in other places. I must say it puzzles me. Faulkner did not have a sister. Why does the topic engage him so much? I should point out that in *Flags in the Dust* and in *The Sound and the Fury*, Horace in the one and Quentin in the other have weak fathers and therefore have no model of manhood to allow them to become fully men themselves. Without a strong father the son is left to construct his entire moral code for himself, and so given the rude, implacable nature of biology incest in such circumstances is natural. As I have said several times, Freudian critics have found ample field to graze in Faulkner, and the issue of incest is a major part of Freud's construction of this psychological theory.

But I think a stronger case can be made for Faulkner as someone deeply interested in the implications of Charles Darwin's theory of evolution by natural selection. The Scopes monkey trial took place in Dayton, Tennessee, in July 1925. Faulkner left for Europe while the trial was going on, but he could not have escaped the national furor over Charles Darwin. Tennessee passed a law against the teaching of evolution in the public schools—including the universities—of the state. Most southern states did the same. The issue was what it remains today. Did the human race evolve from lower animals by adapting to nature, to the environment? Or did God create human beings in His own image? The natural corollary is this: do our morals, our totems, and our taboos, come from God, or are they merely

human constructions driven by a combination of social utility and irrational-
ity? The continual focus of the debate over Darwin in the 1920s was just
this: Are we animals? That focus, the intensity, was driven, too, by Freud's
emphasis on human beings being torn always between sex and death, the
need to reproduce to keep the species alive even if the individual must die.
It is worth noting in this regard that Faulkner uses animal imagery for
human beings throughout his work.

It has to be said that in Faulkner the women do not suffer the pangs of
conscience over the act of sex as do the men. They think about life in a
more accepting way, often making their own morals up as they go along.
Narcissa Benbow is concerned with respectability. Therefore when she gets
an obscene letter from Byron Snopes, she is most afraid of what people will
think of her if anyone discovers that she has received such a communication from a man. She feels filthy as a result. But she does not throw
the letters away. Why? Is it possible that she is titillated by them? We are
not told.

Later on in one of his finest short stories, Faulkner comes back to those
letters. It is more than ten years after the death of Narcissa's husband. The
story, "There Was a Queen," tells of how the letters were stolen from her
house the night after she and Bayard were married and how they turned
up in the hands of a federal agent investigating crimes by Byron Snopes.
The federal agent comes to Jefferson, has dinner with Narcissa and Miss
Jenny—who is now ninety years old and lives in a wheelchair. Miss Jenny
is horrified that he is a Yankee and a Jew and refuses to eat with him. Then
for the first time in her life Narcissa leaves her son and goes to Memphis
for two nights. With aplomb she explains herself to Miss Jenny. The federal agent has blackmailed her. She sleeps with him to get the letters back.
She tells the old woman:

> "That's why I had to go to Memphis. I had that much regard for Bory
> and you to go somewhere else. And that's all. Men are all about the
> same, with their ideas of good and bad. Fools." She breathed quietly.
> Then she yawned, deep, with utter relaxation. Then she stopped
> yawning. She looked at the rigid, fading silver head opposite her.
> "Don't you understand yet?" she said. "I had to do it. They were
> mine; I had to get them back. That was the only way I could do it.
> But I would have done more than that. So I got them. And now they
> are all burned up. Nobody will ever see them." (*Collected Stories* 741)

Narcissa feels that the whole thing is dirty. She returns from Memphis
and goes, taking her son, to a creek, where she sits with him in the cold

water as though to cleanse herself of the filth of sex. But when the cleansing is over, she feels no torments of conscience. Sex is something men want. Women have power because they can give sex or withhold it. As far as Narcissa is concerned, sex is a commodity, something to be bartered for something she wants, and it is by no means the fate worse than death that the moral mythology of the South and the nation hold about sex outside of marriage. By giving her body, Narcissa gains the letters, and with them burned she gets what she most wants, the appearance of respectability. Is all this a symbol of the hypocrisy of the South or the nation? I don't know. But it is an indictment of the cult of respectability that the Southern woman cultivates. And we may have here something of the author's frustration and anger that women he loves or at least lusts for withhold from him that gift of sex that he longs to have and that they hold so lightly in their possession.

Narcissa feels no reserve in her almost incestuous relations with the inept and futile Horace. People do not see these exchanges of intimacy. Perhaps Narcissa is simply sexless. She is, of course, named for the young man of Greek mythology who hates the idea of love. Women and nymphs lusted for him, and the nymph Echo became so desperately in love with him that when he made no response to her, she pined away and became only a voice. The women he rejected demanded vengeance from the gods. So when Narcissus bent to drink from a pool, he became enamored by his own reflection and stayed there, in love with it, until he, too, died.

In one version of the myth Narcissus has a twin sister. She dies. He sees his reflection in the pool and thinks that it is hers and sits looking at it until he dies—a powerful myth of the incest taboo in action, presenting the visage of a sister, a doubling, but not allowing any satisfaction.

At any rate, the cold, aloof, and somewhat maternal image of Narcissa may be a key to this book—that most of its leading characters pine away because of either lost love or futile love. Certainly Horace gets plenty of sex. He not only has an affair with Belle—the name means beauty, of course—right under the nose of her husband, Harry (the name suggests the hairiness of an animal). Horace also has sex with Joan, Belle's sister—legally another kind of incest.

What seems evident in all the white families is that something is lacking. Even the serene and self-contained MacCallums living out in their woodsy Arcadia lack a wife/mother. In the supreme irony of the book, Bayard comes on Christmas Eve to a cabin where a black family lives. The family gives him hospitality, and on Christmas morning he shares the Santa Claus of the children. Everything is love and peace, and they give to Bayard a momentary gleam of what life might be in a world of innocence and mutual love and generosity.

> The negroes drank with him again, amicably, a little diffidently—two opposed concepts antipathetic by race, blood, nature, and environment, touching for a moment and fused within the illusion of contradiction—humankind forgetting its lust and cowardice and greed for a day. (393)

The day passes. Time runs on. He gets on a train Christmas night, leaves Jefferson, and plunges on to his doom.

FAULKNER AND BLACKS

The Endemic Problem of Race and Racism in American Society

At this point it's worth saying something about blacks in Faulkner's novels. Faulkner grew up in a client society where blacks and whites were bound up in an inescapable network of dependency, a hierarchy as meticulously put together as any medieval pattern of feudalism.

In dealing with the problem in literature we have to deal with the N word, "nigger," very probably the most obscene word in the English language for its cumulative associations of bondage, inferiority, and contempt when uttered by white people against blacks. The word has such terrible connotations that it has had an ironic effect on whites. White southerners believe that they are not prejudiced if they don't use it. So for the writer, the use of the word poses a doubly ironic problem. Not to use it implies that the South and the nation as a whole were better about race than they were, and yet to use it may condemn the writer as racist.

Faulkner presents blacks in the stereotypical fashion that was part of southern literature until very recently. Some things portend the future. Caspey has come home from the war with new ideas. He is surly to old Bayard, and the old man picks up a piece of stovewood and knocks him at his father Simon's feet. Simon tells him, "I kep' tellin' you dem new-fangled war notions of yo'n wa'n't gwine ter work on this place. [. . .] You go'n and git dat mare, en save dat nigger freedom talk fer town-folks: dey mought stomach it. Whut us niggers want to be free fer, anyhow? Ain't we get ez many white folks now ez we kin suppo't?" (87).

There is a kind of raw humor here that gives us a lot of difficulty today. I won't make any effort to explain away the unforgivable. I would say that in this instance with the early development of a young man's literary career, the unforgivable should be applied to the whole culture and not laid solely on Faulkner's back.

I don't think we get much satisfaction in trying to find in Faulkner racial attitudes that would achieve the ideal of democracy where all men—and women—of whatever color and origin are considered equal, or if not considered individually equal are at least considered equal in their opportunities to be thought worthy of respect and capable of morality and intelligence on the same level of any other individual regardless of color. In March 1949 when the film *Intruder in the Dust* opened in Oxford, Faulkner gave a picnic at his house for all the members of the cast. But he could not invite the Puerto Rican actor Juano Hernandez, who played Lucas Beauchamp, because the mores of Oxford, Mississippi, would not permit it (Blotner 503).

Faulkner always prized and praised his black "mammy," Caroline Barr, "born to slavery sometime around 1840" (Blotner 76). Faulkner dedicated *Go Down, Moses* to her:

> To Mammy
> Caroline Barr
> Mississippi
> [1840–1940]
> Who was born in slavery and who gave to my family a fidelity
> without stint or calculation of recompense and to my childhood an
> immeasurable devotion and love

All that is very well and good. It's at least not the typical attitude of southerners towards blacks in the 1870s, 1880s, and with a crescendo in the 1890s. Then increasingly the black man in particular was assumed to be a dangerous savage, a wild beast, a brute always lusting after white women, and a danger to any white woman of any age. In 1889 Philip Alexander Bruce of Virginia wrote of black men in particular:

> "They are aroused and stimulated by its foreignness to their experience of sexual pleasure, and it moves them to gratify their lust at any cost and in spite of every obstacle. This proneness of the negro is so well understood that the white women of every class, from the highest to the lowest are afraid to venture to any distance alone, or even to wander unprotected in the immediate vicinity of their homes; their

> appreciation of the danger being keen, and their apprehension
> of corporal injury as vivid, as if the country were in arms." (*The
> Plantation Negro as a Freeman* qtd. in Williamson 156)

This remained the stereotype of the southern black male until the advent of the Civil Rights movement of the 1960s, and it was the basis on which southerners excused their use of lynching and other violence to keep the black man "in his place."

It is certainly to Faulkner's credit that he never stooped to the stereotype of violence. One cannot say as much for Margaret Mitchell in *Gone With the Wind*, published to great acclaim in 1936, the subject of a flamboyant and spectacular movie in 1939/40. Mitchell's book is an attack on black freed slaves and the "Yankee" military government of Georgia after the War.

> The former slaves were now the lords of creation and, with
> the aid of the Yankees, the lowest and most ignorant ones were on
> top. The better class of them, scorning freedom, were suffering as
> severely as their white masters. Thousands of house servants, the
> highest caste in the slave population, remained with their white folks,
> doing manual labor which had been beneath them in the old days.
> Many loyal field hands also refused to avail themselves of the new
> freedom, but the hordes of "trashy free issue niggers," who were
> causing most of the trouble, were drawn largely from the field hand
> class. (GWTW 433–34)

And thus, a little later, Mitchell wrote, "Here was the astounding spectacle of half a nation, attempting at the point of bayonet, to force upon the other half the rule of negroes, many of them scarcely one generation out of the African jungles" (435).

In *Gone With the Wind* the Ku Klux Klan comes to the rescue of the white women threatened by violence. All these stereotypes were convenient for whites in the North and South. The North having freed the slaves now turned its back upon them, leaving them to the violence of white southerners who traded on the notion that, left to themselves, the freed slaves would become violent because of their nature. It was against their brute and bestial stereotype of the black male that Mark Twain created the sweet and docile Jim in *The Adventures of Huckleberry Finn*. And it is to William Faulkner's credit that in none of his works does he ever descend to this crude stereotype.

Yet in Mammyism and in the image of Dilsey in *The Sound and the Fury*, we find an interesting and sometimes troubling reciprocity between some stereotypes of Faulkner and the most standard variety we find in Margaret Mitchell. Take his affecting dedication to "Mammy Caroline Barr" in *Go

47

Down, Moses. That dedication would not sound out of place if it had been put on a monument addressed to a beloved old hound dog in a pet cemetery. Mitchell and Faulkner both play on the stereotype of obedient and loving loyalty of black people to white, and even in Faulkner we have the occasional suggestion that black people need white people to take care of them.

Dilsey in *The Sound and the Fury* is at least partly built on that stereotype. She is the loyal servant, staying on with the Compson family that is weary and decadent and sunk in failure and futility. Dilsey is the pet who feels herself attached to the household because she has always been there, and she is as much a part of the Compson family as the children. Margaret Mitchell would have been proud of her. But Mitchell could not have understood the Compsons because they have let down the side. The Compsons have something squalid about them. They are nothing like the people like the O'Haras and the Wilkeses and all the other plantation owners in her epic who acquire manners as they get money and who have a sense of decency and propriety and somehow know how to farm successfully. So to the romantic myth of the South, Dilsey fits. But the Compsons do not.

Because the Compsons are such a vile lot, weak father and self-pitying mother, Dilsey gets to play another role. She is able to be the moral center of the novel. She becomes the real mother of the family. When baby Quentin, Candace's daughter, is brought home in her cradle, Dilsey takes charge and puts the baby in Candace's old room, but Caroline Compson, the feeble mother, does not want the baby to sleep in the room where the very air may bring her the corruption lived by her mother. "And where else do she belong," Dilsey says. "Who else gwine raise her cep me? Aint I raised ev'y one of y'all?" (20).

But Dilsey also knows how to manipulate the family. She gives Mr. Compson a toddy when he needs it—against the protest of Mrs. Compson, who understands that drink is killing the family. But Dilsey understands that Mr. Compson sober is not less futile than Mr. Compson drunk. So she plies him with whiskey to keep him quiet, so he won't be a bother.

Dilsey is honest. She recognizes Jason's evil and stands up to him, and although he hates her, he cannot touch her because he recognizes her moral superiority. Although she is black, he knows she commands the fortress of virtue, and he knows he cannot harm her. Dilsey is not given a section where her own consciousness dominates as it does each of the sections where the consciousness of one of the brothers rules the action and the progress of the book. It's an interesting omission. Faulkner does not often try to get into the consciousness of a black character. He stays outside so that we usually know what a black person *says* and what a black person *does*, but we do not know what a black person *thinks*.

Faulkner often does that sort of thing. Multiple points of view will revolve around a character who does not have a point of view of her own. Several characters in *The Sound and the Fury* are like that. We never get into Caddy's head. We are left to imagine her situation. It is dismal. So I am not sure if we can make much of Faulkner's standing apart from Dilsey. She serves as the moral compass of the book. Jason hates her because she does stand up against him. She is the mirror in which he sees an unmistakable image of his own evil.

And here we are on ground that we will explore time and again in Faulkner's stories and novels—the revelation that blacks give of the evil of whites: "a nigger," says Quentin, "is not so much a person as a form of behavior; a sort of obverse reflection of the white people he lives among" (*The Sound and the Fury* 53).

In *Light in August* the enigmatic figure of Joe Christmas is never clearly known to be of black descent. He may be Hispanic, but he is thought to be black by many people, and invariably he becomes the catalyst—if we can call him by so unchangeable a term—to bring out obsessive evil in other people. By the time we get to *Go Down, Moses*, we discover just how deep the evil is in whites, an evil that seemingly requires a black person to be revealed.

We should say that, in these early novels, the black men do not stand out as clearly as the black women. The black children show a sort of innocence. But then we may also say that blacks in all of Faulkner seem to have a quality of innocence that Faulkner continually plays on. Even when Caspey comes back from the World War in *Flags in the Dust*, he demonstrates a certain innocence or at least naïveté when he thinks he can bring back with him to Mississippi the liberties that he enjoyed in France as a soldier. He got his white there, he says. But old Bayard quickly knocks him through the back door by hitting him in the head with a piece of stovewood, a wellnigh tragic foretelling of the force whites would use to push down black aspirations in the two decades between the world wars. Faulkner came back to lynch law, the implacable threat of force against blacks, several times in his novels and stories. Yet he retains a confidence in the integrity of the black people whose innocence gives them an honesty that makes us believe in them when we see them and hear them.

True, the innocence of the blacks often opens them to being comic figures of a type that was once the stock of comedy—the black servant like

Rochester in the old Jack Benny films and radio broadcasts, and yet the comedy often lay in the doggedness of the black to see reality when the white person could not.

Luster in *The Sound and the Fury* is a finely drawn black character. Faulkner does not sentimentalize him. He is not the Jim of *Huckleberry Finn.* He treats Benjy with a mix of care and cruelty—as you would expect almost any young child to do with a retarded man, the only grown-up whom he can boss around and treat cruelly without fear of retaliation. Faulkner is moving here to see Luster as a real child, akin to the cruelty and yearning in children as they are. We cannot treat any race or ethnic group fairly in fiction unless we deliver good and bad characters in that group. It is not a reality that allows blacks to make great plans for the future. It is a reality that lets them survive day by day.

THE SOUND AND THE FURY

Now let's work our way more completely into *The Sound and the Fury*. The first important quality to recognize about the book, I think, is that it is a long tone poem and that to make any sense of it, we have to read it over and over. As we understand slowly what is happening, we realize that Faulkner introduces the story to us in the same way that the details of life are given to us as we live, and that to make sense of life we must go back over its details again and again to think about cause and effect and meaning. I believe that the sense of the book is implicit in the title. It is, of course, from Shakespeare's *Macbeth*, the soliloquy where Macbeth declares that "Life's but a walking shadow. [. . .] / [. . .] a tale / Told by an idiot, full of sound and fury, / Signifying nothing" (V.v.24, 26–28). Faulkner gives us the idiot in Benjy Compson. And in a great tour de force Faulkner gets inside Benjy's head.

Detail by detail the story unfolds and creates for us the decline of an old southern family. As I have already said, the Compsons have never been much. In the Appendix he wrote for the book in 1945—long after the original inspiration had left him—Faulkner called Jason "Jason IV" and described him as "the first sane Compson since before Culloden and (a childless bachelor) hence the last" ("Appendix Compson 1699–1945" in *The Sound and the Fury* 233). Culloden was the battle—rather a massacre—in Scotland in 1746 when the Scots were slaughtered by the English. The Scots were trying to put the grandson of James II on the throne of England—or perhaps trying to separate Scotland from England. The English army slaughtered them in a battle that lasted forty minutes, and the whole enterprise of Bonnie Prince Charlie, the Pretender in whose name the Scots fought, became a symbol of madcap romance. Faulkner implies that Jason is sane because he has no romance. And he is obviously the last of the Compson men because Quentin has killed himself. So we have in *The Sound and the Fury* the loss of a family, and since a southern family of aristocratic myth reproduces itself and therefore produces genealogy, the end of the Compson family is oblivion, and their genealogy finally signifies nothing. When Faulkner provided that strange "Appendix" of 1945, he created a genealogy, seeing the Compsons as the natural outgrowth and chancy proliferation of a clan doomed, as he says, to longevity, the assumption being that all the males had their eyes lifted up to eternal fame and so could not bother themselves with the necessary trivia of the daily life and so neglected the soundest of all proverbs, that God is in the details.

Jason is unlike any of his romantic forebears in that he does care for the details. His world is all tied up with money. It's striking that from Jason we get precise amounts of money. He has supposedly paid Earl one thousand dollars to go into business with him in a hardware store. The prejudice in the old South against the money grubber, the person in trade, is intense. But Jason goes into it with a certain skill and, throughout his parts of the book, shows how much he knows about precise amounts. He is a cheat. He has not put the thousand dollars in Earl's business. He has apparently used the thousand dollars to buy him a car. Even as a child, Jason is the treasurer of a partnership making kites and selling them for a nickel apiece (58). And he is probably stealing the money. He speculates in cotton futures, steals from Quentin, the daughter of Candace, because he feels that so much wrong has been done to him that he has the right to do wrong to others. His father sold part of the Compson land to a golf course so Quentin could go to Harvard. But as he repeatedly says, no one has sold land to let him go anywhere, and he feels a continual sense of grievance about life. The sense of grievance makes him apparently care nothing at all about who loves him. While Quentin and Candace and Benjy and Quentin, who is the daughter, all wrestle with some form or other of love, Jason is content to get his love from prostitutes. Love is a commodity. One pays, and one gets all one wants. That seems to be part of Faulkner's intent here. Jason is "the first sane Compson since before Colloden" because he cares nothing at all about feelings.

Faulkner continually doubles in his novels. The pairing of opposite characters is one of the qualities that give his novels form. In *Flags in the Dust* we see the contrast between Bayard Sartoris and Horace Benbow. We see the minor contrast between Loosh Peabody and the cold doctor Alford, old medical practice and new, scientific medical practice, between Aunt Jenny du Pre and Narcissa Benbow.

In *The Sound and the Fury* we see the doubling in all sorts of ways. Quentin the brother of Caddy lusts after his sister and dreams back on her virginal innocence. Yet on the day that he decides he will kill himself he falls in with a young Italian girl who follows him, and Quentin does his best to be rid of her, and she won't go. All the time Quentin is with her, his mind darts back to being with Caddy. But whereas Caddy left him for Dalton Ames and for who knows how many other lovers, the little Italian girl sticks with Quentin, who is delayed in his own intended suicide because he cannot get rid of her. And just as Quentin has accosted Dalton Ames, the little Italian girl's brother Julio accosts Quentin. But whereas Quentin was entirely ineffectual, Julio succeeds in beating Quentin and redeeming his sister—who like Caddy has seen nothing wrong with being with a man from "outside," a stranger. And doubtless the most important doubling in the book is that Benjy and Quentin are both obsessed with love for Caddy. Benjy loves her purely. She is the only person who truly loves him. Quentin loves her in a perverted, mad way because he represents the honor of the family and therefore the worth of his own identity. Quentin might be cured if he could just run off and become a rootless Hemingway character.

Gerald Bland is also a doubling, a rich young Harvard student with a possessive mother, an ability to fight, and a success with women of which he boasts relentlessly—all approved by his mother, a woman utterly unlike the withdrawn Caroline Compson in personality but much like her in values.

Faulkner is always doing this sort of thing, doubling characters so that we are forced to look at them more carefully to see what it is he wants us to see. It is a pattern of repetition akin to the repetitions in his words, his style, a repetition that says to us, "This is important, and I am going to tell you this again and again so you can see how important it is." And as I never tire of saying, Faulkner's repetitions are part of the pattern of life.

Another of his repetitions is the almost casual way that women treat sex when compared with men—unless, of course, the man is someone like Jason, who sees sex entirely as biological release and who never has any intention of having a child to carry on the Compson line. Quentin is obsessed with the notion that sex and love are the same thing. He seems to imagine that when Dalton Ames seduces Caddy, he has interposed his love, Dalton's instead of Quentin's. But for both Dalton Ames and for Caddy, sex is nothing much more than recreation. We get some idea that Quentin has taken his ideas of sex from his mother, Mrs. Compson, who is surely the most truly reprehensible person in the novel.

Jason speaking of his mother says:

> how the hell can I do anything right, with that dam family and her not
> making any effort to control her nor any of them like that time when
> she happened to see one of them kissing Caddy and all next day she
> went around the house in a black dress and a veil and even Father
> couldn't get her to say a word except crying and saying her little
> daughter was dead and Caddy about fifteen then only in three years
> she'd been wearing haircloth or probably sandpaper at that rate. (138)

Everything to the Compsons is an either/or. If Caddy does not live up to the grand expectations of a southern lady, she is not a member of the family at all. If Benjy is not worthy of being a Bascomb, his name must be changed. And if Quentin cannot possess Caddy and cannot stop thinking of her body and the honor it represents, he must kill himself.

Jason makes fun of his mother, seeing her as the saint who must suffer for the sins of her daughter. She's going to take on the ascetic practices of the medieval monks, wearing a coarse shirt of hair next to her skin to mortify the flesh, and Jason carries it much further and suggests that Mrs. Compson may start wearing sandpaper. She feels it her responsibility not to love any of her children but to suffer painfully and more or less in public because she thinks Caddy has brought disgrace down on the whole family.

Throughout all the Compson clan we find a passion for respectability that crushes any attention to the individual. Mr. Compson wanted his wife to let Caddy come home after Caddy's husband, Herbert, threw her out into the street, but Mrs. Compson, with her passion for the appearance of respectability, will not permit it. Yet we see the reality that Faulkner reasserts in many diverse ways. Neither the Compsons nor the Bascombs have any respectability at all. It's all done with mirrors and manipulation. Maury Bascomb is a drunk, a womanizer, and futile beyond all the telling. But when Benjy is born, he is named Maury, and then when it is discovered that Benjy is an idiot, the name is changed to have no family significance whatsoever.

Again this is a repetition because in *Flags in the Dust* Narcissa Benbow refuses to give her son any of the traditional names that have been typical of the Sartoris clan. She calls him Benbow Sartoris. Miss Jenny is amazed. "'And do you think that'll do any good,' Miss Jenny demanded. 'Do you think you can change one of 'em with a name?'" (432). *Flags in the Dust* ends on a grand crescendo of prose, probably overwritten, intended to make us feel some sort of tragic grandeur in the dead and remote ideals of chivalry that the Sartoris clan has tried to embody: we are tools in the hand of God.

> The music went on in the dusk; the dust was peopled with ghosts of glamorous and old disastrous things. And if they were just glamorous enough, there would be a Sartoris in them, and then they were sure to be disastrous. Pawns. But the Player and the game He plays—who knows? He must have a name for his pawns, though, but perhaps Sartoris is the name of the game itself—a game outmoded and played with pawns shaped too late and to an old dead pattern, and of which the Player Himself is a little wearied. For there is death in the sound of it, and a glamorous fatality, like silver pennons downrushing at sunset, or a dying fall of horns along the road to Roncevaux. (*Flags in the Dust* 432–33)

With *The Sound and the Fury* the mood is decidedly darker. It is as if Faulkner had examined the suicidal tendencies of young John and Bayard Sartoris and found their glamor and gallantry wanting and translated that death wish to a whole family and made a deliberate effort to take all the glamor away. In this conclusion to *Flags in the Dust*, we have one of the most explicit references to God that we have in all of Faulkner—the God of destiny who destroys men so that even in their destruction, somehow the grandeur of human life is exhibited. These are Shakespearean heroes who demonstrate their manhood by showing their contempt for death. Something in these characters, the Sartoris clan, seems to shout at me the recollection of the seventeenth-century English poet Richard Lovelace.

To Lucasta, on Going to the Wars

Tell me not (sweet) I am unkinde,
    That from the Nunnerie
Of thy chaste breast, and quiet minde,
    To Warre and Armes I flie.

True; a new Mistresse now I chase,
    The first foe in the Field;
And with a stronger Faith imbrace
    A Sword, a Horse, a Shield.

Yet this Inconstancy is such,
    As you too shall adore;
I could not love thee (Deare) so much,
    Lov'd I not Honour more.

But now the Player is tired of the game, and chivalry is over. When we come to Quentin Compson in the terrible loneliness of his fate before he kills himself at Harvard, we have no sense of a God directing the drama to show the tragic destiny of humankind. Faulkner seems to want us to believe that something exalted demonstrated itself in the fates of the Sartoris twins. I said earlier that the death wish of young Bayard Sartoris is not enough for me to see his fate as tragic. But I am not sure that Faulkner shared that view. He believed in tragedy.

In Quentin Compson's fate the god of the piece has become time, and the motivation for Quentin's suicide is his fatal longing for the body of his sister Caddy. Quentin himself is the obverse of a chivalric figure. I suspect he was named for Quentin Durward, in Sir Walter Scott's novel of that name, published in 1823 and always a favorite among southerners. Southerners loved Scott and his tales of chivalry so much that Mark Twain blamed Scott for the Civil War. Durward was made a Scottish archer in the service of Louis XI of France. He is a person of sterling bravery and honor, and he finally wins his true love, the Countess Isabelle de Croye, by saving her from many dangers and by demonstrating his great heart and his courage and his honor. Quentin in Faulkner's *The Sound and the Fury* is the opposite of everything represented by Quentin Durward. Quentin Durward saves Isabelle de Croye from marriage to Count Campo-Bosso and kills another rival, William de la Marck.

And it's worth pointing out the immense interest in chivalry in the South in the nineteenth century: the tombstone over the grave of William Alexander Percy in Greenville, replica of one in England showing the knight in armor; the tombstone in the cedar grove of Faulkner's own cemetery.

But then later on Faulkner, in his Appendix written in 1945, said that Quentin "loved not his sister's body but some concept of Compson honor precariously and (he knew well) only temporarily supported by the minute fragile membrane of her maidenhead as a miniature replica of all the whole vast globy earth may be poised on the nose of a trained seal" (229). It is as though Faulkner trivializes Quentin's suffering, himself the author finding it mad, Quentin reading into Caddy's body all the romantic notions that a man in fantasy can pour into the body of a woman he desires. When I read Quentin and read Faulkner about Quentin and when I read about the Compson family's obsession with respectability—the appearance of respectability—I see Quentin driven by that chimera, that destroying and mythological delusion, but I see something else. I see Darwin and Freud coming together in Quentin's mind. He has no fear of God that I can see, no sense that when he has a shuffled off this mortal coil the thoughts of what dreams may come must give him pause.

Time is another force that defeats the ineffectual Quentin. Not only does time make all values worthless because none of them is absolute; once time passes, it is irrevocable, but memory plays time again and again in our heads as though to mock us for what we might have done if only we had had the wit or the courage. It removes the impulsive way of our actions and replaces impulse with contemplation when contemplation is too late.

Quentin is driven apparently by the same sense of family that drives his mother and Jason, and Caddy lies at the center of it. One may ask this question: suppose Caddy takes sex as casually as she seems to take it, acting like a dog in heat and attracting men indiscriminately? What if she said to Quentin, "What's the big deal? Let's go to bed?"

Darwin held that human beings are a higher form of animal—higher only in that our brains give us a superior capacity to survive. Freud held that our most fundamental desires are sex and death, that we sublimate our sexual desire and create civilization. But in the figure of Caddy, she seems to use sex as a tool and does not sublimate anything. Caddy seems willing to do anything to get out of that family, and who can blame her? But there is something else about Caddy. She seems to like sex, going against the nineteenth-century Victorian mentality that a *lady* does not like sex. Faulkner has Quentin use animal metaphors, speaking of the boy met at a track and field meet in high school probably: "That pimple-faced infant she met at the field-meet with colored ribbons. Skulking along the fence trying to whistle her out like a puppy" (57). So if sex is for Caddy only an animal impulse, what happens to all the other values that human beings have assembled into this mysterious and fragile thing called civilization? What is it to be human? Here is Quentin caught in the either/or dilemma that I have mentioned earlier as part of the Compson fate: either we are human beings with a set of absolute values founded on something absolute, something more firm than convenience, or else we are nothing.

Quentin is painfully and terribly aware of the immediate sensations of life, of consciousness. And yet he is unable to live without some great, over-reaching abstraction that gives an absolute value to life, an absolute meaning to all the values wrapped up in all the restrictions of civilization. Quentin's father tells him: "you are confusing sin and morality women dont do that your mother is thinking of morality whether it be sin or not has not occurred to her" (62). "Morality" here is only appearance, and if we can get away from the eyes of the world and get away with incest, what does it mean to be humans?

Faulkner had a hankering to create tragedy with Quentin. Quentin is crushed by fate, and his fate is his inability to live in a world where there are no values, no right and wrong. It seems an unworthy tragedy to the more worldly among us. But that may be that most of us have become like

Jason, so filled with business, with being busy, that we do not come to terms with the great issues of life. We do not even think much about them. We fill our lives with the real opiate of the people—which is being busy. And yet Quentin does think about them. He contemplates the heart of darkness and dies because he sees the horror, the horror.

In some respects the whole book comes to a climax in the last scene. Luster, driving Benjy into the square, starts to the left, and Benjy begins to bawl, to roar. It is Jason who leaps into the carriage—not one of those newfangled automobiles, not even a new 1928 Model A Ford, for it is 1928, and the automobile has been around for a long time. But the Compsons are still in a carriage, and Luster drives it to the left. Ben protests. Jason restores the appearances. The carriage goes to the right

 trapped in time

> With a backhanded blow he hurled Luster aside and caught the reins and sawed Queenie about and doubled the reins back and slashed her across the hips. He cut her again, into a plunging gallop, while Ben's hoarse agony roared about them, and swung her about to the right of the monument. Then he struck Luster over the head with his fist.
>
> "Dont you know any better than to take him to the left?" he said. He reached back and struck Ben, breaking the flower stalk again. "Shut up!" he said. "Shut up!" He jerked Queenie back and jumped down. "Get to hell on home with him. If you ever cross that gate with him again, I'll kill you!"
>
> "Yes, suh!" Luster said. He took the reins and hit Queenie with the end of them. "Git up! Git up, dar! Benjy, fer God's sake!"
>
> Ben's voice roared and roared. Queenie moved again, her feet began to clip-clop steadily again, and at once Ben hushed. Luster looked quickly back over his shoulder, then he drove on. The broken flower drooped over Ben's fist and his eyes were empty and blue and serene again as cornice and facade flowed smoothly once more from left to right, post and tree, window and doorway and signboard each in its ordered place. (191)

The impulse towards circularity is here in Faulkner, the circle being a traditional symbol of both time and life itself, a repetition that has no ulti-mate moral value. In the end of *Flags in the Dust* Faulkner speaks of *The Player*, a God who may be tired of the game played at chivalry by the Sartoris men. Now the moral values of life and chivalric civilization seem to be mindless, a tale told by an idiot and symbolizing nothing. "Benjy, fer God's sake," Luster shouts. So, is God simply making us suffer for completely arbitrary reasons? Are any of the sexual taboos more than sound and fury?

It's all arbitrary. Yet Benjy the idiot is used to it. To go to the right represents order. And he is content not because right is right but because it is traditional. It has always been this way. Just like the rest of civilization, it looks familiar because it has always been this way. Quentin's moral problem that has made him kill himself is nothing but an arbitrary decision of society that has become familiar and thus orderly through long use. Jason the sane Compson has restored them.

A note about Benjy as Christ figure: the issue comes up frequently in discussions of Joe Christmas. And it is evident in Faulkner's novel *A Fable*. It's hard to know what to make of symbolic uses of Christ in Faulkner. I don't believe that he was religious in the conventional Protestant or Catholic sense. He seems to use the Christ figure to see how far innocence can be pushed. We have no trouble seeing that Benjy is an innocent. But how far can Joe Christmas be innocent? How far do violence and innocence come together? To what point can we be sympathetic with the violent man or woman and feel that despite his violence, he or she has been misjudged or mistreated? Just how bad can someone be before we are unwilling to see Christ in him?

[handwritten margin note: repetition of time, trapped]

AS I LAY DYING

WILLIAM FAULKNER

AUTHOR OF

THE SOUND

AND THE FURY

AS I LAY DYING

And now we turn to one of Faulkner's finest novels, *As I Lay Dying*, published in 1930, during the remarkable period when Faulkner published five
novels in four years. It is important to say first about *As I Lay Dying* that
all apart from the *meaning* of the novel, it is, as Cleanth Brooks declared,
"a triumph in the management of tone" (141). It was written in forty-seven
days (Gray 151)! The title comes from Homer's *Odyssey*, the same book that
inspired James Joyce to write *Ulysses* in the years after World War I. And
it has affinities with *The Waste Land* of T. S. Eliot. All three of these works
testify to the lost generation mentality that questioned all values and that
left the survivors of the war more aware than ever that life was haunted
by death and that there was no real meaning to any of it.

Both Faulkner and Joyce took as their starting point Odysseus's journey down into the land of the dead. All the shades Odysseus meets in the
world beyond the grave are impotent. They cannot touch each other. They
try. But their bodies simply pass through one another as though there were
nothing there. Agamemnon speaks:

> [. . .] 'twas Aegisthus wrought
> My death and doom, and slew me with the aid
> Of my accursed wife, when he had bidden me
> Unto his house and made a feast for me,
> E'en as a man will slay an ox at stall.

[. . .]

[. . .] But in mine ears
Most piteous rang the cry of Priam's daughter,
Cassandra, whom the treacherous Clytemnestra
Slew at my side, while I, as I lay dying
Upon the sword, raised up my hands to smite her;
And shamelessly she turned away, and scorned
To draw my eyelids down or close my mouth,
Though I was on the road to Hades' house.
So, true it is, no thing can be more awful
Or shameless than a woman who lays up
Such thoughts of wickedness within her mind,
E'en as she too devised a monstrous deed,
Her wedded husband's murder [. . .]. (Book XI)

But I am not at all sure that Faulkner means any more by this title than a general reference to family disloyalty. The Bundrens, man and wife, have no feeling for one another, and their family hangs together only from inertia, not from any true bond of love. Addie seems to love Jewel more than the others because he is her son by the minister, Whitfield, the only spontaneous thing she seems ever to have done.

We have here Faulkner's fourth novel out of his first five that dwell at length on death—the death of at least one major character and the effect that death has on others. Death seems to brood in Faulkner as the force that stirs the rest of the book to life. None of these people except Vardaman seems to be crushed by Addie's death, although Darl is affected by it. Some of the characters seem almost relieved by it. Dewey Dell will get to go to town. Anse will get new teeth. Jewel—it's difficult to know what will happen to him, and Cash seems so utterly absorbed in the mechanical process of making first a coffin and then a trip that he manages to fend off thoughts of death altogether.

The most powerful image in *As I Lay Dying* is the stench of Addie's body, the horror that it causes as the coffin-laden wagon moves through the countryside. This is an image from the Middle Ages, the Renaissance— the *memento mori*—for no matter what glory and grandeur we ascend, we ultimately become food for worms. The novel has as much religion in it as any work of Faulkner's—and religion is impotent against death. Once again it seems to me that a Darwinian impulse is at work here.

Faulkner seems determined to tell us that his characters have little hope for a life after death. Throughout the book death seems devoid of any real Christian hope. Cora notes Addie's pride and says, "Her eyes are like two candles when you watch them gutter down into the sockets of iron candle-sticks, but the eternal and the everlasting salvation and grace is not upon her" (8). But only a little while before, Cora says that for three weeks she has been going to visit Addie, who lies on her death bed, so Addie "would not have to face the Great Unknown without one familiar face to give her courage" (22). Later when Cora recalls wrestling with Addie to bring her to God, Addie says, "I know my own sin. I know that I deserve my punishment. I do not begrudge it" (167). Addie has a stoic resignation towards whatever comes. Cora sounds like a woman caught, as most religious people are, in the twilight zone between faith and doubt. God is to be feared. He is God the judge, God the avenger of sin. But can He do anything to help? And at a certain moment Addie says to Cora, "He is my cross, and he will be my salvation. He will save me from the water and the fire. Even though I have laid down my life, he will save me" (168). Cora realizes suddenly with horror that Addie is not talking about God; she is talking about Jewel. All this works out because Jewel does save her body from the river and from the burning barn. It is like many a scene in Shakespeare where the characters receive omens that they do not understand from oracles, and we are left to watch the strange means by which prophecy is surprisingly fulfilled. So here Addie has the look of one of the Greek oracles, such as the one at Delphi, and we feel ourselves in the hands of fate.

The theme here is the wasteland where feeling is constricted and warped and sometimes devoid of any kind of love. Life is a meaningless circle, as in the buzzards in Darl's speech: "Motionless, the tall buzzards hang in soaring circles, the clouds giving them an illusion of retrograde" (95). It seems again to be the myth of the eternal return, and yet in the Greek myths that return has a hope to it. The green of spring will always come after winter's death.

We may see a glimmer of hope in Cora. She may be the Koré of the ancient Greek myth of Demeter and Persephone. Koré is the virgin raped by Hades but allowed to return to her mother earth six months a year. If such a relation is intended for Cora, it has to be loosely construed because Koré was a virgin—though she seems not to have remained so. We may assume perhaps that Cora represents the continual reassertion of the ordinary life after the death of one member of the community. It may or may not be symbolic that Cora is preoccupied with eggs when we meet her. The eggs are the Greek symbol of life, endlessly repeated on the Greek symbol of the egg and the arrow, of life and of death. Cora will have her eggs no matter what. They provide her the barter by which she can get other things to make cakes. Addie is by far the more interesting figure both because her fate lies at the heart of the novel and because she is a mother who seems to care little for her children. In her we see the mate of Mrs. Compson in *The Sound and the Fury*, both of them mothers who deprive their children of love.

And one can even point to a similarity between Caddy and Addie. No matter that Faulkner called Caddy his heart's darling. She abandoned her daughter Quentin to Jason and went off to save herself at young Quentin's expense. She does not mother her daughter, and one can ask if she does not imitate, replicate her own mother's abandonment of her. Addie in a similar way abandons poor Dewey Dell to Rafe and to pregnancy, and in her efforts to get an abortion, something to get rid of the baby growing inside her, Dewey Dell seems ready to repeat the cycle that appears to go on and on.

We meet Addie in her one soliloquy when she is a teacher who after school can dismiss the children. She must teach and then "go down the hill to the spring where I could be quiet and hate them" (169). It's a reversal of expected roles. The stereotypical teacher is supposed to love her children, and the female goddess in Greek mythology (or muse) is supposed to be a kind spirit at springs giving good things to anyone who comes. Addie hates life: "I would hate my father for having ever planted me" (170). And of the children she says, "I would look forward to the time when they faulted so I could whip them" (170). She seems to have no mother instinct. She has no living relatives. All of them are in the graveyard—in Jefferson. And in the end in a final abandonment, she will not be buried in New Hope where all her children and Anse will most probably be buried. She will insist on being taken back to Jefferson to lie with her dead family. When Cash the first-born came, she saw him as violating her aloneness. She cannot touch her children with an embrace. She can touch them only with a switch.

Addie hates the words that bind, the abstractions. When Cash came, Addie

> knew that living was terrible and that this was the answer to it. That was when I learned that words are no good; that words dont ever fit even what they are trying to say at. When he was born I knew that motherhood was invented by someone who had to have a word for it because the ones that had the children didn't care whether there was a word for it or not. (171–72)

The message here is not unlike that of *The Sound and the Fury*, where all our values, especially our sexual values, are arbitrary traditions repeated again and again so that their very familiarity seems to give them meaning. But when we examine them, we discover that they have no absolute value. They are words based on other words, and the relentless repetition of those words makes it seem that they have meaning when they do not: "And that sin and love and fear are just sounds that people who never sinned nor loved nor feared have for what they never had and cannot have until they forget the words" (*As I Lay Dying*, 173–74).

Words throughout the book have a terrible ability to make things go wrong. And they cannot reflect reality. Addie seems to be in agony because she is a prisoner of words that cannot begin to capture the reality of being a mother or the reality of being the wife of Anse Bundren. But those who do place faith in language often find themselves deluded by their misguided beliefs in language's controlling power. Anse repeatedly announces, "I give her my promised word" (111) to justify a journey which costs Jewel a horse, Cash a leg, and Darl his freedom. Cora worries about losing the cost of the eggs that went into the cakes, for it was on her "say-so" that they bought the hens (5). Her daughter Kate resents the lady who changes her mind about buying them, insisting, "She ought to taken those cakes when she same as gave you her word" (6). This comic undercutting of the power of the word reveals Faulkner's skepticism regarding language's ability to represent "truth" and delineate human experience, reflecting his modernist agenda and tying him to another great modernist practitioner, Robert Frost. Whitfield's attempt to "frame" the words of his confession conjures up the final lines of Frost's "Oven Bird": "The Question that he frames in all but words / Is what to make of a diminished thing" (Clarke 37). Addie, like Narcissa Benbow Sartoris, has no faith in the abstractions of words. And Addie takes vengeance on Anse by having her affair with Brother Whitfield—vengeance because Anse has died, that as Dr. Peabody (who is eighty-seven in *Flags in the Dust*, seventy in *As I Lay Dying*) says:

> I can remember how when I was young I believed death to be a phenomenon of the body; now I know it to be merely a function of the mind—and that of the minds of the ones who suffer the bereavement. The nihilists say it is the end; the fundamentalists, the beginning; when in reality it is no more than a single tenant or family moving out of a tenement or a town. (43–44)

Anse "did not know that he was dead," in Addie's words (173) and therefore had no idea of how he corrupted everyone around him. His death is a reality as powerful as the smell of Addie's corpse, and yet almost everyone is accustomed to it. The name "Anse" has perhaps some affinity to the southern word "hants" for ghosts. If an "h" can disappear in the unpredictable ways that "h" comes and goes in southern dialects, Anse may be a name that describes a phantom life.

But in the tale of life and death, Faulkner seems to give us a reverse parody on the story of Eve and her fall as recorded in the book of Genesis:

> Now the serpent was more subtil than any beast of the field which the Lord God had made. And he said unto the woman, Yea, hath God said, Ye shall not eat of every tree of the garden? [. . .] For God doth know that in the day ye eat thereof, then your eyes shall be opened, and ye shall be as gods, knowing good and evil. And when the woman saw that the tree was good for food, and that it was pleasant to the eyes, and a tree to be desired to make one wise, she took the fruit and did eat, and gave also unto her husband with her: and he did eat. (Genesis 3:1, 5–6)

When Addie looks back on her life, speaking after she is dead, the only thing that she does not regret is her affair with Whitfield. She has discovered that the only way to be human is to sin, and she feels that life itself is punishment.

> I believed that I had found it. I believed that the reason was the duty to the alive, to the terrible blood, the red bitter flood boiling through the land. I would think of sin as I would think of the clothes we both wore in the world's face, of the circumspection necessary because he was he and I was I; the sin the more utter and terrible since he was the instrument ordained by God who created the sin, to sanctify what sin He had created. While I waited for him in the woods, waiting for him before he saw me, I would think of him as dressed in sin. I would think of him as thinking of me as dressed also in sin, he the more beautiful since the garment which he had exchanged for sin was sanctified. I would think of the sin as garments which we would remove in order to shape and coerce the terrible blood to the forlorn echo of the dead word high in the air. Then I would lay with Anse again—I did not lie to him: I just refused, just as I refused my breast to Cash and Darl after their time was up—hearing the dark land talking the voiceless speech. (174–75)

Note that God created the sin! That is Calvinism, the notion that for His own pleasure God did everything. Addie demands freedom, a kind of existential moment, and she finds it in a willingness to be free of God or at least of the concept of God. Cleanth Brooks has written that the principal theme of the book may be "the nature of the heroic deed" (142–43). If so, Addie is the most heroic of all.

Throughout this course I have argued that Faulkner continually assumed popular myths as though he were observing some vulgar religion held by the unseeing masses and dissected those myths by attacking them with other myths, myths from the ancient and primitive worlds where a more innocent or at least a less artificial breed of men and women went to nature and the subconscious to explain a chaotic world and to impose on that world some sort of meaning, meaning that would make the world more predictable and therefore more comfortable.

The popular myths that Faulkner relentlessly assaults are those held by authority and pushed by authority onto the populace at large, or else they are myths adopted by the populace at large as a means of evading reality. Faulkner's novels—like the novels of almost any great writer—create a world of the imagination where authority is continually undermined by the "reality" of the work of art. It is hard to have a great novel (I think) that merely affirms the values and the view of reality that authorities such as government, established religion, and public opinion think that we should all have. Fundamentalists of any religion do not write great novels. Neither do politicians. It is, on the contrary, completely in the stream of American life that presidential candidates and other politicians denounce the arts for violence, for obscenity, for blasphemy, and for a lack of concern for family values. Art that attempts to uphold all the values of its time may strut and fret its hour on the stage, but in time it usually dies away. Real art affronts, condemns, mocks, and ultimately raises doubts about the values of *hoi polloi* and the eternal forces of order. The United States offers a rich and wide province for the writer, the artist, the photographer just because our puritanical heritage has been transmogrified into such a hyperventilated self-righteousness in our public and political life that the artist has so much to undermine. And as Pat Buchanan has declared again and again, we are indeed locked in a cultural war in this country and see the evidence of this conflict every time we have a presidential election.

And as I have said repeatedly, the great artists and the great writers in this country have been rebels against the self-righteous and hypocrisy of American official culture, and since we are without any doubt the most self-righteous and the most hypocritical of any of the great industrial nations, our writers and our artists have immense opportunities for greatness. (I should scarcely have to say that mere protest and the mere desire to undermine do not make for greatness. Otherwise, Ross Perot and Ralph Nader and a host of others would be great artists, and they manifestly are not.)

So here Faulkner delivers a delicious ultimate symbol of the writer's calling, a poor white crowd of family members carrying a rotting and stinking corpse across a rainsoaked landscape and affronting the entire community. The rituals of religion require us to pretty up the corpse, to make it look "natural," which is to say "asleep," and to get it into the ground or else into the fires of cremation before it begins to stink and to remind us all of the animal nature of our being and the inevitability of our mortality. Many people in Faulkner's novels find themselves in various states of denial. The greatest denial of all is the denial of death, the denial of the kind of beings that we truly are. And the community is outraged because its illusions are thrown in its face and shattered in a cloud of stench.

Again I return to one of the themes that I find persistent in Faulkner—his assertion of simple Darwinism against the illusions of the social Darwinists. As I have said, the social Darwinists of the later nineteenth century were captivated by the term "the survival of the fittest." This term was, I think, coined by Herbert Spencer, a British philosopher, who made the "fittest" those most fit to rule others. But as I have said before, the "fittest" in pure Darwinist thought are merely those who survive. Life itself is the aim of nature—not glory. We see throughout the novel that Anse Bundren is a parasite. Yet he survives. We want him to come to a bad end. But he triumphs. He manages to be a complete failure in everything but succeeding in getting other people to do his work. Anse claims that if he sweats, he will die. Anse will avoid all work, as if he were avoiding also the biblical curse on humankind: For in Genesis 3:17–19 God says to Adam,

> cursed is the ground for thy sake; in sorrow shalt thou eat of it all the days of thy life; Thorns also and thistles shall it bring forth to thee; and thou shalt eat the herb of the field; In the sweat of thy face shalt thou eat bread, till thou return unto the ground; for out of it wast thou taken: for dust thou art and unto dust shalt thou return.

Anse has an excuse for everything. Sometimes he blames his troubles on the rich profiteers who profit from the farmers. "Nowhere in this sinful world can a honest, hardworking man profit. It takes them that runs the stores in the towns, doing no sweating, living off of them that sweats" (110). Yet we know that Anse does not sweat and that by some strange enchantment he has managed to get other men in his community to do his work for him. Then at the last of this brief speech he manages to shift the burden of his cares from storekeepers and (we presume) other capitalists. He discovers the bridge out at Samson's store. And he says, "I am the chosen of the Lord, for who He loveth, so doeth He chastises. But I be durn if He don't take some curious ways to show it, seems like" (111).

As we might expect, Anse is inept in quoting scripture. The verse he cites is Hebrews 12:6–8:

> For whom the Lord loveth he chasteneth, and scourgeth every son
> whom he receiveth. If ye endure chastening, God dealeth with you
> as with sons; for what son is he whom the father chasteneth not?
> But if ye be without chastisement whereof all are partakers then are
> ye bastards and not sons.

I suspect that Faulkner's allusion to this scripture may be a key to Anse in a couple of ways. On the one hand, it is a traditional means of explaining how a loving God can allow bad things, even terrible things, to happen to His people. God in the Bible—both in the Hebrew Bible and the New Testament—punishes His own so that He may elevate them to a higher level of grace or mercy. In that framework all the bad things that happen to us are sources of testing to see if we are worthy, and we are supposed to accept the bad with a trusting heart. All this in a psychological way keeps us from losing faith in God when we experience apparently meaningless suffering. We may not understand it, but God does.

All that is part of the Calvinism of fatalism by which so many of the poor in the South live out their lives. What is to be will be. *Qué será será.* It is a resignation that may lead to the laziness and inertia that we find in Anse. But we find that same sort of resignation before Providence in others. In Tull's speech about Addie's funeral, we find Faulknerian italics that seem to reflect the voice of the community ruminating about fate as applied to the growing of crops—a realm where the humors of the gods have mysteriously displayed themselves for as long as agriculture has existed. Who can control the weather on which all crops depend?

> *I don't mind the folks falling. It's the cotton and corn I mind.*
> *Neither does Peabody mind the folks falling. How bout it, Doc?*
> *It's a fact. Washed clean outen the ground it will be. Seems like*
> *something is always happening to it.*
> *Course it does. That's why it's worth anything. If nothing didn't*
> *happen and everybody made a big crop, do you reckon it would be*
> *worth the raising?*
> *Well, I be durn if I like to see my work washed outen the ground,*
> *work I sweat over.*
> *It's a fact. A fellow wouldn't mind seeing it washed up if he could*
> *just turn on the rain himself.*
> *Who is the man can do that? Where is the color of his eyes?*
> *Ay. The Lord made it to grow. It's Hisn to wash up if He sees it*
> *fitten so.* (90–91)

This passage, spoken by Tull and Peabody or perhaps Tull and others at Addie's funeral, is almost pure agricultural religion—a dependence on the gods, a feeling of impotence before their mysterious whims. And it may or may not be important that, in some planting and harvest festivals, a woman is sacrificed to assure survival.

At any rate we find a fatalism all through the book. These characters see everything in the hand of God. Whitfield seems hypocritical to us when he bursts out with rejoicing and thanks God that Addie has died and there-fore left him absolved of the requirement that he confess his sin to Anse and ask for forgiveness. He has expected Addie to have confessed her sins, an old idea that goes back at least to the Middle Ages and probably beyond when confession was made to a priest and necessary if the dying person was to have any hope of gaining paradise. In the Protestant tradition of the priesthood of all believers, confession could be made to anyone, but most particularly it was to be made to the person against whom the sin was com-mitted. So Addie could be expected to confess to her husband her adultery, and the fact that she does not is as clear a sign as we have that she has no fear of the life after death and probably no belief in it. She dies proudly silent about her "sins," dies in her satisfaction at secret revenge against a husband she detests.

So when Whitfield comes on the scene, he knows that his secret is safe, that he can continue being a minister, and that no one will suspect that he has sinned with the dead woman. And like all the other characters who say anything about God, he takes God to be a fatal force that directs life so that we poor mortals are only tools in the divine hand.

Whitfield:

> I have sinned, O Lord. Thou knowest the extent of my remorse and the will of my spirit. But He is merciful; He will accept the will for the deed, Who knew that when I framed the words of my confession it was to Anse I spoke them, even though he was not there. It was He in His infinite wisdom that restrained the tale from her dying lips as she lay surrounded by those who loved and trusted her; mine the travail by water which I sustained by the strength of His hand. Praise to Thee in Thy bounteous and omnipotent love; O praise.
>
> I entered the house of bereavement, the lowly dwelling where another erring mortal lay while her soul faced the awful and irrevo-cable judgment, peace to her ashes.
>
> "God's grace upon this house," I said. (179)

Well, as I have said before, we have more religion in this novel than in any other by Faulkner except the Christ-driven *A Fable*, where he went into metaphorical extremes to make a point about war and innocence. But the religion here seems to be a fatalism that blesses or blames God for everything, and it points to a notion of destiny that may be simply fatalism, a consolation of sorts that we cannot do anything to change our fate.

I have said on several occasions that Faulkner wrestles throughout his early novels with the tension, even the contradiction between consciousness and memory. Consciousness is the moment of now, always dissolving into the past, real but intangible and almost incapable of analysis. Memory is the way we shape consciousness into meaning, the pattern of a life. In consciousness we are free to make all sorts of decisions, do all sorts of things within our natural human and individual limitations. But memory has no real freedom. Memory repeats itself again and again, batters us, taunts us with the possibilities of what we or someone else might have done but did not. In contemplating memory we are likely to console ourselves with fatalism. I might have done this; things then would have been different. Things cannot be changed; therefore, they were meant to be.

Quentin in *The Sound and the Fury* is tormented by what might have been and must kill himself to keep the battering of memory from beating him to death. The Quentin figure in *As I Lay Dying* is Darl, who speaks more than any other character and who understands by a sort of oracular intuition that Jewel is a bastard son. His mother is a horse. Some critics see in the perception by Darl a reference to *Othello* where Iago shouts to Brabantio, "you'll have your daughter cover'd with a Barbary horse [. . .]" (I.i.111–12), referring to Othello, who is considered a sexual machine and an animal because he is black.

SANCTUARY

I think we have to turn now to Faulkner's next novel, *Sanctuary*, written in two versions, as he always claimed because he needed money. He said to one interviewer, "I made a thorough and methodical study of everything on the list of best-sellers. When I thought I knew what the public wanted, I decided to give them a little more than they had been getting; stronger and rawer—more brutal. Guts and genitals" (Blotner 233–34). His publisher [Hal Smith] first told him, "Good God, I can't publish this. We'd both be in jail" (Blotner 239).

But as critics have always noted, we have a lot more here than a horrific gothic tale of rape and other forms of violence.

As a kind of overview of the novel, I want to continue a discussion begun with the last lecture but in fact spreading across this course, and that is Faulkner's preoccupation with fate, predestination, or merely chance that directs these characters. At the close of our last hour I was speaking of the way that fatalism comforts people because it removes the weight of responsibility. If we are forced into something that has unpleasant consequences for ourselves or for others, we can absolve ourselves of guilt or some kinds of sorrow by saying that we did the best we could.

In the *City of God*, St. Augustine dealt with the problem of rape in the manner that was to become the standard Christian teaching. When Alaric and the Visigoths sacked Rome in 410, many Christian maidens were raped, and at a time when virginity was considered next to godliness, some of the rape victims killed themselves by drowning—perhaps a form of rebaptism. I don't know. St. Augustine told them that they should not kill themselves, that they were not responsible for what had been forced upon them, that their purity had not been compromised.

This tolerant assumption was inevitably to collide with the common western patriarchal notion that women were property and that the woman who had had unlawful sexual intercourse was damaged goods, no matter what the cause. Faulkner may have been driven to write a book to make money. But he had to work with his own genius, and the book inevitably became a moral examination of these two contrary ideological forces that have contended with each other for centuries.

Much of this novel turns on fate. These people feel themselves driven and imprisoned by forces which they cannot control. But as many critics have observed, the fate here is more like chance in the novels of Thomas Hardy than it is like the great, driving power of destiny in the Greeks and in Shakespeare. Let's examine this proposition for a moment.

The classic story of Greek fate is the story of Oedipus. An oracle, according to Sophocles, foretold that the baby about to come into the world would kill his father. The father, Laius, had the child exposed. In the story as Sophocles told it, the child was given to shepherds by the servant whom Laius had ordered to abandon the baby in the wilds. The shepherds took the boy to their childless king who raised him as his own son. Oedipus grew up, and for reasons that vary in the myths, he left the court of his stepfather and went wandering. He came upon Laius, some say, at a crossroads near Delphi on the road to Thebes. The two quarreled, and Oedipus killed this man whom he did not know to be his father. Shortly afterwards Oedipus answered the riddle of the sphinx, killed the sphinx, freed the Thebans, and married Jocasta—his mother. In the version of Sophocles, a plague then strikes Thebes, and the oracle of Delphi starts a train of circumstance that reveals that Oedipus has indeed killed his father and committed incest with his mother. Jocasta thereupon kills herself. Oedipus is banished and in some accounts is blinded and dies.

In the version by Sophocles, *Oedipus, the King*, Oedipus blinds himself immediately by snatching up the brooches from his wife's robe and driving them into his own eyes again and again:

> Till bloody tears rain down his beard—not drops
> But in a full spate a whole cascade descending
> In drenching cataracts of scarlet ruin.

It is a complex story, different in the tragedies from the more ancient stories in the epics. The tragic vision shows two qualities. We are in the hands of fate, the lap of the gods. Yet in the end fate conspires to punish those who break the moral taboos and by punishment to vindicate a code of morality for the world. This happens while the characters driven by fate fully join their wills in the process by which fate draws them along. Oedipus does not resist killing his father. He rushes fiercely to the act. His will is one with fate.

Two things happen in the Oedipus cycle. Oedipus himself is humbled and recognizes something grand about human existence—that our greatest pride must end in humility and that the most glorious of our qualities are not sufficient to keep us from suffering, pain, guilt, and death. The greatest of us must bow to forces that confound and destroy us. The young grow old, the strong become weak, the healthy sicken and die. All this is, as André Malraux had it in the title to his greatest book, *La Condition humaine*, man's fate.

But there is something else. The classical tragedy vindicates the moral principles by which society organizes itself. Classical tragedy is an affirmation of an absolute moral order.

That principle holds in Shakespeare. Desdemona is brought to her death by the accident of losing a handkerchief. Iago cunningly uses the lost handkerchief—which his wife Emilia has found—to deceive Othello into believing that Desdemona has betrayed him with young Cassio. Othello murders Desdemona, but when Emilia exposes her husband Iago's perfidy, Othello kills himself. It is a bloody play, and although we may reflect that Desdemona dies without ever knowing what has provoked her husband's murderous rage, for the audience the moral code is affirmed. Iago is caught in his villainy. He feels no guilt at all. But at play's end we know he will be tortured and then killed, and we know that people who conspire as he does against others will be punished in this world if not in the next. Be sure your sins will find you out. And by the way, we know that people should not let passion blind them to reason— the old stoic wisdom of the ancient world.

But then we come to Faulkner's tragic vision in *Sanctuary*, and throughout we have only one piece of tragedy. The proud are humbled. Temple Drake's flighty character makes her fall in with a drunken fool like Gowan Stevens, with whom she has, we assume, allowed herself to take liberties on the level of the animal lust of sex. In consequence, she gets herself raped by a lunatic who is impotent and who in his rape must use a corncob. We do not recognize the means of the rape until the end, when the corncob is adduced in court. Faulkner, in one of his typical exercises of withholding information, does not tell us this detail until the last or almost the last so that, as in "A Rose for Emily," we are forced to review the whole story from the end backwards. And that is part of this continual habit in Faulkner to use devices that force us into reconsiderations that make us dart backward and then forward in our minds to dwell on what he tells us. So Temple is humbled, but unlike Desdemona, she does not finally have force as an excuse for what happens to her. In a reversal of tragic roles, Temple wills not revulsion against Popeye but an attachment to him. Here are two evils that somehow come together in this rape, and Temple accepts not merely the consequences of the evil but the evil itself and makes it her own. She is now an Addie Bundren carried to an absurd extreme.

In *Othello*, chance brings destruction on the innocent Desdemona. In *Sanctuary* chance brings destruction on the guilty Popeye. But as though mocking the moral order of tragedy—or perhaps merely showing us how romantic and mythological that moral order is, Faulkner has Popeye die for a murder he did not commit. In a huge irony, Popeye becomes the innocent one, and Temple lies on the witness stand, and for her lie an innocent man dies. A fearful symmetry is that the jury that condemns Lee Goodwin to death is out eight minutes, and the jury far off in Alabama that condemns Popeye to death is also out eight minutes. A strange kind of order in the midst of chaos. But in the end no great moral purpose is affirmed by these deaths of men who, if not exactly innocent in the broadest sense, are innocent of the crimes of which they are convicted and killed. We are back to *The Sound and the Fury*, where the narrator of our stories sees human life going in endless circles where good and evil are nothing more than convenient constructs of the mind, and in the waste land of their dissolution human beings can only look to their own survival.

Now we must consider Temple Drake from a closer vantage point. The most common attitude towards her is that she is a reversal of true southern womanhood in some respects, the extreme manifestation of the stereotype in others. Utter chance puts her in the home of Lee Goodwin the bootlegger and moonshiner somewhere in the wild countryside outside Jefferson.

All the stereotypes go crashing down here. These people who live in the unspoiled country are not noble savages living in Eden. They are like Temple and Gowan Stevens, living in their own rural version of T. S. Eliot's *Waste Land*, which so much influenced Faulkner. The men where she is a prisoner are, as Eliot says, able to say:

I was neither
Living nor dead, and I knew nothing,
Looking into the heart of light, the silence.
Oed' und leer das Meer ["Barren and empty is the sea," from Richard
Wagner's *Tristan and Isolde*]. (lines 39–42)

In some respects Pap with his inability to see or hear or even taste his food, a man limited to sitting in the sun and letting the hours pass, is the epitome of all these people, dead to life. Temple could get away. But she will not walk. She is used to being driven. She presents herself as helpless before the possibility of walking out by herself. Ruby tells her to leave, to walk away, and Temple will not do it. She finds herself completely helpless in this world of bleak poverty and marginal life.

And not only helpless, but her young sexuality excites every man in the place. The character called Van, the feeble-minded Tommy, and Popeye all want her—in different ways. And even Lee is aroused by her despite his chivalrous effort to defend her from the predator instincts of the others. She brings not only sex but upper-middle-class sex to the wilderness, and the men see possessing her in a complex of ways that a Marxist critic might read as class war. To possess Temple, to violate her, is to tear down some of the barriers that stand between the bourgeoisie and the lower classes—represented in part by Lee Goodwin, who has fought in the war—in World War I—and who represents the old wisdom that war is always the rich man's war and the poor man's fight.

But I doubt that Faulkner had such an explicit intention. We have here a certain realism that is part of the way southern life, especially southern rural and small-town life, was up until the time of the mall and the shopping center and the monotonous urban developments where houses sit back from the street and the highway in sterile isolation unconnected by sidewalks. Faulkner's South was a place where rich and poor, black and white, moved in fluid juxtaposition with one another, knowing each other often by name and family, able to pass the time of day with one another and to inquire about relations and to talk crops and weather, and yet kept in clearly distinct spheres walled off from each other by an incompletely expressed set of rules that establish clear patterns of superiority and inferiority. The rules are not to be broken. The superior people are not to become too "familiar," as the term was, because such familiarity will encourage the inferiors to forget their proper place.

Both Horace Benbow and Gowan Stevens violate this elemental rule of southern life. They find themselves in a frightening situation, and they try to get out of it by talking to their captors as if they were all equals, as if affability will be their salvation. Ruby Lamar hears Horace chattering away to these silent and probably uncomprehending men. The narrator says:

> She listened to the stranger's voice; a quick, faintly outlandish voice, the voice of a man given to much talk and not much else. "Not to drinking, anyway," the woman said, quiet inside the door. "He better

> get on to where he's going, where his womenfolk can take care
> of him." (13)

Horace tells these men his confidential news, the problems with his marriage, believing that revelations of these intimate details will establish some bond of humanity between him and these silent, sullen men. It's a kind of syllogism. We share our most intimate thoughts with our dearest friends. So if we share our intimate thoughts with people, they must be our most intimate friends, even if we have just met them. And Horace becomes the denizen of the Waste Land because none of his intimate thoughts is worth much. He opens the book of his life to these people, and it is full of blank pages or else with pages inscribed with futility and trivia.

Gowan Stevens is a younger, more pretentious, and far more alcoholic version of Horace. He picks up the town boys in his car as he offers them a ride, takes them on, talks to them as though they are his equals—and raises in the one called Doc a foretaste of the anger and violence that he will soon raise in the men at the Old Frenchman's Place. These men know full well that the familiarity is pretended and that their social classes cannot meet on terms of equality, and their natural reaction is anger and then violence.

Temple herself tries to restore some of the balance in her talk with Ruby in the kitchen. She tries on the one hand to say that a common humanity binds these people and her together.

> "I'm not afraid," Temple said. "Things like that don't happen. Do
> they? They're just like other people. You're just like other people. With
> a little baby. And besides, my father's a ju-judge. The gu-governor
> comes to our house to e-eat—What a cute little bu-ba-a-by," she
> wailed, lifting the child to her face; "if bad mans hurts Temple, us'll
> tell the governor's soldiers, wont us?" (56)

The combination here of fear, threat, pleading, and an insincere appeal to equality only infuriates Ruby. Ruby sees Temple's world as artificial and effete. Her own world is superior, a more natural world not because it is an Eden but because it is so much closer to the animal impulses that are untamed by the artifices of genteel society. And we are again in the world of Thomas Hobbes or Charles Darwin where, in Ruby's view, the real man knows what he wants and gets it, and the female of the species appreciates being the object of a real man's desires. She sees Temple for what she is—a woman created by her society and made to be without substance.

> "Oh, I know your sort," the woman said. "Honest women. Too
> good to have anything to do with common people. You'll slip out at

night with the kids, but just let a man come along." She turned the meat. "Take all you can get and give nothing. 'I'm a pure girl; I dont do that.' You'll slip out with the kids and burn their gasoline and eat their food, but just let a man so much as look at you and you faint away because your father the judge and your four brothers might not like it. But just let you get into a jam, then who do you come crying to? to us, the ones that are not good enough to lace the judge's almighty shoes." Across the child Temple gazed at the woman's back, her face like a small pale mask beneath the precarious hat. (57–58)

But if Ruby sees Temple for what Temple is, the men see her as something to be possessed. Here, as always in Faulkner, we do well to pay attention to the title and to the names of the characters. *Sanctuary*. Temple Drake. A student of Cleanth Brooks has probably given us the best explanation of the title—found in a passage from Joseph Conrad's novel *Chance*:

A young girl, you know, is something like a *temple*. You pass by and wonder what mysterious rites are going on in there, what prayers, what visions? The privileged man, the lover, the husband, who are given the key of the *sanctuary* do not always know how to use it. For myself, without claim, without merit, simply by chance I had been allowed to look through the half-opened door and I had seen the saddest possible desecration, the withered brightness of youth, a spirit neither made cringing nor yet dulled but as if bewildered in quivering hopelessness by gratuitous cruelty; self-confidence destroyed and, instead, a resigned recklessness, a mournful callousness. (Conrad, *Chance* 311 of Uniform edition, qtd. in Brooks 136; Brooks's italics)

One can argue from this that the Temple here is the entire soul of the young woman. But I think the name "Drake" seems related to "mandrake," a narcotic plant with a long root resembling the penis and supposed from ancient times to arouse sexual passion, an aphrodisiac. It was supposed to heal a woman of barrenness, and it was said to scream when you pulled it out of the ground.

So I surmise that the "Temple" in Temple Drake is a symbol of the female's genitals, and that she functions here as a possibility for these men, a romantic illusion that bliss and sexual intercourse go together so powerfully that if any man can enter that temple, all troubles will vanish away. The word "sanctuary" calls to my mind at least the medieval and Shakespearean notion that a felon who takes refuge in a church cannot be captured or apprehended by the forces of the law. So I would surmise that what stirs these men is the romantic notion that if they can only have sex with

Temple, all their cares will be over and they will be free from the world outside.

Well, again Faulkner undermines all this romance by making Temple like sex. She upsets the entire southern code by discovering passion in rape. I think this is a place where all of us have a difficult time with this book, given the sensibility that is so much a part of our contemporary culture. The thought that we can accept with equanimity the way that Temple sinks into degradation must give us pause.

But Faulkner is not writing to please our moral sensibilities, and he does not expect us to take his characters as exemplary. He is involved as Ruby Lamar is involved in tearing away the trappings of civilization and placing human beings in the animal world where males fight for the female in heat and where sexual intercourse itself can have trappings of violence. I will not defend Faulkner's view of women. But I would argue that his larger assumption is not merely about women and their capacity for evil. It is rather a statement about human nature at its core.

And we have a powerful suggestion that sex is not something blissful and romantic to Popeye but purely a medium of exchange, a symbol of possession and power rather than anything truly sexual. He rapes Temple with a corncob. Everyone knows that. But what seems unknown among fastidious urban critics is that in the rural South corncobs were used as toilet paper. In the North the privy might have a Sears-Roebuck catalogue. In the South the privy was more likely to have a pile of corncobs in the corner. So when Popeye used a corncob to rape Temple, almost anyone of these characters would have seen it as a symbol of excrement. Since we learn that a man—we don't know which one—watches her relieve herself in the morning, we know that excrement is attended in the book. (Ruby has given her leaves from a catalogue to wipe herself.)

In many respects, Popeye turns out to be a sort of reverse hero in this book, a romantic, and a fool of fate. He wants to have feeling of his own. But that does not seem possible. He is truly dead, but possessed with the demon of wanting to experience life. He can have his feelings only by watching Temple have sex with Red. It must have given Faulkner some amusement to name his gangster "Popeye" and to make him small and impotent at a moment when all his readers would have associated the name "Popeye" with the comic character Popeye the Sailor Man who ate spinach and did amazing feats of strength and who was relentlessly pursued by a skinny girl named Olive Oyl. Then there were the gangster movies so popular in the 1930s. Popeye discovers that he can make Temple submit and perhaps even care for him in her own perverse way. But he cannot finally possess her. She has a passion for Red that she never has for him. Popeye can shoot Red. He cannot have sexual intercourse himself, but he can use the phallic symbol of the pistol to kill rather than to love. So in him murder becomes a surrogate for love, and we have an obvious Freudian connection.

We should say in some extenuation of Temple's plight that she knows men largely as violent abusers. We often overlook the babbling comment Temple makes to Ruby once she has seen that Ruby is not going to buy her combination of familiarity and threat:

> "My brother said he would kill Frank. He didn't say he would give me a whipping if he caught me with him; he said he would kill the goddam son of a bitch in his yellow buggy and my father cursed my brother and said he could run his family a while longer and he drove me into the house and locked me in and went down to the bridge to wait for Frank. But I wasn't a coward. I climbed down the gutter and headed Frank off and told him. I begged him to go away, but he said we'd both go. When we got back in the buggy I knew it had been the last time. I knew it, and I begged him again to go away, but he said he'd drive me home to get my suitcase and we'd tell father. He wasn't a coward either. My father was sitting on the porch. He said 'Get out of that buggy,' and I got out and I begged Frank to go on, but he got out too and we came up the path and father reached around inside the door and got the shotgun. I got in front of Frank and father said 'Do you want it too?' and I tried to stay in front but Frank shoved me behind him and held me and father shot him and said 'Get down there and sup your dirt, you whore.'" (58)

Now Temple has apparently seen her father kill Frank, a man who apparently wanted to marry her. So when she calls Popeye "Daddy" several times in the book, the word "Daddy" may be a simple identification with violence rather than a term of endearment.

Richard Gray has pointed out the concern with watching and being watched in the novel. If this somewhat chaotic story does have any major theme, it is this. As in Benjy's trip around the square in *The Sound and the Fury*, the appearances finally win out over the realities—whatever those realities are. Once again Narcissa Benbow Sartoris becomes the guardian of the appearances. She is if anything the much more evil woman in this book than Temple. She is willing to see Lee Goodwin die for a crime he did not commit. She conspires with the District Attorney Eustace Graham to help defeat Horace. We don't know where the District Attorney got so much information. Cleanth Brooks works out possible sources for the story of the corncob and all the rest. But we are in the land of conjecture when we try to figure it out. What seems clear is that Narcissa starts the train of events that leads to the revelations at the trial that in turn lead to the lynching of Lee Goodwin.

Temple in the end faces the court in a sort of apathy. Horace wants her to testify that Popeye and not Lee Goodwin murdered Tommy and raped her. But it is as though she is in the thrall of the strongest man in the room—and that is Eustace Graham, the district attorney. The name "Eustace" is appropriate here since St. Eustace was a hunter who was converted when he saw a vision of Christ crucified between the horns of a stag. Faulkner may again be working on the Christ mysticism he loved so much—just how far do we push innocence? That question, it seems to me, is what Christ images in Faulkner are all about.

Yet all through the book the theme of appearances is powerful. The novel begins with Popeye watching Horace drinking from a pool that reflects his image like that of Narcissus. Again and again through the book Temple looks at her own face in various mirrors. Tommy watches Temple undress, and a man watches Temple relieve herself in the woods. As if to hammer the theme at us, Popeye's last words to the sheriff on the gallows are, "Fix my hair, Jack."

Brooks says this is "Faulkner's bitterest novel" (127). I agree. Everything here testifies to an absence of real feeling. The honesty of Ruby does not prevail against mob violence or the respectability of church ladies. Temple feels proud of herself for what she endures, for what she survives. But in the end she is once again in her father's hands, in Paris, looking into her face reflected in her compact, then seeing the gray Paris sky, "lying prone and vanquished in the embrace of the season of rain and death" (317). It is the world of Prufrock, "When the evening is spread out against the sky like a patient etherised upon a table." Popeye has already shared her death in that he makes no effort to save himself from the noose.

But in that world of death, the highest form of life is to commit evil.

LIGHT IN AUGUST

And now we come to one of Faulkner's most dense and interesting books, *Light in August*, published in October 1932, when he had lost a daughter, Alabama, born in the spring and living only nine days.

If we teach Faulkner in a writerly way, we have to notice several qualities about this book that put it at a level of structure and style that leaves me, at least, struck with wonder and appreciation at how he pulls it off. Most noticeable I suppose is the style in which certain words are repeated again and again and yet never make the sentences cumbersome or monotonous. These are Faulkner's favorite words. They appear in all his books, but in this one they seem to pour out in unusual profusion as if his head was swimming with them as he wrote—*myriad, tireless, savage, doom, rigid, passive, cold, furious, fatality, impotent, urgent, profound, inscrutable, calm, still, ceaseless, gesticulant, flat, implacable, rapt, dead, quiet, desperate, abject, dumb, grave, reckless, outrage.*

They are intense words repeated again and again so that they give tone to the book, to the mood of the action so that it is both active and dark, a book lightened by flashes of innocence as Lena Grove moves in sublime calm through it all. The words both capture and batter the scene. Faulkner in his repetition does what I have mentioned earlier. He keeps them present in our consciousness. Some writers tell us one time a description of a scene, some character, and they expect us to keep the description in our minds and call it up every time we think of the character. But if we have a character or a mood described only one time, we quickly forget it as we read on. Jane Austen solved the problem by rarely giving any specific description of what her characters looked like. But Faulkner solves the problem by telling us about these characters time and again so that at a given moment we associate the description with the character. We are told time and again that Joe Christmas wears serge pants, just as we are told in *Sanctuary* that Popeye wears his hat at a slant. The serge pants become Joe Christmas's demand for respectability even in his profession of bootlegger, even in his state of not knowing who he is or where he comes from.

The other quality that makes us pay attention to the writerly characteristics of this novel lies in its structure. Once again Faulkner plays with time, happy to break up, indeed to shatter the traditional idea of chronology in the novel, a tradition where we have a linear progression of plot with occasional clearly marked flashbacks. But Faulkner does not clearly demarcate time. From section to section he plays with time, shifting it around so that in the first few pages as Lena moves towards Jefferson, we have a shifting of present and past tenses moving in and out of each other almost with the softness of light. And that is the way the human consciousness works. We cannot walk across the yard or eat our meals or talk with a friend without a continual swift interplay between our consciousness, this moment, this dissolving instant of the present on the one hand and on the other the equally swift but perhaps less transient shooting of memory across the surface of what we are and hear and taste and feel and smell.

The time of the story is also against the common tradition of the novel. As Lena comes into Jefferson in the wagon where a man has given her a ride, the man sees smoke.

> It is the man now who does not hear. He is looking ahead, across the valley toward the town on the opposite ridge. Following his pointing whip, she sees two columns of smoke: the one the heavy density of burning coal above a tall stack, the other a tall yellow column standing apparently from a clump of trees some distance beyond the town.
> "That's a house burning," the driver says. "See?" (26)

That passage is at the end of chapter one, page 26 of the original edition. On page 278 Lena steps down in Jefferson, and between these two pages we have whirled back in time, and Joe Christmas and Joanna Burden have had their love affair, their strange, paradoxical fling with loveless sex, and Joe has killed her and set fire to her house and run away.

Lena and Joe Christmas never meet. Their stories run along parallel to one another throughout the book, and were we in the nineteenth-century novel, these two important characters would have some sort of confrontation with one another. But in this novel they seem only to be images of contrary forces that work in a sort of yin and yang through human society. Joe Christmas is the wild and tormented questioner who demands to know the solutions to puzzles that cannot be solved. Lena Grove is the placid life force of nature that flows on through all living things and propagates the race though the earth rumbles and riots sweep towns and fires burn down houses and consume the uplifted hopes and ideals of civilization. They do not have to meet each other. Faulkner merely exhibits them, marks their effect on the community where they both pass through as aliens and transients. Faulkner makes Lena at home in the world, a manifestation of the female principle, a mother bearing a child and, as one of the barren characters in the novel, Gail Hightower, says, bringing luck back to this place. Lena Grove is, in some sense, Eve before the fall, having no real sense of how much evil there is in the world, assuming the best in everyone, seeing the world as a friendly place where people will take care of her—and, remarkably enough, it does take care of her. It meets her expectations. Lena Grove—Lenis, linis—soft, mild, smooth. And grove—the sacred groves of mythology where the trees are like gods. Michael Millgate says she brings out the best in Jefferson (129).

Joe Christmas, on the other hand, is the wild man, a figure with some of the qualities of Popeye in *Sanctuary*. The greatest attention to Joe Christmas has been fixed on his identity. Is he part black? He never knows. And we never know. He puzzles over his own origins, and his savage grandfather Doc Hines, the Calvinist, is obsessed with the possibility that he is. But the fact is that we never know, and neither does Joe Christmas. He is suspended in a cloud of wondering. Faulkner said, "'that to me was the tragic, central idea of the story—that he didn't know what he was, and there was no way possible in life for him to find out'" (Blotner 301).

Joe Christmas has often been made a Christ figure by critics. As Christ figure, we see that Joe Christmas is left on a doorstep on Christmas Eve—the holiest night of the year (133). Faulkner himself seemed to play with the idea and then back away from it. He changed Joe Christmas's age from thirty-three to thirty-six in the typescript of the novel when he was revising the handwritten manuscript. Christmas is too violent. But like Benjy he is abused and castrated, and then other qualities remain. He is named Joe Christmas, after all—the name Joseph—his passivity before death, the way in which the community led by Percy Grimm seems to take out on him all its hatreds and its fears, its imagined terror before the consequences of letting any white woman be killed by a black man without responding with violence. Joe Christmas recalls in death the ironic comment at the crucifixion of Jesus that it is expedient that one man die for the people. And don't forget that Joe Christmas, like Jesus, comes into the world as a bastard. Mary tells Joseph that she is pregnant by the Holy Ghost, the agency of God, so that even in the officially pious Middle Ages Joseph was often depicted as a buffoon. The initials for Joe Christmas, J. C., are the same as for Jesus Christ.

But there is something else here, too. That is the sense of priesthood imposed on Christ in the anonymous letter to the Hebrews in the New Testament. There the writer picks up the story of Melchisedec, who in the book of Genesis was the king priest of Salem and to whom Abraham paid homage. The writer of the letter to the Hebrews was trying convert the Jews to Christ, and he picked up this story as a foretelling of the priesthood of Jesus and made of Melchisedec a quasi-divine figure, perhaps an apparition of Christ himself. The writer made much of the fact that Melchisedec was not said to have any genealogy in the book of Genesis. He was:

> King of Salem, which is, King of Peace; without father,
> without mother, without descent, having neither beginning
> of days nor end of life; but made like unto the Son of God,
> abideth a priest continually. (Hebrews 7:2–3)

We may pause here and ask ourselves if Joe Christmas can possibly be a priest. Can that be part of his type as a Christ figure? Several times in the book he is referred to as being a monk-like character, and it may well be that he mediates to the people of Jefferson some sort of entree to approval by the fierce, angry, and cruel God who stands back of the Christian religion. What kind of God is it that at one time demands animal sacrifice and then as the culmination of revelation and redemption demands the crucifixion of His Son in expiation of the sins of the world when God himself has created the world where sin is possible? These are questions that in the Mississippi of 1931 might not be directly posed, but they seem to linger in the heart of this book. When Percy Grimm castrates and kills Joe Christmas at the climax of the book, he prefaces the act, in the narrator's words, with pregnant meaning:

> "Jesus Christ!" Grimm cried, his young voice clear and outraged like
> that of a young priest. "Has every preacher and old maid in Jefferson
> taken their pants down to the yellowbellied son of a bitch?"
> He flung the old man aside and ran on. (439)

The brutal harshness of the God of the Bible comes storming off these pages in both the characters of McEachern and Hines. Both of them exhibit attributes of the God of the Bible that most liberal Christians and Jews would rather forget. McEachern will beat Joe Christmas into submission with the same alacrity with which Joshua slaughtered the people of Jericho or Elijah killed the three hundred priests of Baal.

Doc Hines is the God who predestines everything. When young Joe Christmas asks him, "Is God a nigger, too?" the mad old man declares: "He is the Lord God of wrathful hosts. His will be done. Not yours and not mine, because you and me are both a part of His purpose and His vengeance" (362). That's the grim God of John Calvin. As he did in *Flags in the Dust*, Faulkner speaks late in the book of God as the Player, capitalizing the "P" in player to indicate that he is speaking of God. "But the Player was not done yet" (439). The sentence comes when Grimm has shot Joe Christmas, just before Grimm bends over the dying man and cuts off his genitals with a butcher knife.

Faulkner is usually taken in these passages about McEachern and Hines to be attacking bigotry in religion. But it is worth pointing out that some Christian traditions—including the Puritan tradition that gave us Harvard University—held precisely the doctrines that both McEachern and Hines profess and practice. So I am saying that Faulkner may have intended in all this a frontal assault on Christianity itself. That assumption is made plausible, I think, by a comment Faulkner made about *Light in August* at the University of Virginia:

> [I]n August in Mississippi, there's a few days somewhere about the middle of the month when suddenly there's a foretaste of fall, it's cool, there's a lambence, a luminous quality to the light, as though it came not from just today but from back in the old classic times. It might have fauns and satyrs and the gods and—from Greece, from Olympus in it somewhere. It lasts just for a day or two, then it's gone, but every year in August that occurs in my country, and that's all that title meant, it was just a pleasant evocative title because it reminded me of that time, of a luminosity older than our Christian civilization. (Gwynn and Blotner 199)

But now if we see Faulkner rejecting some of the people whose interpretation of the Bible is literal and literally bloodthirsty, we still can have characters in his work who are Christ figures of one sort or another. That idea may be especially potent if we think of Jesus in human terms as an innocent young man who moves shadow-like and elusive behind the veil thrown over his historical shape, a veil created by legend and theology and the words of the New Testament itself, and if we see that young man with historic existence somehow arrested by the Romans and crucified as a rebel and dying in utter loneliness on the cross and crying out those words that seem more authentic to me than anything else in the New Testament, "My God! My God! Why hast thou forsaken me?"

Here we have sacrificial suffering of the innocent, a sacrifice to the blood lust of some who must kill if they are to keep their own belief system alive. We have already seen that in Faulkner the belief systems of his community and his world are arbitrary and that people conform to them not because those systems are grounded in something absolute but rather because the community accepts them and closely watches each of its members to see to it that everyone conforms. If an occasional victim must be sacrificed to that system, the community is thereby preserved.

But the other side of this business of the Christ figure is innocence. Christ is assumed to be innocent. The Christ figure must be innocent. No doubt that thirty-three-year-old Benjy in *The Sound and the Fury* is innocent. But what about Joe Christmas? I wonder if Faulkner is here pushing the definition of innocence to the limit? He drew back because he seems to have found Joe Christmas too violent for innocence. But still the question remains: just how bad can we be and still be innocent? We may ask the question of Popeye. We may ask it of Joe Christmas.

Joe Christmas certainly starts out innocent—the hapless child born to a girl named Milly, unloved and brutalized daughter of the fanatic Doc Hines—information revealed slowly, deliberately as Faulkner gives us first a Joe Christmas lost and on the move and violent; thus, in chapter six we are suddenly thrust back into his childhood in the orphanage when he eats the toothpaste. He has been slipping into the dietitian's room and eating a measured coil of toothpaste, but in this day he finds himself surprised by the dietitian and her doctor friend who come into the room for a quickie. So while they are having sex, Joe Christmas is eating toothpaste from the phallic-like toothpaste tube, and he vomits and reveals himself: "the thin, furious voice hissed; 'you little rat! Spying on me! You little nigger bastard!'" (114).

It is all chance—the kind of chance that changes a life. It has none of the grand fatalism of classical tragedy because it does not radically change his life. He is already in an orphanage. The dietitian calls him a "nigger." But although she hates him because she is sure he is going to tell, she does not kill him or perhaps even change his life in any major way. She merely changes the place of his lovelessness and loneliness. What happens to him remains on the level of incident. He is kidnapped by the janitor, taken to an orphanage for black children in Little Rock, brought back again, and at last farmed out to the brutal Scotch-Irish McEachern father and his sentimental wife. McEachern tells him of his new home, "'You will find food and shelter and the care of Christian people [. . .]. And the work within your strength that will keep you out of mischief. For I will have you learn soon that the two abominations are sloth and idle thinking, the two virtues are work and the fear of God'" (135). In time McEachern beats Joe for the child's stubborn refusal to learn the catechism. The description of the beating is one of the most brutal scenes in American or any other literature:

McEachern was waiting, holding the strap. "Put it down," he said. The boy laid the book on the floor. "Not there," McEachern said, without heat. "You would believe that a stable floor, the stamping place of beasts, is the proper place for the word of God. But I'll learn you that, too." He took up the book himself and laid it on a ledge. "Take down your pants," he said. "We'll not soil them."

Then the boy stood, his trousers collapsed about his feet, his legs revealed beneath his brief shirt. He stood, slight and erect. When the strap fell he did not flinch, no quiver passed over his face. He was looking straight ahead, with a rapt, calm expression like a monk in a picture. McEachern began to strike methodically, with slow and deliberate force, still without heat or anger. It would have been hard to say which face was the more rapt, more calm, more convinced.

He struck ten times, then he stopped. "Take the book," he said. "Leave your pants be." He handed the boy the catechism. The boy took it. He stood so, erect, his face and the pamphlet lifted, his attitude one of exaltation. Save for surplice he might have been a Catholic choir boy, with for nave the looming and shadowy crib, the rough planked wall beyond which in the ammoniac and dryscented obscurity beasts stirred now and then with snorts and indolent thuds. McEachern lowered himself stiffly to the top of a feed box, spread kneed, one hand on his knee and the silver watch in the other palm, his clean, bearded face as firm as carved stone, his eyes ruthless, cold, but not unkind.

They remained so for another hour. Before it was up Mrs. McEachern came to the back door of the house. But she did not speak. She just stood there, looking at the stable, in the hat with the umbrella and the fan. Then she went back into the house.

Again on the exact second of the hour McEachern returned the watch to his pocket. "Do you know it now?" he said. The boy did not answer, rigid, erect, holding the open pamphlet before his face. McEachern took the book from between his hands. Otherwise, the boy did not move at all. "Repeat your catechism," McEachern said. The boy stared straight at the wall before him. His face was now quite white despite the smooth rich pallor of his skin. Carefully and

deliberately McEachern laid the book upon the ledge and took up the
strap. He struck ten times. (140–41)

I said last time that the notion of a Christ figure entails sacrifice, expiation, the sacrificial victim innocent or pure before the plunge of the sacrificial knife. I said that the god to whom the sacrifice is made in this book is
the fierce deity of these fanatics, McEachern and, as we discover, Doc Hines,
who is the child's grandfather. Now, is this child anything other than innocent? How long does the innocence last?

Here is the child scourged as Jesus was scourged. And the child was
silent before his tormentor as Jesus was silent before his. "He was led as a
sheep to the slaughter, and like a lamb dumb before his shearer, so opened
he not his mouth" (Acts 8:32, quoting Isaiah 53:7).

We may ask the question of Joe Christmas, the same question of Popeye:
what part does fate that we cannot control play in making us do the evil
that we do?

> The tragic vision is in its first phase primal, or primitive, in that it
> calls out of the depths the first (and last) of all questions, the question
> of existence: What does it mean to be? It recalls the original terror,
> harking back to a world that antedates the conceptions of philosophy,
> the consolations of the later religions, and whatever constructions the
> human mind has devised to persuade itself that its universe is secure.
> It recalls the original un-reason, the terror of the irrational. It sees man
> as questioner, naked, unaccommodated, alone, facing mysterious,
> demonic forces in his own nature and outside, and the irreducible
> facts of suffering and death. Thus it is not for those who cannot live
> with unsolved questions or unresolved doubts, whose bent of mind
> would reduce the fact of evil into something else or resolve it into
> some larger whole. Though no one is exempt from moments of tragic
> doubt or insight, the vision of life peculiar to the mystic, the pious, the
> propagandist, the confirmed optimist or pessimist—or the confirmed
> anything—is not tragic.
> Nor is the tragic vision for those who, though admitting unsolved
> questions and the reality of guilt, anxiety, and suffering, would be-
> come quietist [sic] and do nothing. Mere sensitivity is not enough.
> The tragic vision impels the man of action to fight against his des-
> tiny, kick against the pricks, and state his case before God or his fel-
> lows. It impels the artist, in his fictions, toward what Jaspers calls
> "boundary-situations," man at the limits of his sovereignty—Job on
> the ash-heap, Prometheus on the crag, Oedipus in his moment of
> self-discovery, Lear on the heath, Ahab on his lonely quarter-deck.

> Here, with all the protective covering stripped off, the hero faces as
> if no man had ever faced it before the existential question—Job's
> question, "What is man?" or Lear's "Is man no more than this?" The
> writing of a tragedy is the artist's way of taking action, of defying
> destiny, and this is why in the great tragedies there is a sense of the
> artist's own involvement, an immediacy not so true of the forms, like
> satire and comedy, where the artist's position seems more detached.
> (Sewall 4–5)

Here is the ancient moral confrontation of fatalism and freedom, of compulsion and responsibility, and Faulkner leaves us no clear answer. In the fatalistic qualities that in the narrative drive Joe Christmas on his way, we see some evidence of real tragedy. The tragic figure *believes* that he is acting freely, making decisions, fashioning the stuff of his life. Joe Christmas thinks he is free, that he can shape his destiny. Joanna Burden, wild in her passion for him, begins to speak of having a child, and suddenly the idea of marriage inserts itself, and Joe Christmas must consider his life—security, ease, never having to move again as long as he lived. But his response is, "'No. If I give in now, I will deny all the thirty years that I have lived to make me what I chose to be'" (250–51). But did he really have any choice?

Tragedy in the end is about death, and the shadow that death throws on the brightest hours of life. The tragic vision examines every moment of life to ask, "Is this all my life is?" For Joe Christmas life is to be without love, and Joanna Burden gives him passion in sex with wild abandon, but she cannot give him love because she is like all the other people in his life to whom he has been bound by some cord of obligation. She sees him not as a person but as a sentient, living object to be directed according to her own desires and need.

She is a New Englander—a woman in the New England stereotype devoted to doing good, to propagating benevolence, charity, to lifting the inferior to a better life. (Joanna was one of the women in the Gospel of Luke who found the empty tomb and proclaimed the resurrection to the apostles and also one of the women who followed Jesus and contributed to the support of his ministry. It is the female name for John.) And in typical Faulkner style, she gets a genealogy. It goes back to Calvin Burden, fanatical son of a New England minister, Nathaniel Burrington (228). Calvin changes his name and incarnates the fanatical—and stereotypical—New England condemnation of slavery that has in it not love but fury and hatred. Nathaniel Burrington was a Unitarian—a church united in fanatical confidence of its hold on the best way to be moral, and Calvin inherits a passion equivalent to that of any fanatical Methodist.

When the boy was about five, Burden killed a man in an argument
over slavery and had to take his family and move, leave Saint Louis.
He moved westward "to get away from Democrats," he said. (229)

The older Calvin Burden looks at the Mexican woman who is Nathaniel II's
wife to be and their son and thinks immediately of intermarriage as the way
to lift up the inferior, as the way to raise black people, the first thing a New
Englander (in Faulkner's stereotypical view) thinks of:

The father sat, gaunt, grizzled, and austere, beneath the lamp.
He had been listening, but his expression was brooding, with a kind
of violently slumbering contemplativeness and bewildered outrage.
"Another damn black Burden," he said. "Folks will think I bred to a
damn slaver. And now he's got to breed to one, too." The son listened
quietly, not even attempting to tell his father that the woman was
Spanish and not Rebel. "Damn, lowbuilt black folks: lowbuilt because
of the weight of the wrath of God, black because of the sin of human
bondage staining their blood and flesh." His gaze was vague, fanatical, and convinced. "But we done freed them now, both black and
white alike. They'll bleach out now. In a hundred years they will
be white folks again. Then maybe we'll let them come back into
America." He mused, smoldering, immobile. "By God," he said suddenly, "he's got a man's build anyway, for all his black look. By God,
he's going to be as big a man as his grandpappy; not a runt like
his pa. For all his black dam and his black look, he will." (234)

The old man moves with the younger Nathaniel to Jefferson during reconstruction, and John Sartoris shoots both the one-armed grandfather and
the young Calvin Burden, who is not old enough to vote, and in the story
as Joanna Burden tells it, seasoned with her imagination and that of Joe
Christmas, Colonel Sartoris looks like a coward. And Joanna Burden was
born fourteen years after her brother Calvin and her grandfather Calvin
were killed. Her mother was not the mother of her brother Calvin but a
mail-order bride, so to speak, a woman sent for impersonally by her father
when his first wife had died. Joanna is born, a disappointment to her father,
and she is led out to the graveyard in the cedar grove to see her grandfather's grave and her brother Calvin's and to receive the family doom and
commission. Joanna Burden's command from her father:

"'Remember this. Your grandfather and brother are lying there,
murdered not by one white man but by the curse which God put
on a whole race before your grandfather or your brother or me or
you were even thought of. A race doomed and cursed to be for-

ever and ever a part of the white race's doom and curse for its sins.
Remember that. His doom and his curse. Forever and ever. Mine.
Your mother's. Yours, even though you are a child. The curse of
every white child that ever was born and that ever will be born.
None can escape it.' And I said, 'Not even me?' And he said, 'Not
even you. Least of all, you.' I had seen and known negroes since I
could remember. I just looked at them as I did rain, or furniture, or
food or sleep. But after that I seemed to see them for the first time
not as people, but as a thing, a shadow in which I lived, we lived,
all white people, all other people. I thought of all the children coming
forever and ever in the world, white with the black shadow already
falling upon them before they drew breath. And I seemed to see the
black shadow in the shape of a cross. And it seemed like the white
babies were struggling, even before they drew breath, to escape
from the shadow what was not only upon them but beneath them
too, flung out like their arms were flung out, as if they were nailed
to the cross. I saw all the little babies that would ever be in the
world, the ones not yet even born—a long line of them with their
arms spread, on the black crosses. I couldn't tell then whether I saw
it or dreamed it. But it was terrible to me. I cried at night. At last I
told father, tried to tell him. What I wanted to tell him was that I must
escape, get away from under the shadow, or I would die. 'You cannot,' he said. 'You must struggle, rise. But in order to rise, you must
raise the shadow with you. But you can never lift it to your level. I see
that now, which I did not see until I came down here. But escape it
you cannot. The curse of the black race is God's curse. But the curse
of the white race is the black man who will be forever God's chosen
own because He once cursed Him.'" Her voice ceased. (239–40)

It is an awful declaration of the condescension of the New England heritage as Faulkner sees it, a resolution to do good without compassion, love,
or understanding, and at a given moment Joanna Burden seems to feel her
sexual passion for Joe Christmas because she thinks he is black, and she
may be in love with her own immolation rather than with himself. She made
their love affair a madness where she plays a part that sees him not as a
person but as a member of a class, a forbidden class so that she can feel
the thrill of something akin to sin.

He is a man on whom identity is imposed. Joanna Burden imposes the identity of *Negro* on him, an identity that comes complete with fantasies of rape.

Sometimes the notes would tell him not to come until a certain
hour, to that house which no white person save himself had entered in

years and in which for twenty years now she had been all night alone; for a whole week she forced him to climb into a window to come to her. He would do so and sometimes he would have to seek her about the dark house until he found her, hidden, in closets, in empty rooms, waiting, panting, her eyes in the dark glowing like the eyes of cats. Now and then she appointed trysts beneath certain shrubs about the grounds, where he would find her naked, or with her clothing half torn to ribbons upon her, in the wild throes of nymphomania, her body gleaming in the slow shifting from one to another of such formally erotic attitudes and gestures as a Beardsley of the time of Petronius might have drawn. She would be wild then, in the close, breathing half-dark without walls, with her wild hair, each strand of which would seem to come alive like octopus tentacles, and her wild hands and her breathing: "Negro! Negro! Negro!" (245)

And then, when she ages as if life has been burned out of her and falls into fantasies of religious fanaticism and improvement, Joe Christmas kills her. But remember!!! She has tried to kill him first because he will not acquiesce in her imposition of identity on him. She has pointed an old cap-and-ball pistol at him, pulled the trigger, and can claim no reprieve merely because the pistol has misfired. Later, he has taken the pistol and run away with it after slashing her neck with the razor with which she intended to kill him and then to kill herself.

Despite all these efforts to impose identity upon him, Joe Christmas still does not know who he is. Within the context of the story, that terrifying absence of identity means that he does not know whether he is black or white—and he buys without protest the southern stereotype that if he has any black ancestor, he must be black himself, altogether black without hope of mitigation.

On that level, Joe Christmas is tragic in that as part black he has bought the white stereotype of the black as inferior—an attitude made familiar to us by Thurgood Marshall's use of white and black dolls to show what segregation was doing to the consciousness and self-confidence of black children. When black children were given a choice between white dolls and black dolls, they chose the white dolls, and when they were asked why, they said, "Because white is better." Joe Christmas reminds us of Malcolm X and his description of his efforts to conk his hair, to straighten it so it would look more like a white man's hair. And here is Joe Christmas plunging into a revival at a black church, cursing the people, cursing their God, raging against the church that incarnates and encapsulates the black experience of submission.

But in the larger, tragic sense, Joe Christmas is a mirror of ourselves, the seeker of an identity that can never be found in this life. We cannot tell our own story until death. We cannot answer the question of who we are until we meet death, and the essence of that question contains the essence of the tragic dilemma.

In the end of tragedy, the rhythms of social life are restored, and the peace that has been disrupted comes again. At the end of *Hamlet*, Fortinbras takes charge of the realm of Denmark. At the close of *Macbeth*, Malcolm comes home for the exiles of Scotland, promotes those who have helped defeat Macbeth, and announces a return to measure. At the end of *Lear*, the old king is dead and at peace, and Edgar and Kent take over a realm in woe—in Albany's words, "the gor'd state sustain" (V.iii.320). The world must be restored, for if it is not, tragedy has no stage on which to exhibit its lessons.

So in Faulkner Joe Christmas has been savagely killed by the storm trooper Percy Grimm—the namesake of Hotspur, all impulse and honor—but in Grimm's case, he has not experienced the thrill of battle so that he burns with a lust to kill Joe Christmas. Joe Christmas, in his sacrificial death, affirms the values of the society that has killed him with Grimm as its instrument.

But then also we have Lena Grove serenely making her way north into Tennessee, having entirely disrupted the methodical life of the stable and pedantic Byron Bunch. He is clocklike in his efficiency. He is honest. He remembers dates with a neat and orderly progression of memory that is akin to his pocket watch and as prescribed in his circular motions as the gears and hands of the timepiece itself. Byron Bunch has his life, all the loose strands gathered together in a bunch and thereby kept orderly. But he is also Byron, the greatest of the nineteenth-century romantics and adventurers, and he seems predisposed to go off into romance when the occasion arises, and arise it does in the wandering Lena Grove. She innocently undermines everything, and Byron becomes her protector, the double, one may suggest, of Joe Christmas who knows "love" only as sex and violence. Byron wants sex, but he is willing to give up his whole old life so he can be with Lena. He is not going to rape her; he is going to win her. When he declines to run away at the last, the furniture dealer who tells the story to his wife describes how Byron returned:

> "And he come around to the back of it [the truck] and he stood there, and her not even surprised. 'I done come too far now,' he says. 'I be dog if I'm going now.' And her looking at him like she had known all the time what he was going to do before he even knew himself that

he was going to, and that whatever he done, he wasn't going to
mean it.
"'Ain't nobody never said for you to quit,' she says." (479)

For most of us the ultimate tragedy of Joe Christmas is that as far as his identity is concerned, it is no more than a word. What is it to be a member of the white or black race? Here is an opposite problem from what Faulkner usually considers in his novels to date. In them, people like Narcissa Benbow are eager to keep up appearances, no matter what the reality. But here we have an appearance that allows no clear definition of race, and yet we have a man cursed by nothing more than a word that has no real content. What freedom do we have when so much meaning, condemnation, is poured into our birth by a word that we have no voice in defining?

PYLON

We now come to Faulkner's novel *Pylon*, often called his second worst novel. (*Mosquitoes* is considered his worst.) It has many flaws—the stilted dialogue, the weight Faulkner puts on a woman having sex with two men as if this were a shocking and even titillating abnormality, the little boy who cannot know who his biological father is, the trick of never giving us the reporter's name, the too obvious effort to link the novel to T. S. Eliot. The two men who share the woman, Laverne, are not very interesting. It also becomes tedious to see Faulkner making elaborate efforts to rename Louisiana and New Orleans. New Orleans becomes New Valois; Louisiana becomes Franciana. Canal Street becomes Grandlieu Street. For some of us, all that is distracting. Faulkner went two and a half years between *Light in August* and the publication of *Pylon*. During that time he went out to Hollywood to write screenplays. He hated being in Hollywood, but he needed the money desperately, and he had to make do.

Yet none of these flaws keeps the novel from being interesting. *Pylon* came out in March 1935 and captures a romantic attitude towards flying that Faulkner had had since childhood. The Wright Brothers flew at Kitty Hawk, North Carolina, in 1903, when Faulkner was six. By the time he had turned twenty, and the United States had entered World War I, fliers were already regarded as the knights of the air, and the thrill of leaving the earth in those flimsy and tiny machines created in Faulkner's own imagination a band of heroes worthy of emulation. In May 1927, Charles Lindbergh made the first non-stop solo crossing of the Atlantic by air, landing in Paris after flying thirty-six hundred miles from Roosevelt Field on Long Island in a little over thirty-three hours. He was called the "Lone Eagle," and he was an instant hero all over the world but especially in America. Lindbergh flew in a tiny machine. These flimsy craft created in Faulkner's imagination a band of heroes worthy of emulation for their courage but also symbolic of alienation, for the men who flew them were not normal human beings. Or at least they did not seem normal to people who watched them soar aloft into the thin air that was the realm of birds rather than the domain of human beings so that every take-off and landing seemed to defy the natural and to threaten those who made them with violent death.

The fliers Faulkner wrote about in *Pylon* were like many of his characters in that they were on the margins of society, outcasts who live day by day. At the University of Virginia in 1957 Faulkner said some things that help us interpret the book:

> To me they were a fantastic and bizarre phenomenon on the face of a contemporary scene, of our culture at a particular time. I wrote that book because I'd got in trouble with *Absalom, Absalom!* And I had to get away from it for a while so I thought a good way to get away from it was to write another book, so I wrote *Pylon*. They were ephemera and phenomena on the face of a contemporary scene. That is, there was really no place for them in the culture, in the economy, yet they were there, at that time, and everyone knew that they wouldn't last very long, which they didn't. That time of those frantic little aeroplanes which dashed around the country and people wanted just enough money to live, to get to the next place to live again. Something frenetic and in a way almost immoral about it. That they were outside the range of God, not only of respectability, of love, but of God, too. That they had escaped the compulsion of accepting a past and a future, that they were—they had no past. They were as ephemeral as the butterfly that's born this morning with no stomach and will be gone tomorrow. It seemed to me interesting enough to make a story about, but that was just to get away from a book that wasn't going too well, till I could get back at it. (Gwynn and Blotner 36)

As you remember, Faulkner enlisted in the RCAF in his vain effort to get into World War I, and his first novel was about an airman, Donald Mahon, who has been fearsomefully scarred in aerial combat. By the time he wrote *Pylon* Faulkner had also written about John and young Bayard Sartoris in *Flags in the Dust*, and he had learned to fly himself. He participated in the dedication and inauguration of the Shushan Airport in New Orleans in February 1934. By then he owned his own small plane. One of the biggest heartbreaks of his life was the death of his younger brother Dean in an air crash a few months after *Pylon* was published. Faulkner had encouraged Dean to take flying lessons. Faulkner had sold his brother the airplane in which Dean was killed in November 1935.

Richard Gray has made the interesting point that *Pylon* shows the effects of Faulkner's connection with motion pictures, that its broken quality seems to mirror what Gray, following Marshall McLuhan, calls "the discontinuous landscapes of urban life: a fractured, disjunctive mixing of disparate media and messages, alive with implication and rumour" (198). The use of headlines, of fragmentary messages, reflects the influence of John Dos Passos, whose work we know Faulkner admired. (And it is obvious that Faulkner's chapter "Night in the Vieux Carre" is a reflection of Joyce's "Ulysses in Night Town," the episode with Circe in *Ulysses*.)

Pylon represents one of the few times that Faulkner wrote about a metropolis. He includes Memphis in several books and stories, but it is always a Memphis reflected against a small town or a rural world not far away. And Memphis was scarcely more than a second-rate city compared to New Orleans. But Gray also points out that throughout the book we have a mixture of modernity and nostalgia.

While he wrote *Pylon*, Faulkner was struggling with *Absalom, Absalom!* As we shall see, next to *The Sound and the Fury, Absalom, Absalom!* was his most complicated work and also one of his greatest. He seemed to turn from *Absalom, Absalom!* almost in relief, away from its cramped, almost smothering atmosphere of history and doom, into the wild, free air where none of these people is truly bound to a past and where for a few moments at least the possibilities seem as limitless as the sky itself.

One of the most important differences between *Pylon* and *Absalom, Absalom!* is here, in this dealing with time. *Absalom, Absalom!* grows out of a conversation between Quentin Compson and his roommate, Shreve McCannon (MacKenzie in *The Sound and the Fury*), in a dorm room here at Harvard on a cold winter night sometime in the winter of 1909–1910 because that is the school year when Quentin is here, and we know from *The Sound and the Fury* that Quentin kills himself on June 2, 1910. So when he published *Absalom, Absalom!* in 1936, the book looked back almost three decades, and *Absalom, Absalom!* is an effort to make sense of events that took place before, during, and after the Civil War. But *Pylon* takes place almost at the same time the book is published—certainly within a few months of the events it describes. The book gives us the confusion of the city, the disparate clashing voices of modern times where sounds, sights, smells, tastes, and touches run together in confusion.

> Now they could cross Grandlieu Street. There was traffic in it now;
> to clash and clang of light and bell trolley and automobile crashed and
> glared across the intersection, rushing in a light curbchannelled spin-
> drift of tortured and draggled serpentine and trodden confetti pending
> the dawn's whitewings—spent tinseldung of Momus' Nilebarge clatter-
> falque. Ordered and marked by light and bell and carrying the two
> imitationleather bags and the drill mealsack they could now cross,
> the four others watching the reporter who, the little boy still asleep
> on his shoulder, stood at the extreme of the curbedge's channelbrim,
> in poised and swooping immobility like a scarecrow weathered grad-
> ually out of the earth which had supported it erect and intact and now
> poised for the first light vagrant air to blow it into utter dissolution.
> He translated himself into a kind of flapping gallop, gaining fifteen or
> twenty feet on the others before they could move, passing athwart
> the confronting glares of automobiles apparently without contact with
> earth, like one of the apocryphal nighttime batcreatures whose nest or
> home no man ever saw, which are seen only in midswoop caught for
> a second in a lightbeam between nothing and nowhere. (Introduction,
> "Night in the Vieux Carre," *Pylon* 68)

We can see Faulkner here trying to do something radically different from what he was doing in *Absalom, Absalom! Absalom, Absalom!* is all about past and future—Thomas Sutpen striving to create a dynasty, to have his name imprinted in the Mississippi land to endure forever, and we get in that book the story of his life and his death in the futile and tragic effort to accomplish his dream.

But these people have little past—until Faulkner succumbs to his inner demand to create a past and a genealogy for Roger Shumann, the pilot. In the novel, two contradictory philosophies of life collide with each other. One is cumulative—human life as a collection of building blocks, the days like bricks to be laid on top of each other so that a unified structure *rises*, that it becomes something to be seen by the ages, a monument to a life that *was*. Life is *progressive*, and if you build life aright, you accumulate fortune and name and fame so that like Colonel Feinman in *Pylon* you can have an air-port named after you. But this kind of careful cumulative life is what T. S. Eliot calls a "waste land" because it is so carefully calculated that it lets us sink into the machinery of modern mass culture without feeling, indeed without the ability to have any passion at all.

In Eliot's poem "The Love Song of J. Alfred Prufrock," which Faulkner incorporates as the last chapter of *Pylon*, the narrator assumes always that there will be time, time enough to dare, but the time ends measured out in coffee spoons, a man growing old and powerless in his respectability as the days accumulate and his ability to dare dissolves in age and indecisiveness:

> And indeed there will be time
> To wonder, "Do I dare?" and "Do I dare?"
> Time to turn back and descend the stair,
> With a bald spot in the middle of my hair—
> (They will say: "How his hair is growing thin!")
> My morning coat, my collar mounting firmly to the chin,
> My necktie rich and modest, but asserted by a simple pin—
> (They will say: "But how his arms and legs are thin!")
> Do I dare
> Disturb the universe?
> In a minute there is time
> For decisions and revisions which a minute will reverse.
>
> For I have known them all already, known them all—
> Have known the evenings, mornings, afternoons,
> I have measured out my life with coffee spoons;
> I know the voices dying with a dying fall
> Beneath the music from a farther room.
>   So how should I presume? (lines 37–54)

The fliers in *Pylon* live life and time in another way. They are always looking at watches, always wanting to know the time because time is short, and every time they fly they risk losing all their time in death. They live every day for itself without attention to the past or to the future. Because they are indifferent to continuity, they fascinate the reporter who lives in a repetitive job that continuously seeks to hold onto events in the moment by putting them in words published in a newspaper that is "ephemeral," passing away despite the heaviness of lead type, the alchemy of words, the labor of writing.

The fliers are above these masses in the waste land of earth, the tawdry and tacky modernism of the airport, built to honor Colonel Feinman so that even the beacon flashes FFF in Morse code. The fliers with their *ménage à trois* have left behind the conventional and binding values and the conventional morality of earthlings, living without emphasis in a three-sided marriage that would be a scandal to people like McEachern or Doc Hines in *Light in August*. And it's scandal to Doctor Shumann, Roger's father, in *Pylon*. Indeed Dr. Shumann is cut out of the same tin as Doc Hines.

Yet just as Joe Christmas lives in an illusion of freedom and yet is bound, so do these people live in illusion. They are bound to the progression of one

107

airplane race after another, one contest after another just like the rest of these people. The title "pylon" has some significance here because it calls up one of Faulkner's recurring themes—the circle, the endless return, the continual repetition of our circles of life. The pylon in an air race is the tall metal pole topped with a flag that marks each corner of a racing course in the kind of contests that Faulkner describes here. The planes must fly on the outside of the pylons set at intervals across the land, and to gain advantage they must cut the corners as sharply as possible, turning the planes on their sides and banking so steeply that they may stall and crash, and because they are running with their engines flat out, the engines can explode. Ultimately the pylon is a symbol of a journey that does not go anywhere, part of the myth of eternal return that no matter how energetically and with what power and resolve we enter on life in history, we end in going in arbitrary circles not unlike the circled journey around the courthouse in Jefferson that Benjy insists must always be done to the right. Cycles exist in several places in the novel—the reporter's cycle of being hired and fired, the drunkenness and sobriety of various characters, birth and death, and in the end Laverne tells Doctor Shumann that she will have another child and that she knows the jumper is the father, and she and the jumper will go away together, very much as Lena Grove has gone away with Byron Bunch in *Light in August*. The woman who bears a child in Faulkner carries the world.

The pylon can have other meanings. It can be an obvious phallic symbol if one wants to give it a Freudian interpretation, and it can also be the pylon that stands in stone outside an Egyptian temple, a monument to the dead. So Faulkner may be playing with the idea of sexuality as a temple where we gain sanctuary from a world where one does not fit. I'm not sure.

The reporter is a remake of Gail Hightower, and maybe also of Byron Bunch. He is associated throughout the book with images of death. The editor tells him that his prose has all the facts but no life. Jiggs describes him early: "Tall guy. Says he is a reporter. That looks like they locked the graveyard up before he got in last night" (31). And a little later on someone else calls him a "skeleton" (31).

Throughout the novel, Faulkner evokes T. S. Eliot and the conviction that modern urban society is a waste land. Early in the book we read in the newspaper of the dedicatory monument raised to American aviators and ". . . Colonel H. I. Feinman, Chairman Sewage Board Through Whose Undeviating Vision and Unflagging Effort This Airport was Raised Up and Created out of the Waste Land at the bottom of Lake Rambaud at a Cost of One Million Dollars" (25–26).

Here it is—the combination of money, the equation of money with sewage, the manipulation of nature, the words "waste land" all combined in one brief burst of words. And yet there is high irony here because the airport supposedly created out of "waste land" by which the makers of the airport mean "unprofitable wilderness" has, in fact, become part of the waste land of T. S. Eliot's poem, the "unreal city" where all the "real" impulses of human nature are stifled under the robotic power of conformity.

As Olga W. Vickery has pointed out in one of the earliest and finest books about Faulkner's novels, the reporter is part of that lifeless world. It is a world where things happen, where facts are dumped on us in such profusion that we smother under an avalanche of information, but we are unable to find life in it (145–47). And the reporter is there, perfect denizen of this blasted and hollow world, always looking out at a world that he can collect but never where he can be at home. Here is how the reporter appears:

First Fatality of Air Meet
Pilot Burned Alive

Beyond it, backflung, shirtsleeved, his bald head above the green eyeshade corpseglared too, the city editor looked at the reporter fretfully. "You have an instinct for events," he said. "If you were turned into a room with a hundred people you never saw before and two of them were destined to enact a homicide, you would go straight to them as crow to carrion; you would be there from the very first: you would be the one to run out and borrow a pistol from the nearest policeman for them to use. Yet you never seem to bring back anything but information. Oh you have that, all right, because we seem to get everything that the other papers do and we haven't been sued yet and so doubtless it's all that anyone should expect for five cents and doubtless more than they deserve. But it's not the living breath of news. It's just information. It's dead before you even get back here with it." Immobile beyond the lamp's hard radius the reporter stood, watching the editor with an air leashed, attentive, and alert. "It's like trying to read something in a foreign language. You know it ought to be there; maybe you know by God it is there. But that's all. Can it be by some horrible mischance that without knowing it you listen and see in one language and then do what you call writing in another? How does it sound to you when you read it yourself?"

"When I read what?" the reporter said. Then he sat down in the opposite chair while the editor cursed him. He collapsed upon the chair with a loose dry scarecrowlike clatter as though of his own

skeleton and the wooden chair's in contact, and leaned forward
across the desk, eager, apparently not only on the verge of the grave
itself but in actual sight of the other side of Styx: of the saloons
which have never sounded with cashregister or till; and that golden
District where gleam with frankincense and scented oils the celestial
anonymous bosoms of eternal and subsidised delight. (44–45)

It is worth pointing out, as a slight digression, that the reporter here plays a role common in Faulkner's work—the observer like Gail Hightower or Gavin Stevens, who is at a distance from the real world, trying without great success to make sense of it. But there may also be a commentary on Faulkner himself. As I said, he wrote this book because he got stuck on *Absalom, Absalom!* He wrote, I think, to get some distance from the problems he was having in writing the much greater book. What the editor fears is a terrifying prospect that every writer knows, that somehow he may tell a story that has everything in it that a story seems to require—plot, tension, and even some clarity—but does not have that mysterious quality called *life*. We can pick up almost any piece of writing, read a few paragraphs, and know if it has a vitality that will interest us. Yes, tastes are different, and Faulkner's taste was demanding—much more demanding than our own. I suggest that we see him here in the reporter, wondering if after such a run of spectacular novels, he had written himself out.

Vickery has pointed out that part of the deadness is that our symbols have lost their power (147). Mardi Gras (Fat Tuesday) is traditionally the last day of revel, license, and carnival before midnight brings in the solemn days of Lent and reflection and sorrow for our sins that caused Christ to die his horrible death. But Faulkner saw what is evident to anyone who has ever attended the Mardi Gras festival in New Orleans or New Valois, as it is here. It is only a festival, nothing more than a riotous entertainment devoid of any religious or mythological significance whatsoever. Madam Sosostris, the "famous clairvoyant" in Eliot's *The Waste Land*, does not find the "Hanged Man" the symbol of a suffering Christ who has vanished from the earth. She says, "Fear death by water." This is the suffocating, choking death that stops breath. And at the end of *Pylon*, the penultimate chapter, we have the subtitle "Lovesong of J. A. Prufrock," and the search for Shumann's body in the water of the lake. It is also Eliot's powerful poem about meaninglessness, with life evaporated from our symbols. Human beings in that world are corrupted by one another and death by drowning, death by suffocation. Noyades Street, where the reporter lives, means the street of the drowned.

> I grow old . . . I grow old . . .
> I shall wear the bottoms of my trousers rolled.
>
> Shall I part my hair behind? Do I dare eat a peach?
> I shall wear white flannel trousers, and walk upon the beach.
> I have heard the mermaids singing, each to each.
>
> I do not think that they will sing to me.
>
> I have seen them riding seaward on the waves
> Combing the white hair of the waves blown back
> When the wind blows the water white and black.
>
> We have lingered in the chambers of the sea
> By sea-girls wreathed with seaweed red and brown
> Till human voices wake us, and we drown. (lines 122–33)

In Eliot, a man growing old finds his life devoid of daring, isolated from nature, unable to hear nature sing to him as it sang to our pagan ancestors. Eliot and Faulkner after him are making a bitter comment on Wordsworth's lament in his sonnet:

> The world is too much with us; late and soon,
> Getting and spending, we lay waste our powers;
> Little we see in Nature that is ours;
> We have given our hearts away, a sordid boon!
> This Sea that bares her bosom to the moon;
> The winds that will be howling at all hours,
> And are up-gathered now like sleeping flowers;
> For this, for everything, we are out of tune;
> It moves us not.—Great God! I'd rather be
> A Pagan suckled in a creed outworn;
> So might I, standing on this pleasant lea,
> Have glimpses that would make me less forlorn;
> Have sight of Proteus rising from the sea;
> Or hear old Triton blow his wreathe'd horn.

Wordsworth could at least write some poetry that swept him up into intimations of immortality against a world of increasing doubt. But both Eliot and Faulkner contemplate with a bleaker vision a world where people do not even know that they doubt, where they are hollow without even knowing they are hollow. New Valois becomes a symbol of that world where no sense of mystery exists, where facts prevail, and one set of sensational facts is displaced by another that comes along tomorrow with the relentless repetition of a clock. Vickery comments that "*Pylon* has more references to specific hours of the day and night" than any other Faulkner novel (146). Yet it is meaningless time. It is mere progression, not a *kairos*, not an epiphany or a revelation. New Valois becomes only a maze, chaos without any of the sacred mystery that Rudolf Otto described in his book *The Idea of the Holy*. It is not Delphi, not Jerusalem. And the water of the lake where Shumann has crashed, died, and vanished is no baptismal water of purification and redemption. It is filled with human debris, a burial ground. The narrator tells us:

> The seaplane slip, dredged out, was protected from the sluggish encroachment of the lake's muddy bottom by a sunken mole composed of refuse from the city itself—shards of condemned paving and masses of fallen walls and even discarded automobile bodies—any and all the refuse of man's twentieth century clotting into communities large enough to pay a mayor's salary—dumped into the lake. (171)

The deaths of pilots, the risks, are not in the name of honor but only of money. When Shumann's plane is disabled, he managed to fly in another plane that everyone knows is unsafe, lethal. It is much the same situation that Bayard Sartoris encountered with the poorly designed plane that kills him in *Flags in the Dust*. But Bayard exhibited throughout a death wish. Shumann needs the money. He is like other people in the town consumed with the need for money in a world where money is the currency of all values. Day after day in repetitive motions they risk death to give jaded and hollow people a thrill that they have paid to see, and if they die, the death is deprived of all significance, pagan or Christian. Such is the bleak world of this book.

The reporter is perhaps the central character in the book—of dubious parentage like Joe Christmas and without a name, very much the eccentric in Faulkner's myriad characters who have names and past histories. The reporter is the ideal objective observer, the man to report the facts, to remain detached. But he does not remain objective and detached. He enters the actions because first he makes romantic heroes of these people. He is the Tom Sawyer–like child who looks at the steamboat men on the Mississippi River with envy and longing only to discover when he becomes a pilot on the river himself that the Mississippi and its boatmen and even its sunrises and sunsets have lost all their mystery.

The reporter intervenes because he is fascinated with these people. He takes them home with him. He makes them drink and talk when they ought to be sleeping. And he is the one who works out the scheme of forgery and fraud that allows Roger Shumann to fly the plane that becomes lethal to the pilot. The reporter is brave. He is willing to risk his life by going up with Roger Shumann in the plane so Roger can test it. But the test they give the plane is not the same as a race around pylons at top speed, and when the race comes, the plane cannot stand the stress, and the pilot not only dies but is never found.

I believe that we have a sort of message here from Faulkner, an affirmation that Faulkner is making to himself, perhaps in the conception of *Absalom, Absalom!* At the time Faulkner wrote *Absalom, Absalom!* he must have recognized that it was a tragic and perhaps (to use one of his favorite words) a bleak book. He was working as a screen writer, relatively anonymously. Hemingway, with his glorification of the hero and heroic death and a certain flair for tragic and romantic love, sold thousands of copies of anything he wrote almost as soon as the books hit the bookstores. Thomas Wolfe, the North Carolina writer now almost forgotten, was also a big seller, younger than Faulkner, past his best work already, doomed to die in 1937, but still popular.

I think it entirely possible that we have in the reporter a sort of moral fable addressed to the writer. When the writer meddles in the lives of his (or her) characters and tries to wrench them into something they are not, he can only mess them up. The reporter tries to force these characters into a heroic mold, and he breaks them. They are just as desperate for money as any of the grubby people of New Valois, and as Colonel Feinman and his backers who have put up the money to build a million-dollar airport.

As usual in Faulkner, such redemption as we find is in the woman who bears children and endures. Laverne, the woman in the *ménage à trois*, finally gives up one of her children so she can sink back into a real family, a real marriage with Jack the Jumper, the known father of the child she carries in her womb when Roger Shumann is killed. Her name—Laverne—means "the green," and she is a symbol of the ever-bearing spring that despite the cruelness of April's cold and cruelty inevitably comes to fructify the earth. She is capable of true passion because she is aware of death. When she is about to make her first parachute jump, she comes back into the cockpit—aptly named here—and somehow manages to make love to Roger the pilot in what seems to be pure act, stirred by the awareness that she is about to risk her life and enter into death where no act, no passion, is possible.

As Richard Gray points out, Laverne is like so many of Faulkner's women, somewhat androgynous, boyish looking, cutting her hair short, dressing like a man (199), like Drusilla in *The Unvanquished*, doing mannish things. But while Drusilla is a fighter, Laverne is a mechanic, a parachutist, and very clearly a mother and a woman who has sex with men and enjoys it. When she makes the parachute jump in Kansas, which we know about through flashback, her skirt comes unfastened, and she enrages (and doubtless titillates) the spectators by descending bare-bottomed to earth. She is not ashamed to show herself nearly naked. She has no hesitation in being the lover of two men who know of each other and don't mind sharing her. The people of New Valois would rather spend their sexual energy slipping away from spouses to prostitutes. But then is there any symbolism in how Laverne is dragged through the mire at the end of her jump? Do we have a scene reminiscent of Caddy's muddy drawers in *The Sound and the Fury*? It is possible, but it may be that the filth is only in the eyes of the spectators who make her sex something dirty.

The sexual relations here stand in sharp opposition to the orgy of Mardi Gras, where sexual license is the order of the day—or the night. In New Valois it is a liberty without love, longevity, or commitment, the bought love of prostitutes. In *Pylon* one of the few things not bought is sex or the love or commitment that Laverne gives to both men—a commitment that the reporter sees, admires, and probably does not understand since he believes she might, with the same freedom, give her love to him. But we know that his fantasies are preposterous. A woman as alive as Laverne is not going to give her body to walking death.

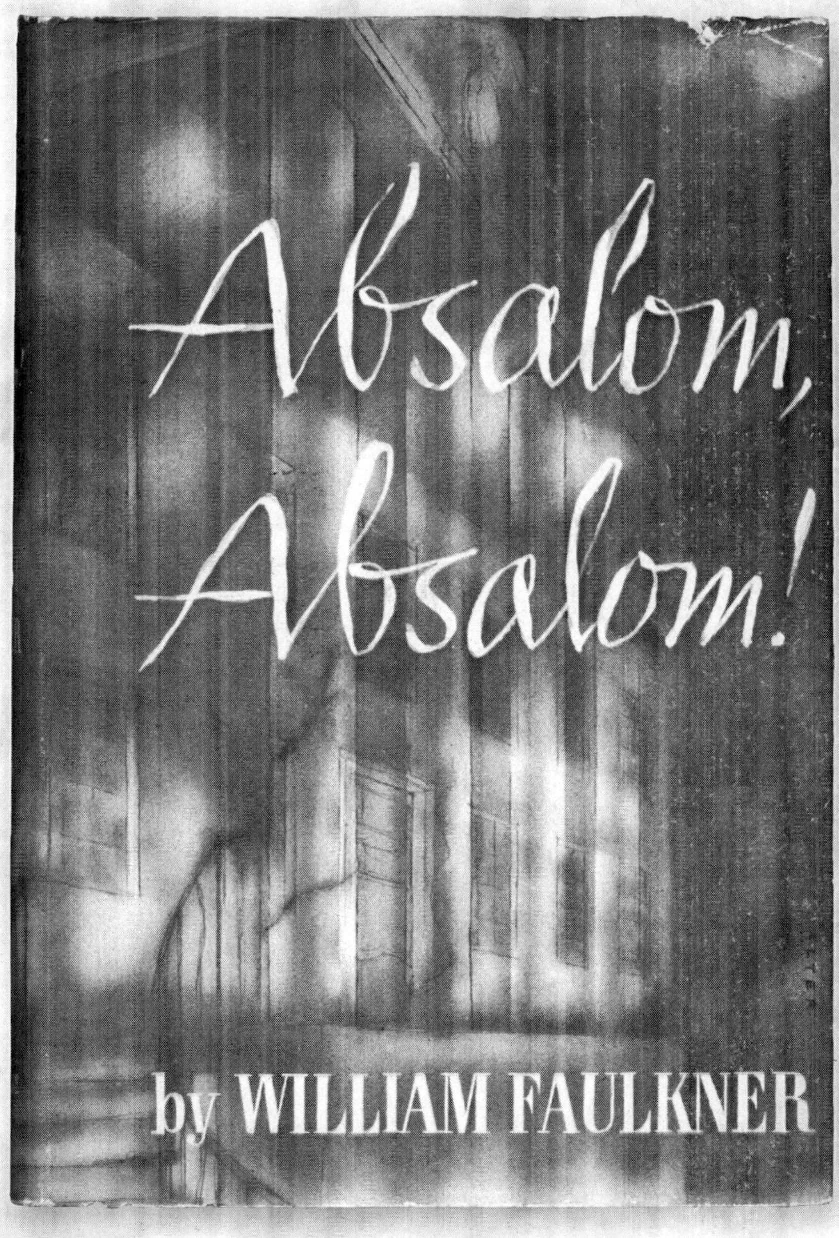
Absalom,
Absalom!
by WILLIAM FAULKNER

ABSALOM, ABSALOM!

Now it's time to tackle one of the most difficult and complex of all Faulkner's novels, *Absalom, Absalom!,* to which he returned after he finished *Pylon*. To my mind it is a beautifully written and constructed book that has bewildered most people at first reading and then bewitched those who are disposed to like Faulkner. Yet it has never enjoyed great popular favor. When he finished reading the galleys, he wrote a friend, "I am going to undertake to sell this book myself to the pictures [. . .]. I am going to ask one hundred thousand dollars for it or nothing, as I do not need to sell it now since I have a job" (Blotner 375). *Gone With the Wind* had just been published, a sensation so enormous that it immediately brought with it a wave of speculation about who would be cast as Scarlett O'Hara. But Faulkner's book was something else. It did not sell more than about seventeen thousand copies—good sales but nothing to compare with *Gone With the Wind*. Many critics rank it among the greatest books in American literature. But in a review in *The New Yorker* Clifton Fadiman called it "the most consistently boring novel to come my way during the last decade" (62).

But those of us who love the novel are swept up into its torrent of words, its construction, its symbolism. It is a novel we can read time and again and always find new things in it. It is, as Faulkner himself suggested, a tragedy. It is also akin to *Moby Dick*, and it hints of Nietzsche. Sutpen seems to be something different, opposite, from the protagonists in many other of Faulkner's novels.

Most obvious, Sutpen is not a wounded war hero who comes into the book obsessed with an outmoded chivalry that leads him to a valiant but futile death. He is not a Donald Mahon, wounded and oblivious to the world around him, the incarnation of the noble sacrifice in a futile and bitter business. He goes to war. But from what we seem to see of him, he does his bit efficiently, dutifully, but with none of the gallant flair that marks the military career of John Sartoris. Nothing about him suggests the warrior who must have his war and must fight because fighting is the ultimate reason for his existence. He is no Bayard Sartoris with a death wish. We are told enigmatically that during the war his troop deposed John Sartoris and put Sutpen in his place as colonel of the regiment. We may suspect from what we know of Colonel Sartoris elsewhere—in *The Unvanquished*, for example—that Colonel Sartoris's gallantry with its overlay of chivalry was too reckless for men who knew that such attitudes could get them killed. Later on when Colonel Sartoris becomes a leader in the Ku Klux Klan or some similar band of fighting men resolved to ward off by violence the rule of carpetbaggers, scalawags, and freed slaves, Sutpen defies them and refuses to join their violent enterprise. He has no illusions about war. He has no desire to continue war when peace has come. His only interest is to take care of his land.

Neither is Sutpen one of those passive, irresolute characters, the paralyzed intellectual like many of the talkative people in *Mosquitoes* or like Horace Benbow in *Flags in the Dust* and *Sanctuary* or like Gail Hightower in *Light in August* or like Quentin Compson in *The Sound and the Fury*. He is not the observer like the reporter in *Pylon*. No, Sutpen is the active, aggressive, driven *agent* resolved to be master of his fate. He has one goal—to found a dynasty—and he pursues it with a fervor that subsumes every other object to an inferior place. He wills to prevail. His will rules his character. He is no indecisive Hamlet, finding excuses not to do what he feels he must do.

We are told that Sutpen has fathered Clytemnestra, named her after the murderous wife of Agamemnon, the woman who inspired the title *As I Lay Dying*. But since he was self-educated, it is just possible that Sutpen got her name wrong. Maybe he intended to name her Cassandra, the daughter of Priam and Hecuba of Troy who is the woman murdered with Agamemnon, the woman whose cries Agamemnon heard as he lay dying. Cassandra was a prophet, a kind of oracle, continually prophesying the fall of Troy, but because she resisted the blandishments of the god Apollo, he spat in her mouth, and no one would believe her. When Troy fell, she was dragged from embracing an image of the goddess Athena and raped by Ajax. Then she went by the casting of lots to the booty of Agamemnon, who took her home with him. Ajax was arrogant to the point that he angered the gods. They drove him to madness, and in the tragedy of Sophocles, he killed himself.

These words seem to be floating images in Faulkner, not precisely attached to one idea but suggesting the Greek sin of hubris, arrogance, doom, death, and, especially in the case Ajax, self-destruction. In such a floating image, we do not seek to find a precise connection between every part of the image and every part of the story the writer tries to tell. These images rather create a mood, and as usual in Faulkner, it is a dark and tragic mood.

The title furthers this mood. Absalom was the son of King David of Israel, and he rebelled against David in David's old age. The story of Absalom and his rebellion takes up more than six long chapters in the book we call Second Samuel in the Hebrew Bible that Christians call the Old Testament. It is one of the longest stories in the Bible with far more time given to Absalom than to Adam and Eve or Ishmael and Isaac. King David had a large harem, and Absalom was the son of one of his wives. His son Amnon was the son of another. David also had a virgin daughter named Tamar, and Amnon lusted after her, and having beguiled her into his chamber by pretending to be sick, he raped her. Having raped her, he hated her, and the author of the book says, "Then Amnon hated her exceedingly; so that the hatred wherewith he hated her was greater than the love wherewith he had loved her" (2 Samuel 13:15). And he cast her aside. Scandal ensued. Absalom bided his time. Two years after the rape, Absalom invited Amnon to a festival in the country, and having got him drunk, Absalom had him killed. Absalom then fled beyond the borders of Israel, and the Bible says that David mourned for him but felt that for this murder he must leave him in exile. But because of his love for him, David brought him back after three years, and Absalom built a popular following and rebelled against his father. In the battle that followed, the forces of David under his general Joab prevailed against Absalom's army, and Absalom fled on the back of a mule, and his head caught in the branches of an oak tree, and the Bible says, "He was taken up between the heaven and the earth; and the mule that was under him went away" (2 Samuel 18:9). David had commanded Joab and his army to do no hurt to Absalom, but Joab took three darts and thrust them into Absalom's heart so that he died. When David heard of it, he uttered one of the great laments of the Bible:

> And the king was much moved, and went up to the chamber over the
> gate, and wept: and as he went, thus he said, O my son Absalom, my
> son, my son Absalom! would God I had died for thee, O Absalom, my
> son, my son! (2 Samuel 18:33)

It should be mentioned, too, that in the course of this story, a "wise woman," an oracle of some sort, came to David to speak to him about life

119

and death. She declares the tragic wisdom of the ages: "For we must needs die, and are as water spilled out on the ground which cannot be gathered up again; neither doth God respect any person" (2 Samuel 14:14).

As I say, these are floating images, and Faulkner uses them to create a mood. He does not sketch his story neatly on top of the images so that every part of the image has some relation to the novel Faulkner writes. They provide a mood, and the mood is dark.

Sutpen is a sort of Nietzschean superman who refuses to accept the condition of his birth. We have already seen that Faulkner has in previous books depicted conventional morality as arbitrary, as conformity to society rather than substantially grounded in divine or human nature. He seems to have adopted for his characters both Darwin and Freud. Our human nature demands that we reproduce our species. In this effort Sutpen becomes one of the most Darwinian of his characters, but also biblical in that the Hebrew Bible offers immortality of a sort only to those who propagate children, especially sons. Sutpen lives in society, but Freud has taught that we have society and its mores—its morals and its laws—as a means of sublimating our sexual energy. Civilization represents displaced sexuality. I don't hold to that Freudian view, but it may have been in Faulkner's mind.

One does not have to be a Freudian to believe that values have an arbitrary quality about them. Certainly the previous books Faulkner wrote give us a society whose sexual values are at least arbitrary, often absurd, and contrary to the inclinations of our minds and the desires of our bodies. Yet these values in Faulkner and in reality succeed in holding society together. This successful social glue that society provides—as thinkers as far back as Ralph Waldo Emerson had copiously noted—is bought at the price of our own individuality. We become so immersed by the desire to conform and be approved by our peers that we make no effort at all to explore or to develop that part of us that is unique to our own individual existence, our being in time, unique in that amazing, inexplicable, and miraculous way that we have a selfhood, a consciousness that no one else shares or even knows.

Nietzsche's superman is not amoral. But he defines his morals by his own will. Nietzsche held that it is impossible to imagine a world where what is deemed fair and just to one man can be considered fair to all. He held that those who lived according to conventional morality never discover the freedom that is inherent in individual existence. Nietzsche's superman was not the superman of Nazi ideology.

Yet in Sutpen we have some affinities to the dictators, to the men on horseback, the strong men of the 1920s and the 1930s who used force to take over their countries and to impose their will on whole peoples and to seek to control all the wild vagaries of unpredictable chance that affect the histories of nations. These dictators wanted to make the nation part of a design in history. It is more or less the tail end of Henri Bergson's *élan vital*, the force of an all-conquering energy that can sweep all opposition before it and impose its own order on events. Faulkner's perception—the tragic vision—is that all such efforts are doomed not only to failure but to the destruction of those who undertake them.

We know that Sutpen has a conscience. Faulkner seems to think that we all have that. Sutpen told General Compson that he had an earlier wife, that he had discovered in Haiti that she was an octoroon—that is, that African ancestry composed one-eighth of her blood inheritance. That means that one of her great-grandparents was black. He had to repudiate her. Conscience was to be quelled by his design (211). Sutpen has a kind of innocence about him: "it was that innocence again, the innocence which believed that the ingredients of morality were like the ingredients of pie and cake and once you had measured them and balanced them and mixed them and put them into the oven, it was finished and nothing but pie or cake could come out" (211–12). That, at least, is how Quentin, telling the story, interprets what his grandfather had to say about Sutpen.

Now let's look at the structure. The story unfolds as a collection of narratives gathered in the consciousness of the doomed Quentin Compson. It seems essential to recall that we join the Quentin of this novel to the Quentin of *The Sound and the Fury*, that we make this novel an extension of Faulkner's favorite among his own works. So we know that Quentin will kill himself in June 1910 and that the motive for his suicide will be tied up with his incestuous longings for the body of his sister, Caddy.

At the start of the book, Quentin is summoned by Miss Rosa Coldfield to tell her side of the story of Sutpen. Miss Rosa Coldfield seems to play on the image of the rose, a virgin. But "Coldfield" is a wintry landscape and therefore barren. She has been put away by Sutpen, betrothed to him and rejected. The biblical allusion would be Matthew 1:18–21, where Joseph learns that the woman to whom he is betrothed, the Virgin Mary, is with child. He is ready to put her away privately when God appears to him in a dream and announces that the child was conceived by the Holy Spirit. If Miss Rosa was put away by Sutpen after their engagement was announced, the implication in the community would naturally be that Sutpen had discovered that she was not a virgin. Therefore, she wants to leave her own legacy to Quentin. She wants him to know that she rejected Sutpen because of his obscene proposition.

The obscene proposition, as Miss Rosa sees it, is that Sutpen proposed to marry Miss Rosa on condition that they conceive the child first. The child would also have to be a son. Miss Rosa's outrage roils through her story, seemingly expressed with her last, desperate energy because, when we come to Chapter 6 and find Quentin and his roommate Shreve in their chamber in the "iron cold" of January at Harvard, we learn from a letter sent by Quentin's father that Miss Rosa has died. She is aptly named because she is indeed a cold field, having not a shadow of pity for Sutpen or sympathy and perhaps of understanding.

Then in Chapter 2 the narrator shifts, and it is Mr. Compson sitting on the veranda in a summer of wistaria explaining to Quentin some things about Sutpen that have been handed down in the community, things that Mr. Compson was told by his own father. Then in Chapter 5 we get Miss Rosa's narrative that culminates in Sutpen's indecent proposal. And in Chapter 6, we have Quentin and Shreve in their cold room at Harvard, the letter from Mr. Compson telling them that Miss Rosa has died.

At this point in the narrative, we seem to know several things. Sutpen appeared in Jefferson at age twenty-five in 1833. He manages to possess one hundred square miles of land, that is, a plantation that would be roughly ten miles on each side. There are 640 acres to a square mile, and therefore Sutpen would own something like 64,000 acres of land—a huge tract of land. He gets the land, we discover, from the Indians by chicanery. He comes trailing mystery behind him. In similar mystery, he procures the resources to begin building a great house that symbolically enough seems never finished although we are told that it is. While the house is abuilding, Sutpen lives a wild, animal-like existence, running naked with his horde of wild, black slaves, sometimes fighting with them for the pure sport of it. It is this wildness, this hint of sexual license or licentiousness, that seems to cause the hostility that he stirs up in the community. Not only does he fight with his slaves. He brings in two women slaves and apparently uses them as his concubines, and he engenders Clytie, Clytemnestra, the one who should perhaps have been Cassandra because she is the prophecy of the doom of his hopes. But, as Clytemnestra, she is also an image of the death of the extended life that he—Agamemnon—will bring on himself or have brought on himself.

When he succeeds in marrying Ellen, "the stainless wife and the unimpeachable father-in-law" (39), the wedding is held at night. A hundred people are invited. Only ten show up. Some of his wild slaves are there, holding up burning brands made of pine knots, just as the wild slaves had gone about delivering the invitations. A crowd stands outside the almost empty church, and when the wedding party emerges, the people outside fling dirt and rotten fruit and vegetables at Sutpen (44). I think we are left to infer that these angry citizens feel that something is wrong with Sutpen's attitude towards race, that his cultivation of these wild black men is dangerous to the mores of the community, and that therefore we have a deepening of the motivation Sutpen has to create a dynasty that will overawe this community. So here is a Nietzschean character, one who insists on the freedom of his own will as the source of all his moral values, and yet we find him limited in that he must impress the community. Therefore, in the end just as the aviators in *Pylon* are shown to be bound to the money that corrupts all things in modern society, so is Sutpen shown to be bound to the community that he seems to reject, for he must have a son to carry on his dynasty, and that son must be entirely white because his community will not otherwise be awed.

But let us go on. From his union with Ellen, Sutpen produces two children, Judith and Henry. Judith seems to be named for the apocryphal character Judith who kills Holofernes—another woman's name to symbolize death for a strong man. Sutpen has his son—Henry, bearing the name of eight English kings, the royal name that had been applied to more English kings than any other by the time Faulkner finished writing his book. Sutpen obviously has a strange flair for names.

We also know that Henry came under the spell of an older youth named Charles Bon. But is it Bon (good) or Bond (bondage)? We know that Bon courted Judith, became engaged to her, and seems in truth to have loved her. We seem to be fairly certain from the various narratives that Sutpen investigated Bon by going down to New Orleans. There he discovered that Bon was legally married to an octoroon woman—a woman with one-eighth African blood. This marriage is the first impediment we know to Bon's proposed marriage to Judith. Do we know that the marriage to the octoroon woman was valid? We seem to have that fact. Certainly we know that Henry and his father quarrel about Bon, and in consequence of this quarrel, Henry renounces his birthright. That is, he renounces the dream that his father has for himself as well as his plans for Henry. And then the final, unassailable truth we know is that as the two young men return from honorable service in the Civil War, Henry shoots Bon to death almost at the very doorway of the unfinished Sutpen house, and Bon is buried in the family plot at Sutpen's Hundred with the tombstone announcing that he died on May 3, 1865, and that he was thirty-three years and five months old, indicating that he was also born about Christmas time in 1831—not two years before Sutpen turned up in Jefferson.

So here we have a set of clues in what Cleanth Brooks has called a model of the detective story. This is the material that Shreve and Quentin have to work with as they try to connect the clues and arrive at meaning. They are the detectives, as Brooks says, and detectives turn out to be like historians trying by means of plausible conjectures to fit the evidence together into a story that can be told as a historical narrative (311–12). The history has to be told because it is related to us, to what we are today. We are the cumulative working out of who our ancestors were, and our society is inherited as though we might inherit our fate in the evolutionary product of societies that have lived and died in the eons before we came into our own chancy and unpredictable being.

We have several stories as our evidence. The most solid blocks of evidence that Quentin and Shreve have to work with are the stones in the Sutpen family graveyard that give the names and dates of death and sometimes the birthdates of those who lie there. Much less tangible evidence comes from stories told by Rosa Coldfield and by Mr. Compson, who passes on what his father told him. Driving Quentin and Shreve is the conviction that a previous marriage is not enough to explain the act of murder, Henry's shooting of Charles Bon.

When he was at the University of Virginia in the 1950s, a student asked a question about Sutpen:

> Q. Mr. Faulkner, in *Absalom, Absalom!* does anyone of the people who talks about Sutpen have the right view, or is it more or less a case of thirteen ways of looking at a blackbird with none of them right?
>
> A. That's it exactly. I think that no one individual can look at truth. It blinds you. You look at it and you see one phase of it. Someone else looks at it and sees a slightly awry phase of it. But taken all together, the truth is in what they saw though nobody saw the truth intact. So these are true as far as Miss Rosa and as Quentin saw it. Quentin's father saw what he believed was truth, that was all he saw. But the old man was himself a little too big for people no greater in stature than Quentin and Miss Rosa and Mr. Compson to see all at once. It would have taken perhaps a wiser or more tolerant or more sensitive or more thoughtful person to see him as he was. It was, as you say, thirteen ways of looking at a blackbird. But the truth, I would like to think, comes out, that when the reader has read all these thirteen different ways of looking at the blackbird, the reader has his own fourteenth image of that blackbird which I would like to think is the truth. (Gwynn and Blotner 273–74)

Several points are to be made from this comment by Faulkner. One is that Faulkner esteems Sutpen more than the characters who talk most about him. Note that he does not think any of them has the stature to be able to judge Sutpen. Sutpen is too much for them. So when we read their accounts of him, we see the man glimmering through the individual curvatures of mirrors that reflect *their* lives, their consciousness. We can see that quality especially in Miss Rosa's account by its furious vehemence.

Mr. Compson, on the other side, sees Sutpen, as Michael Millgate tells us, as one of those late nineteenth-century people absorbed in decadence, for whom nothing is new and nothing is forbidden, and for whom no grand purpose nor reason pervades life. Life is to be seen not as a substance but rather as an aesthetic experience. Anything is valuable only in so far as it inspires some sort of ripe feeling, but not passion—merely a sense of enjoyment, pleasure, and perhaps also superiority in knowing that one is enjoying a pleasure that *hoi polloi*, the common herd, may regard as revolting, criminal, or depraved. Mr. Compson mentions Oscar Wilde and Aubrey Beardsley, men who practiced a sort of flamboyant artificiality while they mocked the moral conventions of their times. Mr. Compson must see Sutpen with a certain envy. Mr. Compson is passive, and we know that he eventually drinks himself to death without accomplishing anything. In contrast, Sutpen has a manly vigor, a will, a sheer physicality that makes him a fighter and provocateur of destiny.

Quentin, on the other hand, suffers most, suffers grandly, and sees the entire drama of Sutpen, of Henry, of Charles Bon as a doubling of his own misery. Quentin, remember, held a pistol in his hand, and with it he could have killed Dalton Ames, the violator of his sister's virginity. But he could not pull the trigger. Henry did his best to persuade Charles Bon to do the right thing, to renounce Judith. But when a proud and stubborn Bon—who just may have been in love with Judith—refused to renounce her and refused to break the publicly proclaimed engagement, Henry killed him. As Wash Jones cries out in his role as messenger of death, "Henry has done shot that durn French feller. Kilt him dead as a beef" (106).

Like his father, Quentin is passive in his view of life. He listens patiently to Miss Rosa Coldfield. He says "Yessum" to her several times, the servant's tone obedient and undemanding. He listens just as patiently to his father's rambling monologues. And he lets Shreve interrupt him time and again and take over the story Quentin is telling. To one passive and doomed as Quentin is, Sutpen must have had a sort of epic grandeur, the tragic hero brought down by a combination of his own flaws and by chance.

But what was the nature of the chance? It has seemed to many critics that Shreve and Quentin make up much of the story—and I suspect that Faulkner wants us to consider just that possibility. Then we have Quentin and Shreve arriving at the supposition that Sutpen's first wife was an octoroon woman and that when Bon turned up at Sutpen's Hundred, or even before that encounter, Sutpen realized that, by some vicious and incredible chance, Henry had met Sutpen's son by that first wife, and that son, put away, had now returned and that, as Quentin suggests, the whole edifice of Sutpen's design comes down as if it had been made of smoke (215).

Bon has in this version deliberately come to the University of Mississippi, a small, primitive college in the wilds of Mississippi itself, and he has deliberately seduced Henry, his father's son, his own half-brother. In Mr. Compson's version of the story, Bon corrupts Henry, seduces him not in an overtly homosexual sense but rather gives him an idea of manhood that Henry in his countrified ways always wants to emulate. Henry remains a puritan despite his admiration of Bon's worldly ways. (But then Puritans are always fascinated by the worldliness of others: that fascination keeps them puritanical, I suppose.) All this would seem to be a fantasy that Mr. Compson makes up, trying to make history out of the relics of the past.

Even Mr. Compson realizes he doesn't quite have it all. He tells Quentin:

> Yes, Judith, Bon, Henry, Sutpen: all of them. They are there, yet something is missing; they are like a chemical formula exhumed along with the letters from that forgotten chest, carefully, the paper old and faded and falling to pieces, the writing faded, almost indecipherable yet meaningful, familiar in shape and sense; the name and presence of volatile and sentient forces; you bring them together in the proportions called for; but nothing happens; you re-read, tedious and intent, poring, making sure that you have forgotten nothing, made no miscalculation; you bring them together again and again nothing happens: just the words, the symbols, the shapes themselves, shadowy, inscrutable and serene, against that turgid background of horrible and bloody mischancing of human affairs. (80)

The suggestion here is that the data of history lie inert until someone in the present can put everything together, make connections, and suppositions, and put living flesh on the still, dry bones of the past. The chemical formula drawn from the trunk and spread out to be read makes no sense or does nothing until the chemist acts on it to see if what is written down in truth corresponds to the symbols dry and dead on the paper. The difference, however, is that the chemical formula can be repeatedly tested. The chemist can test it, prove it, again and again, and the precise relation of these symbols to reality can be seen. But events of the human past can never be repeated with any chance of seeing what *really* happened.

Anyway, history always has a cumulative quality, whether done in the folk tone or in scholarly discourse. At Yale in bygone day I heard William Golding say about the deserted island in his novel *Lord of the Flies* that it represented Eden ruined by history. The boys abandoned there by war, cut off from adults, can pick the fruit of the trees and survive with no difficulty until they are rescued by adults—who happened to be locked in what seems to be World War III. But they bring with them a paranoia from the adult world—or it may be part of human nature. They divide against one another. At a moment, a combat high in the air above their island causes a fighter pilot to eject from his aircraft, but he descends silently through the night already a corpse, hanging on the lines of a parachute, and he comes to earth on a high part of the island. The wind fills his chute from time to time, making the corpse move, rise to a sitting position and fall back again. Some of the boys see the motion. Instead of drawing near to it to ascertain that it is a dead man, they assume that it is a god, the Lord of the Flies, and they assume, too, that they must make a blood sacrifice to it. At the end they are chasing poor Piggy, the intellectual among them, to kill him for their god.

Golding told us that afternoon that the parachutist dead but moved by the wind was his metaphor of history. The past is dead. We cannot recover it. We cannot live in it. Yet we continue to sacrifice the present to it. We continue to treat it as a god that must be appeased.

And that is what happens to Thomas Sutpen. He passes through several stages of life. The first is a deprived childhood placed improbably in the wild backwoods of West Virginia, a kind of Eden. It is the first period of his innocence. At ten years old with a drunken father snoring sedately on the back of an ox-drawn wagon, he, along with his family, moved down out of the mountains and into the Tidewater. Note that almost as usual in Faulkner, Sutpen's mother was dead, and the family is set in motion by the women, Sutpen's sisters, one of whom becomes pregnant and is delivered of a baby along the way (180–81). His long childhood journey into the Tidewater is a journey out of Eden—the mountains, the wilderness—into a world that, as Quentin passes on the story that Sutpen has told General Compson, shows the inequalities of society in a fallen world. General Compson describes the passage:

127

" [. . .] doggeries and taverns now become hamlets, hamlets now
become villages, villages now towns, and the country flattened out

now with good roads and fields and niggers working in the fields
while white men sat fine horses and watched them, and more fine
horses and men in fine clothes, with a different look in the face from
mountain men about the taverns where the old man was not even
allowed to come in by the front door and from which his mountain
drinking manners got him ejected before he would have time to get
drunk good (so that now they began to make really pretty good time)
and no laughter and jeers to the ejecting now, even if the laughter
and jeers had been harsh and without much gentleness in them.

"That's the way he got it. He had learned the difference not only
between white men and black ones, but he was learning that there
was a difference between white men and white men not to be measured by lifting anvils or gouging eyes or how much whiskey you could
drink then get up and walk out of the room. That is, he had begun to
discern that without being aware of it yet. He still thought that that
was just a matter of where you were spawned and how; lucky or not
lucky; and that the lucky ones would be even slower and lother than
the unlucky to take any advantage of it or credit for it, feel that it gave
them anything more than the luck; that they would feel if anything
more tender toward the unlucky than the unlucky would ever need
to feel toward them. He was to find all that out later. He remembered
when he did it, because that was the same second when he discovered the innocence." (182–83)

Sutpen's childhood innocence was to assume equality. He was, after all,
in Jefferson's state, Virginia, where the writer of the Declaration of Inde-
pendence had been spawned, Jefferson who wrote, "we hold these truths to
be self-evident, that all men are created equal." But Sutpen the child discovered that whatever creation all men and women are not equal: when he
was sent to the door of a big white house expecting to be shown in, given
a tour, he was instead contemptuously turned away by a black slave. And
at that moment Sutpen lost his innocence and resolved not only to be rich
himself, not only to become a gentleman, but to make his mark on history,
to establish his own empire that would by his own will be impressed on time
as an enduring monument, his Old Testament immortality.

And Sutpen's destiny, his design, is done in by the same influence, the
same force that does in the South itself. That is race. It is not merely race
as appearance, not the sense of race as radical difference between blacks
and whites. No, it is race as a tissue of words and values inherited from the
past, from history, that classifies the Africans as "the other."

Race seems to hit Sutpen twice. When he is in Haiti, he marries a woman
with "mixed blood" whom he then repudiates. He cannot *see* that she has

mixed blood. But in the past she has had an African ancestor, and that past—obscure and almost lost—is what governs Sutpen's decision to repudiate her.

And now we find another piece of the story. The wife Sutpen repudiated in Haiti comes back to be the mother of Charles Bon, who, Mr. Compson suggests to Henry, was named Charles Bon—Charles Good—by Sutpen himself (213). It is all important that we know this piece of the story, for if it is not true, we have no clear evidence for all the fantasies that Quentin and Shreve concoct in their room at Harvard so long after the events. In Chapter 6 we get many of Quentin's memories. Does he share them with Shreve? It seems that he does, and that they are the narrator's summary of a conversation (143). Throughout we have a narrator's voice that rolls majestically on, giving both the substance and at least part of the meaning of their conversation, and sometimes it is broken by a different voice, usually Shreve, who sounds very much like an amazed adolescent. Where does Mr. Compson get that information that Quentin conveys to Shreve late in Chapter 7, well over two-thirds of the way through the novel? Shreve himself is surprised that Mr. Compson has held this information silent for so long. This is a critical passage because it ties important threads in the book together. Quentin says to Shreve of Sutpen:

> He chose the name himself, Grandfather believed, just as he named them all—the Charles Goods and the Clytemnestras and Henry and Judith and all of them—the entire fecundity of dragons' teeth as Father called it. And Father said—
>
> "Your father," Shreve said. "He seems to have got an awful lot of delayed information awful quick, after having waited forty-five years. If he knew all this, what was his reason for telling you that the trouble between Henry and Bon was the octoroon woman?"
>
> "He didn't know it then. Grandfather didn't tell him all of it either, like Sutpen never told Grandfather quite all of it."
>
> "Then who did tell him?"
>
> "I did," Quentin did not move, did not look up while Shreve watched him. "The day after we—after that night when we—"
>
> "Oh," Shreve said. "After you and the old aunt. I see. Go on. And Father said—" (214)

Now the important question comes here: how did Quentin acquire the information that he passed on to his father? Quentin says that he told his father after his night visit to Miss Rosa—the second visit that he made to her in the September days before he went to Harvard in 1909. Shreve seems to assume that Miss Rosa told him. But Quentin does not say that. He says only that he told his father the day after the night visit to Miss Rosa, and it is entirely possible that Miss Rosa did not tell him anything, that he has had a flight of fantasy, and that, starting with Miss Rosa's bitter story, he has made up a connecting link and told it to his father as truth.

Shreve then propounds the story of incest, a story whose seeds Quentin has planted. And it is Shreve who works up a means of explaining the coincidence that brought Bon to the University of Mississippi and in touch with Henry. Bon's mother plotted it all along. That was her vengeance. But that is Shreve's story, and we do not know if it is true. Like so many of our stories about the past, it is plausible enough to make us hope it is true because then we fill in part of the missing knowledge of the past that leaves it always a perplexing puzzle. Or maybe it is dramatic enough to make us want it to be true because then it is part of the mythic grandeur of the past that makes it epic and reduces our own time to an almost sought mediocrity so that we are happily paralyzed because epic is beyond us.

But then the question comes again: who told Quentin that Sutpen was Bon's father? Quentin never says that it was Miss Rosa, and it would seem that if Miss Rosa knew all that she would have made more of it. It is just possible that Henry himself told Quentin the story, that the two of them talked long enough for Quentin to acquire detailed knowledge of the precise dilemma that faced Sutpen when Bon and Henry became friends. And the reigning supposition of the three Compsons is that Sutpen told Henry that Bon was his brother and that Henry by this time had fallen so under Bon's spell—perhaps in love with him in a sexless, slightly homosexual way—that Henry has repudiated his father, repudiated the destiny that Sutpen had crafted for him, and therefore repudiated his birthright.

In the middle of the war, Sutpen comes back to Jefferson on leave, having transported a worthy gravestone of Italian marble for his dead wife, Ellen, and thirty years after he has told General Compson part of his story—the part about going to Haiti, finding a wife, repudiating her—he tells General Compson something of his dilemma, perhaps enough then to let General Compson know that Bon is his, Sutpen's, son.

Quentin and Shreve work out a broad scenario by which Henry and Bon go to New Orleans—but only after Sutpen has been there before them—and ascertain that yes, Bon is the son of the octoroon mistress/wife whom Sutpen has married and then repudiated in Haiti. In the elaborate plot worked out by Shreve, Bon is the tool of his mother's vengeance and her lawyer's mercenary scheming, and in consequence Bon goes to the University of Mississippi as a pawn in an elaborate plot with blackmail and vengeance at the heart of it. The plot works. Bon seduces Henry just as the plot intended. Bon discovers slowly that Sutpen is the missing father. And then Bon foils the plot by wanting not vengeance or blackmail but recognition. And it is just this recognition that Sutpen refuses to give him. So Bon continues his plan to marry Judith—who as an inexperienced and isolated country girl is seduced by this stylish and courtly and slightly epicene character just as Henry is. Bon becomes a romantic character a little like Edmond Dantes in *The Count of Monte Cristo,* both to Judith and to Henry—but more important to Shreve, who rushes ahead with the story and apparently seduces Quentin with it so that by the end of this part of the novel Quentin and Shreve are telling (manufacturing) the story to one another so rapidly that Faulkner no longer makes an effort to tell us which one of them supplies what parts! In that tale Bon takes on a kind of stoic honor, the character from chivalry who assaults the lawyer who thinks only of money. Indeed Bon is so honorable that, in their imagined version of the story, Bon is the one who goes out of his way to reveal to Henry not only the fact that they are brothers but also that Bon has an octoroon mistress and a child by her, that he has duplicated in a grand way his father's past in Haiti—though Bon's theatre of operation is New Orleans —and that he is further prepared to go the second step and duplicate the repudiation of a wife and a son who bear in them a spot of African blood and to marry a woman, his own sister in Bon's case, who is incontestably white. Henry is willing to accept it all—once he has got used to it.

At that point the war intervenes. Henry is the one in this fabricated story who says, "But you will have to wait! You will have to give me time! Maybe the war will settle it and we won't need to" (273). But the war serves to bring Bon one more chance to see Sutpen and be recognized, acknowledged, and still he, Bon, is willing in exchange for this acknowledgment to accept the incest and to go away and never see Judith again (279). But although in this fancy Sutpen sees Bon, he does not acknowledge him. Instead Sutpen calls Henry to his tent and tells him that Bon must not marry Judith, that Henry must prevent it. By now Henry has accepted the idea of incest. But at this moment, Sutpen plays his trump card:

> – *He cannot marry her, Henry.*
> *Now Henry speaks.*
> – *You said that before. I told you then. And now, and now it wont be much longer now and then we wont have anything left: honor nor pride nor God since God quit us four years ago only He never thought it necessary to tell us; no shoes nor clothes and no need for them; not only no land to make food out of but no need for the food and when you dont have God and honor and pride, nothing matters*

except that there is the old mindless meat that dont even care if
it was defeat or victory, that wont even die, that will be out in the
woods and fields, grubbing up roots and weeds.—Yes. I have
decided, Brother or not, I have decided. I will. I will.
*   — He must not marry her, Henry.*
*   — Yes. I said Yes at first, but I was not decided then. I didn't let*
him. But now I have had four years to decide in. I will. I am going to.
*   — He must not marry her, Henry. His mother's father told me that*
her mother had been a Spanish woman. I believed him; it was not
until after he was born that I found out that his mother was part
negro. (283)

So it is not incest that makes Henry kill Bon but that Bon has a spot of African blood. All this tale, spun out in the room at Harvard, may be nothing but fantasy. But it is just possible that Henry told Quentin that he killed Bon for that reason. Bon insists on persisting in his demand that Sutpen acknowledge him. Sutpen refuses. Bon dies, and Sutpen's dream is demolished.

The effect of all this on Quentin, who will commit suicide because he lusts for his sister, must be to make him believe that the South is indeed cursed, that it will accept incest before it will accept miscegenation, that God has indeed cursed it because, in search of a racial "purity," it has compromised and perhaps cast off every moral value. "I don't hate it." Quentin says. Yet Sutpen becomes a symbol of the South, and his downfall is proof enough of the reasons that God has quit the place. And there may just be the suggestion here of tragedy in the classical mode where the tragic protagonist is brought down by the implacable forces of destiny but a higher set of values is thereby proclaimed to be set in the order of the universe. And the value here affirmed is the very equality that Sutpen knew in his Eden, western Virginia, where he was a child and innocent.

I have spoken at some length about *Absalom, Absalom!* as tragedy without defining my terms. It is always a mistake to speak of tragedy as if everyone understands what we are talking about. In fact, "tragedy" is one of the most subtle and difficult of topics, and it has been debated with vigor but without conclusiveness ever since the time of the Greeks who seem to have invented it—although one can make a case, I think, for tragic features in the poetic portions of the book of Job.

In traditional tragedy a great figure passes from prosperity to misery in the course of the drama. Aristotle held that tragedy involves us in terror and pity and that in the end these emotions are cleansed from us by catharsis. For Aristotle tragedy must also have a plot, and it must be treated with the utmost seriousness. The plot involves conflict. And it involves *hamartia*, the tragic error or flaw in the main character that leads to catastrophe. The flaw may be a moral lapse. Or it may be simply a mistake. We may interpret Sutpen in either way. We may see his mistake in assuming that no human being is worth anything when considered in the light of his conception of his destiny. He would seem to be completely amoral. And when he treats Milly Jones as nothing better than an animal, not even as esteemed as a mare, Wash Jones kills him with a scythe. But if we could conjure Sutpen up out of the ground to get him to deliver his own opinion, he would doubtless say that his mistake, his *hamartia*, was to marry the woman he thought to be Spanish when in fact she was African. Tragedy therefore has several dimensions, and it looks different as we consider it from our own point of view.

But I want to argue that tragedy always presents a value system, and the catastrophe comes to the protagonist for violating it. The value system may be the value system of the society, in which case the catastrophe may befall an innocent person as it does Desdemona in a society where a husband is justified in putting his wife to death for unfaithfulness. Or the value system may be that of the writer who repudiates the value system of the person who suffers the catastrophe, as Shakespeare does with Macbeth.

For Faulkner, I think, tragedy comes to the South because of race and violence and perhaps also because of an unfeelingness, a lack of compassion, that is a part of both racism and violence. Look how many characters we have seen so far who seem to have no compassion for anyone—Jason Compson (Quentin's youngest brother) in *The Sound and the Fury*, Percy Grimm in *Light in August*, Popeye in *Sanctuary*, and the onlookers in *Pylon* who see the death of airmen as only an event to talk about, something that happens, that allows them the satisfaction of telling others of their hollow kind that they were there. And now we have Sutpen in *Absalom, Absalom!*

Faulkner has a genius at showing us cold-hearted, single-minded people preoccupied only with their own ends. And we should not forget Caroline Compson in *The Sound and the Fury*.

I do not have to say much about the violence in Faulkner. It is everywhere, and it is violence treated in the most serious and realistic way. It, therefore, satisfies Aristotle's demand that tragedy be about serious business. Nothing here of the cartoon violence of today's action films.

At a certain moment when he has treated the supreme tragedy of the South in the story of Thomas Sutpen, Faulkner seems to draw back. He has in *Absalom, Absalom!* given us a South where incest can be excused but where a faint trace of African blood in Bon is enough to cause Henry to

133

shoot him dead. This is bleak business, catastrophe indeed, and with how much catharsis? Perhaps the catharsis lies only in our release at having spoken the unspoken truth about the South. Racial issues in the South have always gone on among people in "polite society" as an undercurrent of murmuring, euphemism, jokes, and other forms of elliptical discourse where the bare, blunt meaning of what is said is partly concealed and seldom said in overt and unmistakable language. It is at last a sort of catharsis to have Faulkner say the truth clearly: the morality of the South is such that incest between brother and sister can be accepted, but marriage to a man with one-sixteenth African blood is such a taboo that any man who threatens to violate that taboo can be permissibly killed.

The
Unvanquished
by
WILLIAM
FAULKNER

A RANDOM HOUSE BOOK

THE UNVANQUISHED

It is as though Faulkner, having made that pronouncement in *Absalom, Absalom!,* almost exhausted himself, and his next novel is a kind of conglomeration called *The Unvanquished*, published in February 1938—a significant title for the time with the Stalin purges on in the Soviet Union, Civil War in Spain with the Nazis, and the Italian Fascists helping General Franco overcome the Spanish Republicans, war looming everywhere, and the fuses of violence and horror ignited already and sputtering towards the catastrophe of World War II.

Yet *The Unvanquished* is also a collection of tall tales, improbable, sometimes comic, sometimes stark, but all of them reassuring. It is as though the man who later wrote that man would not only endure but also prevail recovered himself after a novel where a dynasty is cut down in the making by a scythe and the story is in large measure told by a boy on the point of suicide. When Faulkner recovered, he set out to write a story where his imagination was allowed to run through comedy and serious drama to a happy ending.

The Unvanquished had been composed as a collection of stories, some published, and in 1937 Faulkner finished off the collection with the longest of the lot. That was "An Odor of Verbena," verbena being a garden flower that, as Drusilla tells Bayard, is "the only scent you could smell above the smell of horses and courage [. . .]" (220).

The climax of the story and of the novel is Bayard's facing the man who has murdered his father, John Sartoris. Ben Redmond has been John Sartoris's business partner and has fallen out with him. John Sartoris is no innocent in all this. He has taunted Redmond, insulted him, diminished his manhood, and Redmond killed him.

Bayard is summoned home from the University. The universal expectation is that he must now kill Redmond. Bayard has already killed. He has shot Grumby to death, the murderer of Granny—not only shot Grumby but cut off his hand and nailed it to Granny's grave. And Bayard has had enough. Urged on by the town, pushed to revenge by Drusilla, who is exalted at the thought of killing a man, Bayard proves his courage by walking unarmed into Redmond's office, letting Redmond fire his pistol, and standing there while Redmond walks out, gets on the train, and leaves Jefferson forever.

All of this calls to mind the Eumenides of classical mythology, the goddesses whose duty was to avenge crime. By punishing crime they helped sustain the social order. They especially punished murderers, sometimes with madness.

Drusilla plays the part of the Furies in this story. When Bayard arrives home after his long ride with Ringo, she meets Bayard with sexually charged words:

> hearing Drusilla now, the unsentient bell quality gone now, her voice whispering into that quiet death-filled room with a passionate and dying fall: "Bayard." She faced me, she was quite near; again the scent of the verbena in her hair seemed to have increased a hundred times as she stood holding out to me, one in either hand, the two duelling pistols. "Take them, Bayard," she said, in the same tone in which she had said "Kiss me" last summer, already pressing them into my hands, watching me with that passionate and voracious exaltation, speaking in a voice fainting and passionate with promise: "Take them, I have kept them for you. I give them to you. Oh you will thank me, you will remember me who put into your hands what they say is an attribute only of God's, who took what belongs to heaven and gave it to you. Do you feel them? The long true barrels true as justice, the triggers (you have fired them) quick as retribution, the two of them slender and invincible and fatal as the physical shape of love?" [. . .] She stood back, staring at me—the face tearless and exalted, the feverish eyes brilliant and voracious. (237–38)

Here clearly she is one of the Furies, passionately urging vengeance on Bayard. But Bayard refuses to obey her. He must prove that he is brave; he faces Redmond unarmed. But he must also stop the cycle of violence. He will not take the weapons he is proffered.

Many critics say that Bayard here responds in a Christian way, and that may be true. But I am inclined to suggest that Faulkner's model here was the story of Orestes as told especially by Aeschylus. Orestes was the son of Agamemnon and Clytemnestra, and when Clytemnestra killed Agamemnon, Orestes was saved from the same fate by his sister Electra, who stole him away to be raised by an uncle. Apollo required Orestes to avenge his father, and Orestes did so, killing both Clytemnestra and her lover Aegisthus. But then the Furies pursued Orestes and drove him mad. Apollo advised him to go to Delphi and be purified, and so he did, and then he was tried and acquitted because Athena cast her vote in his favor. The effect was to stop the cycle of violence.

In part, Bayard's refusal to seek revenge against Redmond was part of Faulkner's family history. His great-grandfather William Clark Falkner was shot down by a former business associate. His son, Faulkner's grandfather, John Wesley Thompson Falkner, refused to seek revenge on the murderer. We do not know the reasons. Yet in reading the story and knowing how much Faulkner loved Shakespeare, it is impossible not to remember *Hamlet* and the carnage that Hamlet's revenge brought on Elsinor.

Throughout these stories Faulkner seems to purge himself and by extension his own construction of the South from the romantic vision of the Civil War being propagated by, among others, the United Daughters of the Confederacy, during the period about the time Faulkner was born.

The Yankees in this book are gentlemen to a fault. They have such respect for Granny Millard that she is able to become one of the most successful horse and mule thieves in literary history. She is murdered not by the Yankees but by one of the brigands on the Confederate side, the sort thrown up like garbage from the storm caused by any war. The most important moral development noted by Bayard and Ringo is that Granny Millard becomes an out and out liar. She has been a woman of impeccable virtue, the emblem of gallant southern womanhood. But the war turns her morality upside down. Yet despite her death at the hands of a southern bushwhacker the novel remains generally upbeat.

I suspect that writing *The Unvanquished* was a great relief to Faulkner. In *Absalom, Absalom!* he had written one of the darkest and most tragic tales in American literature. He always liked children, and they loved him. His idealization of the power of the innocence of children is evoked in the tale of how Ringo and Bayard run Grumby to earth and kill him. It is a romantic tall tale. It must have been a relief to Faulkner after creating a child as helpless and confused as Vardaman in *As I Lay Dying* or the child and

139

child-man who was Benjy in *The Sound and the Fury*. These boys have an authority in the book that young boys may have in their fantasies but that they seldom can have in reality. They are Tom Sawyers who become authentic heroes.

Perhaps most important, we find no pain in the relation of black and white characters. Yes, Loosh, the older black slave, knows that Vicksburg has fallen and that the Yankees will win the war. And, yes, we see something of the agony and misplaced hope of slaves following the Federal army—all to no effect since the Federals had no idea what to do with them and found them a nuisance. But the relations of Ringo and Bayard involve no trauma. Ringo remains the loyal black servant different from Mammy in *Gone With the Wind* only in his age and sex. He loves Bayard, remains his servant even when slavery has been abolished, and we find no trace that I can see in the torment of race that agitates the drama of *Light in August* and *Absalom, Absalom!*

Drusilla is the most interesting character in the book. She is a rebel against the conventional place that southern society gave to women. She is also another of the boyish women whom Faulkner creates so often in his novels—the boyishness here being a token perhaps of a free attitude towards sex that one might expect of southern men or boys. Drusilla cuts her hair short. She goes off to fight with John Sartoris in the war, and she only reluctantly comes back to women's expected role when she marries him. She also shows her sexual freedom when she kisses Bayard—and gives to Faulkner yet another chance to exercise his preoccupation with incest. Her name is Drusilla. Drusilla was the name of the sister of Gaius Caligula, the mad Roman emperor of the first century. They were widely thought to have had sex with each other, and when she died, he proclaimed that she was to be worshiped as a goddess throughout the Empire.

Richard Gray has said that Drusilla is a confusing figure and that her last exit "screaming with laughter" makes her just another hysterical woman in the South (235). But I think her true place is not as a typical woman in the South but as one of the Greek Furies who turns at last into the Eumenides, the blessed ones. The Furies could in the wink of a Greek or Roman eye become also the Eumenides, the blessed spirits, who presided over the peaceful cultivation of the land and the fertility of the soil. This is the role that Drusilla took when she left the sprig of verbena on Bayard's bed to approve the courage with which he had faced Remond.

I find the boyishness of these women characters perhaps reflective of an old Platonic idea, that men and women were separated, divided, from one sex and that to exist in harmony they must be reunited.

THE
Wild Palms

A NOVEL BY
William Faulkner

THE WILD PALMS

Now we come to one of Faulkner's slighter novels, published under the title *The Wild Palms*. Later on he wrote a woman friend, one of his lovers whose name was Joan Williams, " [. . .] I remembered how I wrote *The Wild Palms* in order to try to stave off what I thought was heart-break too. And it didn't break then and so maybe it wont now, maybe it wont even have to break for a while yet, since the heart is a very tough and durable substance or thing or whatever you want to call it" (*Selected Letters* 338). He had originally planned to call the book *If I Forget Thee, Jerusalem*, the lament in the 137th Psalm: "If I forget thee, O Jerusalem, let my right hand forget her cunning." It is a sad song of loss and a bitter protest against the captors of Israel who had carried Jerusalem's inhabitants off into exile after the destruction of Jerusalem by King Nebuchadnezzar of Babylon in 587 BC.

By the rivers of Babylon, there we sat down, yea, we wept, when we remembered Zion. We hanged our harps upon the willows in the midst thereof. For there they that carried us away captive required of us a song; and they that wasted us required of us mirth, saying, Sing us one of the songs of Zion. How shall we sing the Lord's song in a strange land? If I forget thee, O Jerusalem, let my right hand forget her cunning. If I do not remember thee, let my tongue cleave to the roof of my mouth: if I prefer not Jerusalem above my chief joy. I remember, O Lord, the children of Edom in the day of Jerusalem, who said, Rase it, rase it, even to the foundation thereof. O daughter of Babylon, who are to be destroyed: happy shall be he, that rewardeth thee as thou has served us. Happy shall he be, that taketh and dasheth thy little ones against the stones.

We have in the Psalm what I have called a floating image or a floating set of images. The words call up some images that will recur in the body of the story. The inept doctor, Harry Wilbourne, loses his cunning in his right hand, the one with which he tries to do a surgical abortion on his lover, Charlotte Rittenmeyer. The death of children is heralded in the Psalm. And the mood of exile fits the whole story as these people are all displaced from anything that might be considered home. As in floating images, we have a sense of mood rather than a direct correlation between the images and the story.

The sharpness of the Psalm itself is arresting. Religious people have trouble with it. I don't recall in all the hundreds of sermons that I heard as a child and a young man that any minister ever preached on the text, "Happy shall he be, that taketh and dasheth thy little ones against the stones." This is not Sunday School talk. This is a well of bitterness springing up from the heart. It adequately reflects Faulkner's mood in this time. He had with *Absalom, Absalom!* reached the summit of his creative life, I think, but the world talked not about this masterpiece of a book but about *Gone With the Wind*. In May 1937 Margaret Mitchell won the Pulitzer Prize for *Gone With the Wind*, but *Absalom, Absalom!* was ignored by all but a few critics, although it did sell around 17,000 copies—not bad in any age for a serious novel. Faulkner thought he could sell the book to the movies for $100,000, but his hopes are only a reflection of how little he understood Hollywood. He later offered it for $50,000, but he was turned down flat. The idea that Hollywood in that period, the 1930s, would film a novel about incest, miscegenation, and murder seems preposterous today, but for Faulkner it meant that once again he was deprived of the financial security that he so desperately wanted. He was reduced to proposing to sell the manuscripts to many of his works including *The Sound and the Fury* and *As I Lay Dying* (Karl 563). He had to spend a lot of time in Hollywood as a screen writer, lonely and far from home, surrounded by people he did not understand and who did not understand him. There he became deeply involved in a love affair with Meta Carpenter, a young woman with what Frederick Karl calls an "uncomplicated" personality—which is to say that she was shallow. She worked in a minor capacity for Howard Hawks, and after refusing Faulkner at first because he was married, she became his lover.

He drank heavily and, according to Meta's recollections, spent a lot of time feeling sorry for himself. He had terrific hangovers and sometimes drank himself to the point of death. He still grieved for his brother Dean, who had been killed in a plane crash, flying a small plane that Faulkner had sold him. He could not gather any inspiration to write for himself in Hollywood, and so he drank more. When he did go back to Mississippi, he found Estelle more removed from him than ever. On June 22, 1936, Faulkner took out an ad in the *Memphis Commercial Appeal* and then a few days later in the local Oxford *Eagle*. It said, "I will not be responsible for any debt incurred or bills made, or notes or checks signed by Mrs. William Faulkner or Mrs. Estelle Oldham Faulkner" (Karl 574).

We might wonder why Faulkner simply did not leave Estelle and marry Meta Carpenter. The times were different. Divorce was still looked on as a scandal. And despite his numerous infidelities, Faulkner remained a puritan. Estelle had already been divorced once. Society could forgive one divorce, or at least it could withhold judgment while frowning on it and dis-approving. But if Estelle had been divorced twice, she would have been regarded by her own narrow society as scarcely more than a whore. I have an intuition that Faulkner was trying to do the right thing, that he felt obli-gated to Estelle on all sorts of levels. He was married to Estelle, and he would stick with her, and he would continue to be a father to his daughter Jill, born in 1933, and even to Estelle's two children by her previous mar-riage to Cornell Franklin. Estelle's children always remembered him fondly. But when I am tempted to think such good thoughts about Faulkner, I recall that he loved Rowan Oak, his house bought on the outskirts of Oxford and named for the Rowan Oak that, according to James Frazer in *The Golden Bough*, guards a house from demons. In a divorce he very likely would have had to give it up. So he may have felt obligated to stay with Estelle from motives that were not entirely praiseworthy. Like most of ours, Faulkner's motives were probably a mixture of good and bad.

The marital situation was not helped in 1937 when he went back to Cali-fornia, this time taking Estelle and Jill with him. Both Estelle and Jill were unhappy there, and Faulkner started seeing Meta again, this time on the sly. Yet still he refused to think of getting a divorce. Frederick Karl suggests that by this time Faulkner hated Estelle (579). But in a while Meta tired of wait-ing for him and married someone else, a pianist named Wolfgang Rebner, whose hopes were large and whose attainments were small. Meta and Faulkner saw each other from time to time. When she was divorced from Rebner shortly after Faulkner published *The Wild Palms*, she met Faulkner in New Orleans, and they became lovers again. But they never returned to the ardor of their liaison in the 1930s, and Faulkner's marriage with Estelle fell into the abyss, although it continued.

So it is against this melancholy background that he constructed the novel that he named *The Wild Palms* after giving up on the title *If I Forget Thee, Jerusalem*. In an essay written some years ago while Faulkner was still alive,

145

Irving Howe called it "probably the most depressing and painful narrative Faulkner has ever written, if only because the self-destruction of its characters proceeds from a desire in itself admirable" (93). It became an experimental novel, and indeed David Minter says that it can hardly be called a novel at all (173). We read the two stories as they are set within the covers of one book, one chapter about a doctor named Harry Wilbourne and his lover, a married woman named Charlotte Rittenmeyer, and then we read a chapter about the "tall prisoner" and his exploits in saving a woman from a great flood on the Mississippi River, the flood of May 1927.

That flood on the Mississippi River was one of the greatest natural disasters of all time. In his wonderful and disturbing book on the flood, *Rising Tide: The Great Mississippi Flood of 1927 and How It Changed America*, John M. Barry describes the break in the levee near Greenville, Mississippi, at 12:30 in the afternoon on April 21:

> The crevasse was immense. Giant billows rose to the tops of tall trees, crushing them, while the force of the current gouged out the earth. Quickly the crevasse widened, until a wall of water three-quarters of a mile across and more than 100 feet high—later its depth was estimated at as much as 130 feet—raged onto the Delta. (Weeks later, engineer Frank Hall sounded the still-open break: "We had a lead line one hundred feet long, and we could find no bottom.") The water's force gouged a 100-foot-deep channel half a mile wide for a mile inland.
>
> It was an immense amount of water. The crevasse at Mounds Landing poured out 468,000 second-feet onto the Delta, triple the volume of a flooding Colorado, more than double a flooding Niagara Falls, more than the entire upper Mississippi ever carried, including in 1933. The crevasse was pouring out such volume that in 10 days it could cover nearly 1 million acres with water ten feet deep. And the river would be pumping water through the crevasse for months. (202–3)

Faulkner tells the two stories in alternating chapters, opening with the story of Charlotte and Harry under the title "The Wild Palms" and then telling the story of the prisoner in "Old Man," going back to "The Wild Palms," and then going back to "Old Man" and so on until the bleak tale is ended. The wild palms in the story make a dry, rasping noise when the wind blows on them in the holiday house on the Mississippi coast where Charlotte and Harry take their refuge. The "old man" in the story is the Mississippi River itself. Faulkner has a black man give the name to the tall convict.

> "What's that?" the convict said. A negro man squatting before the
> nearest fire answered him:
> "Dat's him. Dat's de Ole Man."
> "The old man?" the convict said. (543)

We can almost hear the strong baritone voice of Paul Robeson from *Show-boat* booming back, "Old man river, Dat ole man river." But the flood gives to Faulkner an opportunity to explore a theme that comes up in his books and stories again and again—endurance, simple, dogged endurance against the forces of nature and the flooding power of life itself. In that story, the tall convict reflects the other meaning of the word "tall." He is brave. He endures. He triumphs. And if he is put back in prison at the end and has ten years added to his sentence, well he still triumphs. Or so it seems.

Reflecting Faulkner's own peregrinations between Hollywood and Mississippi, the story is not set in Yoknapatawpha County. It has a lot of metropolitan city scenes in it, scenes set in Chicago. The very name "Rittenmeyer" does not have the southern rural resonance that his other names have—McEachern, Hines, Snopes, Compson, Sartoris, Benbow, and so on. The story of the tall convict is set in the middle of the Mississippi River, which dumps him finally in Louisiana so that despite ourselves we are reminded of Huck Finn and Jim. It is also interesting that Faulkner has nothing in this novel to say about race. The subject that had so possessed him in *Absalom, Absalom!* and that he had tried to sugar over in *The Unvanquished* does not appear here in any major way.

But we should remember that Charlotte and Harry try to escape the city. They go off to Utah, where Harry becomes the doctor for a mining operation and finds himself cheated out of his wages and forced to do an abortion for his boss's wife. Irving Howe has said, just as the tall convict is caught up in the literal flood of the Mississippi, Harry and Charlotte are caught up in "a flood of passion" (98), most of the passion seemingly coming from Charlotte, who lives under the assumption that true love, which includes passion, is more important than anything else. They pay the price for that folly. But is it folly? Yes, but it is also life lived on the edge.

In part the two stories are connected by their account of two separate ways in which a man and a woman can have some sort of connection—one by romantic love and one by simple, unfeeling circumstance. From the very first, the tall convict tries to get rid of the woman he has rescued and the baby he has helped her birth. He wants to set her ashore and get back to his prison. We learn that Charlotte Rittenmeyer's husband, a Catholic, will not give her a divorce. And he gives her carte blanche to come back to him, giving Harry and her a check for enough money to pay her way back on the train whenever she decides to return. In a writerly way we can look at Faulkner doing what writers always do—taking fragments of his own experience and using them in a novel. Faulkner had to face Estelle's father and mother, who always disapproved of him, when Estelle sought her divorce from Cornell Franklin to marry him. Now with Meta Carpenter he talked about divorce from Estelle. He obviously then found himself in a marriage where he had no rewards other than the stability of being able to live in his own house.

In the opening section of "The Wild Palms," Charlotte is bleeding from the botched abortion that Harry has performed on her, and before the book is over, she will die. Abortion itself is considered scandalous. It recalls Hemingway's famous short story "Hills Like White Elephants," where the subject is treated in a much more elliptical way. Indeed Hemingway's short story appeared in a collection published by Scribner's. I suspect that Faulkner read Hemingway's story as he was writing his own. The scenes between Charlotte and Wilbourne are also eerily reminiscent of Hemingway's extremely popular novel *A Farewell to Arms.* In that book, set in Italy in World War I, the protagonist, Frederick Henry, is wounded while fighting with the Italian army against the Germans. He is cared for in the hospital by a nurse, Catherine Barkley, and she becomes pregnant, and later, when Frederick Henry survives the Italian army's disastrous defeat at Caporetto, he joins her in Switzerland, where she dies in childbirth. The book appeared in October 1929, and despite the crash of the stock market in that year, it was wildly popular. It is almost as if Faulkner, in reading it, seeing its romantic appeal and all the tricks Hemingway used to make it popular, decided after a few years of rumination that he would write almost a parody of Hemingway's somewhat sappy story of love, pregnancy, birth, and loss.

It's worth pointing out here for the record that Faulkner was always much more bold in his description of sex than Hemingway was allowed to be. Hemingway's editor was Maxwell Perkins at Scribner's. Perkins was a prudish man, eager not to offend bluenoses. He insisted that Hemingway cut out words such as *shit, fuck, son of a bitch, whore, whorehound, balls, cocksucker,* and *Jesus Christ.* Hemingway argued that he ought to be able to write *cocksucker* as a blank with c—s——r, but Perkins refused to let that scheme pass (Lynn 382). Perkins also refused to let Hemingway include a discussion about how difficult sex was for a girl who, as he wrote, "has always been good" (Lynn 382).

But in Faulkner we have a directness about sex that doubtless would have drawn the blue pencil of Maxwell Perkins. Sometimes, even when he is indirect, we realize that he is talking about matters that seem bold indeed given the temper of the times. In describing Harry Wilbourne and Charlotte Rittenmeyer in the cold of Utah, after she is pregnant and they know that a baby is coming, Faulkner writes:

> They ate together, went through the day's routine, they slept together to keep from freezing; now and then he took her (and she accepted him) in a kind of frenzy of immolation saying, crying, "At least it doesn't matter now; at least you wont have to get up in the cold." (635)

The attentive reader will ask a question here: Why would Harry Wilbourne have to get up in the night when they make love? And we suddenly realize, why, he must get up to put on a condom. And we have forgotten the common cultural outcry against any discussion of birth control in that time, just as we have forgotten that condoms once came with a sort of disclaimer: "Sold for the prevention of disease." The implicit view was that the condom manufacturers did not want people to think condoms were for birth control. They were to protect males from getting syphilis when they went to whorehouses, the assumption being that going to a prostitute was much less sinful than corrupting a "good girl" by having sex with her without the responsibility of children.

In 1932 Hemingway had also published his account of Spanish bullfighting, *Death in the Afternoon.* In it he includes a dialogue between an "author" and an "old lady." The dialogue comes and goes in the book. It's a juvenile sort of thing—at which Hemingway excelled. In one section he wrote of Faulkner with what seems to be an envious glance at Faulkner's freedom. He has been describing his experience of getting into a bullring while drunk and being beaten up by the bulls. The old lady says:

> Then I may take it that you have abandoned the bull ring even as an amateur?
> Madame, no decision is irrevocable, but as age comes on I feel I must devote myself more and more to the practice of letters. My operatives tell me that through the fine work of Mr. William Faulkner publishers now will publish anything rather than to try to get you to delete the better portions of your work, and I look forward to writing of those days of my youth which were spent in the finest whorehouses in the land and the most brilliant society there found. I had been saving this background to write of in my old age when with the aid of distance I could examine it most clearly.
> *Old lady:* Has this Mr. Faulkner written well of these places?
> Splendidly, Madame. Mr. Faulkner writes admirably of them. He writes the best of them of any writer I have read for many years.
> *Old lady:* I must buy his works.

Madame, you can't go wrong on Faulkner. He's prolific too. By the
time you get them ordered there'll be new ones out.
Old lady: If they are as you say there cannot be too many.
Madame, you voice my own opinion. (164)

In Faulkner's story, the time is the late 1930s, about the time Faulkner
wrote the novel. The second section—I can hardly call them "chapters" because the word "chapter" implies a unity that the book does not have—we
meet the "tall convict" at the time of the Mississippi flood. The major action
of "The Wild Palms" sections roves across several years. The major action
of "Old Man" is fairly compact, although we know a few things about the
convict's past. Among other things we know that he has been seduced into
thinking that what he read in books has something to do with reality. He
has read "pulp fiction," a genre that has passed away now, thick, paper-
bound volumes in the format of magazines but printed on pulp paper rather
than on slick paper. They had lurid covers and included melodramatic tales
of adventure, detective stories of "Diamond Dicks and Jesse Jameses" (509).
The tall convict has imagined that he could rob a train in just the way that
Jesse James was said to rob trains in the multitude of stories written about
him. But the tall convict has been caught and sentenced to Parchman Prison
in Mississippi, a vast "prison farm" that still exists. In time when Harry
Wilbourne's hacking at Charlotte kills her, he is sent to Parchman, too, but
we are not told in this novel that Harry and the tall convict ever see each
other. The plight of the tall convict seems to be an ironic statement on the
relation of fiction to "reality." In his fiction Faulkner wrote about a rich and
complex world, but Faulkner himself lived in a world considerably restricted
by his continual need for money. The tall convict does not need money. He
wants only to get home—to prison. Harry Wilbourne needs money at every
turn, and his lack of money is part of his futility.

The two stories thus act in one of Faulkner's favorite devices. We look
at one character—here the tall convict—and see an improbable success
while the other character—Harry Wilbourne—fails catastrophically. But is
the success a real success? And is Harry Wilbourne's failure a real failure?
As always in Faulkner, things are not what they seem. The tall convict is
one of a gang of convicts driven out from Parchman to do what they can to
rescue people threatened by the raging waters of the great flood of 1927.
His own saga begins when he is asked to take a skiff and pick up a woman
sitting on a cypress snag near the shore, and then he is to go pick up a
man who is trapped on the roof of a cotton house with the water rising
around him. Before his adventures are over, he survives the flooding Mississippi, saves the woman. She is pregnant. He delivers her baby and, in gen-

eral, acts heroically—and for his trouble has his sentence in prison extended because, by charging him with trying to escape, the officials at the prison can justify their own earlier bureaucratic supposition that he had been killed. One reason the tall convict is apprehended again by the police is that he insists on returning the boat that is not his property and getting back to Parchman Prison where he belongs. Now when we get to this part of the story, we are in tall tale country, Faulkner giving us a bitter parable about life rather than a story where we can effectively suspend disbelief. Faulkner is expressing, it seems, his bitterness towards a world that does not adequately reward those who labor heroically.

We have another futile man, now a doctor, "Harry Wilbourne." In making Harry an inept doctor, Faulkner may have been reacting against the doctor novels of his own time and of later times where doctors are heroic conquerors of disease. We've already seen how he makes fun of doctors in *Flags in the Dust*. In 1925 Sinclair Lewis, one of the most popular novelists of the day, published his novel *Arrowsmith* about a doctor named Martin Arrowsmith, whose aim in life is to do good and whose victories are won against the titans of commercial medicine who are after publicity and money. In 1938 Thornton Wilder's sweet play *Our Town* was produced, featuring the love story between Dr. Gibbs and his beloved young wife who dies in childbirth and speaks lovingly from beyond the grave to her adoring and bereft husband. I am sure Faulkner could not have known of Thornton Wilder's work while he was writing *If I Forget Thee, Jerusalem*, but it is as if he intended to break into the smugness of his time regarding doctors and show one completely inept.

As though continuing his comments on doctors, he has the tall convict meet a doctor on the steamboat that rescues him and the woman whose baby he has successfully delivered. I should say that they also rescue the skiff that the convict has been floating in on the river because the convict insists that it be brought on board the rescue boat. That doctor, a mild man, so the narrator of the book calls him, makes a statement.

> "There has been conferred upon my race (the Medical race) also the power to bind and to loose, if not by Jehovah perhaps, certainly by the American Medical Association—on which incidentally, in this day of Our Lord, I would put my money, at any odds, at any amount, at any time." (663)

151

The doctor manages to become the cause of a little humor. He insists that the tall convict drink a little whiskey. The tall convict does not want to drink whiskey. He has drunk whiskey one time in his life. When he drank whiskey, he started a fight, and he is afraid he will start a fight again, and he refuses the proffered drink. But the doctor forces his medical authority upon him, and the tall convict drinks. And sure enough he starts a fight and has to be subdued by being clubbed to the deck. He bleeds profusely from the nose. The doctor says, "Anyone ever suggest to you that you were hemophilic?" (658). Now this is a framed story. At the time we get the story, the tall convict is back in prison telling of his adventures in the flood. He is talking to his friend the plump convict. And he says that the doctor asks him, "Anyone ever suggest to you that you were hemophilic?" "Hemophilic" refers to hemophilia, the disease of European nobility (including the son of Tsar Nicholas II) that will not let the blood clot so that a person can bleed to death from the slightest cut or scratch. But the plump convict who hears the story thinks that doctor has asked, "Anyone ever suggest to you that you were homosexual?" "You let him call you that?" the plump convict says (658–59). At this point in the text, we are jerked back to the deck of the steamboat, the tall convict dazed by the beating he has received after that one drink of whiskey, and the doctor tells him, "You put up as pretty a scrap against forty or fifty men as I ever saw. You lasted a good two seconds. Now you can eat something. Or do you think that will send you haywire again?" (659).

I think in this passage Faulkner is stretching. He seems to have supposed that these lines are funnier than they are. The theme of homosexuality is, of course, one of the taboos in American literature. The tall convict, not excessively intelligent, serves as the target of a joke even as we admire him for his endurance, and that is clearly what Faulkner admires, the almost unconscious manliness, the heroism that does not recognize itself as heroism. He is a simple man caught up in events he cannot control, and he goes on. He endures—but always for the sake of going back to prison. Before he met the steamboat and was hauled aboard, he tried to surrender, and he got shot at for his trouble. Says the narrator of the tall convict:

> But he was not thinking of the bullets. He had forgotten them, forgiving them. He was thinking of himself crouching, sobbing, panting before running again—the voice, the indictment, the cry of final and irrevocable repudiation of the old primal faithless Manipulator of all the lust and folly and injustice: *All in the world I wanted was just to surrender,* thinking of it, remembering it but without heat now, without passion now and briefer than an epitaph: *No, I tried that once. They shot at me.* (662)

He speaks of "the Manipulator" capitalizing the "M" as Faulkner had earlier capitalized the "P" in the "Player" in *Flags in the Dust.* He's giving us an idea of God, not a personal God (I think) but the force that rules the universe, that reduces men to petty impotency, and that mocks his efforts. But again, the convict is raging because the Manipulator is hindering him in getting back to prison.

The tall convict gives Faulkner an opportunity to demonstrate some of his superb writing about nature, the wildness of it, a theme that always entranced him. Here is just one place where we are reminded of *Moby Dick*, but the convict is on no ocean but on a madly flooding river:

> Sometime about midnight, accompanied by a rolling cannonade of thunder and lightning like a battery going into action, as though some forty hours' constipation of the elements, the firmament itself, were discharging in clapping and glaring salute to the ultimate acquiescence to desperate and furious motion, and still leading its charging welter of dead cows and mules and outhouses and cabins and hencoops, the skiff passed Vicksburg. The convict didn't know it. He wasn't looking high enough above the water, who still squatted, clutching the gunwales and glaring at the yellow turmoil about him out of which entire trees, the sharp gables of houses, the long mournful heads of mules which he fended off with a splintered length of plank snatched from what he knew not where in passing (and which seemed to glare reproachfully back at him with sightless eyes, in limber-lipped and incredulous amazement) rolled up and then down again, the skiff now travelling forward now sideways now sternward, sometimes in the water, sometimes riding for yards upon the roofs of houses and trees and even upon the backs of the mules as though even in death they were not to escape that burden-bearing doom with which their eunuch race was cursed. But he didn't see Vicksburg; the skiff, travelling at express speed, was in a seething gut between soaring and dizzy banks with a glare of light above them but he did not see it, he saw the flotsam ahead of him divide violently and begin to climb upon itself, mounting, and he was sucked through the resulting gap too fast to recognize it as the trestling of a railroad bridge; for a horrible moment the skiff seemed to hang in static indecision before the looming flank of a steamboat as though undecided whether to climb over it or dive under it, then a hard icy wind filled with the smell and taste and sense of wet and boundless desolation blew upon him; the skiff made one long bounding lunge as the convict's native state, in a final paroxysm, regurgitated him onto the wild bosom of the Father of Waters. (601–2)

The two major women in the drama deserve some attention. Once again they seem unsatisfying. Charlotte is willing to pay any price to have her passion, and she seems not even to dread death. The woman in the skiff who has the baby does not play much of a role. Does she have much feeling at all? I'm not sure. I should also point out that we have more indications of Faulkner's persistent attention to the dirtiness of women. Harry reports to the doctor who is his landlord on the Mississippi coast that Charlotte is bleeding:

> "You say she is bleeding. Where is she bleeding?" the doctor says.
> "Where do women bleed?" the other said, cried, in a harsh exasperated voice, not stopping. "I'm no doctor. If I were, do you think I would waste five dollars on you?" (504)

The very last words of the book carry this linking of women and filth to the ultimate. The plump convict is talking to the tall convict who has had his jail sentence extended ten more years. The plump convict can only think about women:

> The plump convict stood blinking at the tall one, rapidly and steadily. "Yes sir," he said. "It's them ten more years that hurt. Ten more years to do without a woman, no woman a tall that a fellow wants—" He blinked steadily and rapidly, watching the tall one. The other did not move, jackknifed backward between the two bunks, grave and clean, the cigar burning smoothly and richly in his clean, steady hand, the smoke wreathing upward across his face saturnine, humorless, and calm. "Ten more years—"
> "Women, shit," the tall convict said. (726)

But are we to take the tall convict's attitudes as Faulkner's? No, I don't think so. I have already said that the tall convict is expressing all this effort merely to return to prison. He relished prison. Prison offers him security and even comfort compared to what the rest of his life has been. At one point in the book he meditates on the benefits of Parchman. Parchman is now his home:

> He thought of home, the place where he had lived almost since childhood, his friends of years whose ways he knew and who knew his ways, the familiar fields where he did work he had learned to do well and to like, the mules with characters he knew and respected as he knew and respected the characters of certain men; he thought of the barracks at night, with screens against the bugs in summer and good stoves in winter and someone to supply the fuel and the food too; the Sunday ball games and the picture shows—things which, with the exception of the ball games, he had never known before. (607)

The metaphor is all powerful. A man who lives for security like this is in a prison, and in an odd inversion, Faulkner makes the tall convict an emblem of all those respectable people whose ambitions are similar to his. All they want is something to pass the time away. Or as T. S. Eliot wrote in *The Waste Land*:

> Unreal City,
> Under the brown fog of a winter dawn,
> A crowd flowed over London Bridge, so many,
> I had not thought death had undone so many. (lines 60–63)

The tall convict for all his endurance is dead in much the same way that Anse Bundren is dead. He can't think of anything he wants in life except the pleasant, comfortable routines of prison. He does not even know that he has had an adventure. To him it has all been annoyance. I can't imagine that Faulkner ever would have sided with him in his lack of desire for freedom. Faulkner loved freedom, and he sided with those people who live on the edge, who like himself rebel against the middle-class standards and set out to find something in life that people of the waste land can never have. I think his heart is with Harry and Charlotte throughout, although he sees in them the suffering that is part of love, the suffering that he felt so often himself.

In the end, both men are directed in their fate by women. The tall convict goes back to Parchman—where he is at home, esteemed by his friends, given a cigar by the warden, and seemingly left in peace, a peace that rises because he does not have women to plague him. Harry is sentenced to Parchman for a period of fifty years at hard labor. The judge directs the verdict:

> "Gentlemen of the jury, you will find the prisoner guilty as charged
> and so bring in your verdict, which carries with it a sentence at hard
> labor in the State Penitentiary at Parchman for a period of not less
> than fifty years. You may retire." (713)

But of course the story is not over. Charlotte's husband wants his own special revenge. He wants Wilbourne dead, and he brings him a cyanide capsule in the jail so Wilbourne can do the honorable thing and kill himself. But Wilbourne declines the opportunity. He destroys the cyanide capsule and sits preparing to go to prison. He ponders memory:

> But after all memory could live in the old wheezing entrails: and now
> it did stand to his hand, incontrovertible and plain, serene, the palm
> clashing and murmuring dry and wild and faint and in the night but

> he could face it, thinking, *Not could. Will. I want to. So it is the old meat after all, no matter how old. Because if memory exists outside of the flesh it wont be memory because it wont know what it remembers so when she became not then half of memory became not and if I become not then all of remembering will cease to be.—Yes* he thought *Between grief and nothing I will take grief.* (715)

It was a comment that Faulkner had made earlier to Meta, and it reminds us very much of Addie Bundren, her sense that her fornication with Whitfield was the only worthwhile thing in her life, that it was better to have had the memory of it than nothing at all. The thoughts about memory are reminiscent of Proust, the sense that memory is the reality that events create in our heads and that the memories have their own life. And that is finally Faulkner's theme here, that it is better to have something to remember than to have the prosaic, empty lives that are described in T. S. Eliot's *Waste Land*. Better to feel—if only what we feel is suffering—than not to feel at all. It is a vision worthy of Dostoyevsky and indeed it may surpass the Russian's. We are beings who suffer. We are beings who die. Better to suffer for a passion than to live the dead, still lives of men in the Waste Land.

The Hamlet

A NOVEL OF THE SNOPES FAMILY BY

WILLIAM FAULKNER

THE HAMLET

Today I want to talk about *The Hamlet*, one of Faulkner's most popular books—also one of his longer works—but one that always draws from critics the comment that its only thematic unity is the treatment of greed, commerce, and love through many tales—some of them elaborate and partly unbelievable tall tales which were—like *The Unvanquished*—published as short stories and then cobbled together as a novel.

Doubtless the motives of commerce and greed are important here, and we shall have to deal with them. At no place in his work is Faulkner closer to Mark Twain, whose depictions of human nature are filled with the corruptions great and small that greed can effect on the human psyche. And Faulkner's somewhat cold-hearted view of love is also part of his own constant pessimism that human love can be enough to triumph over simple selfishness, which includes lust and barter in "love" as part of the orbit that it sweeps out in the elliptical swing of our self-concern around our egos. Here in his depiction of love I see a Darwinian impulse that I find constant in Faulkner from the beginning.

The store itself is an image of sorts. Varner is in the business of commerce, and when Eula does get pregnant, he has to marry her off. The person willing to take her is Flem Snopes, on his way up in the world of Jefferson and willing to do anything to advance himself and his family. This novel is often called the first of the Snopes trilogy; it is the story of the rise and fall of Flem Snopes and his clan and the rise and not the fall, one thinks, of a different kind of South, the triumph of the lower classes who learn modern ways.

But I would like to suggest that the main character in *The Hamlet* is, as the title indicates, the community itself—a rural, identifiable place (identifiable at least in our imaginations) where a certain unique personality emerges. In some major respects this work resembles Thornton Wilder's sweetly romantic tale, the play *Our Town*, which in 1938 won the Pulitzer Prize and which enjoys in our own day periodic revivals. On another level, some things in the novel remind us of the collection of monologues spoken in Edgar Lee Masters's *Spoon River Anthology*, published in 1915. *Our Town* is set in New Hampshire. *Spoon River Anthology* is written in free verse, and the graveyard where the stories are told is in Illinois. But both works show what it means to live in a specific place and how characters with talents and temperaments that would have developed in one way in New York or Chicago or Boston develop in a different but still recognizable way in a small, rural community. And I might say that the sense of that small rural community was becoming something lost in an America of 1939 and 1940 where the movement into the cities had become inexorable.

Faulkner takes into account the intense, although sometimes almost unconscious feeling that southerners—and perhaps all rural peoples—have for the closed and isolated hamlets that give so many of us our real identities.

Here the "hamlet" in question is Frenchman's Bend. It is little more than a store in the wilderness. It has a cotton gin and a blacksmith shop and a livery barn where men can rent horses, and it has a rundown hotel, and, of course, it has a school house. In this novel the hamlet collects itself around the country store run by Will Varner and eventually usurped from him by Flem Snopes. The country store with its stove in the winter and its porch in the summer was the natural gathering place of men in those frequent intervals in rural life when there is nothing to do but wait for planting time or harvest to give its yield that allows life to go on.

In such places the currency that gains admission to this circle is a man's ability to tell a story. The story does several things. For one, it grants a great deal of authority for the man who tells it. The storyteller is not only showman and entertainer; the storyteller is also interpreter, judge, and prophet. The person able to tell a story is by the nature of narrative forced to provide some meaning and verdict on the stories that he tells. He, therefore, becomes the wise man of the hamlet, able to command respect and attention because he has the power to see in events connections that allow the story to be told, connections that might not be seen and therefore that might not become stories to the inattentive or passive observer. The storyteller always has an active intellect.

In *The Hamlet*, the chief storyteller is V. K. Ratliff, the sewing machine salesman, who travels the county selling his sewing machines, a necessary piece of technology in a society where people make their own clothes, often out of feed sacks. Faulkner told someone that he fell in love with Ratliff—whose name he changed from Suratt to Ratliff because someone named Suratt moved into Oxford. Faulkner was pestered—as any novelist is—by those people who could not make anything up and so who assumed that all stories told in a novel are true and therefore potentially libelous. The name change is in itself token of the kind of intimate and close community that Faulkner wrote about in *The Hamlet*. Ratliff says, "You fellows don't know how good a man's voice feels running betwixt his teeth" (88). But of course they do know; they all know how good it is to tell a story and to be heard. So Ratliff becomes the principal voice by which the community assumes its identity in our eyes and to some extent in its own.

I might say that the women in this novel and in Faulkner in general do not tell stories. They do make judgments on events. But they do not spill out these long and complex and sometimes fabricated narratives. The reasons have much to do with southern society in that time. The men have moments of leisure that allow them to congregate at Will Varner's store, and the leisure and their community give them the opportunity to tell stories. Woman have no such leisure. As the proverb declares, "Men may work from sun to sun, but women's work is never done." Women must do all the work at home—cook the food, clean up the dishes, take care of the children, and, of course, make the clothes. That is the image of women in this novel, women forced continually to construct their own lives around the deeds and words of their men.

The most poignant example here is Yettie Snopes, Mink's wife, whom he has married out of a brothel and by whom he has a couple of children. She remains loyal to him even after he has driven her and the children out of the house when he has killed Jack Houston from ambush. The place of women is also illustrated by the decision of the judge to give the horse that has done so much damage to Mr. and Mrs. Tull to Mrs. Tull.

But *The Hamlet* is also something else. It is an inverted pastoral. "Pastoral" is one of the most popular genres in Western literature, starting at least with Virgil's *Eclogues* and continuing to Robert Frost, whose life in a rural surrounding becomes a place of sweetly simple virtues that contradict the complexities and hypocrisies of town life. Typically the pastoral extols the peacefulness of shepherd life compared to the subtle and malicious competition of the court life of kings and nobles. Marie Antoinette had her pastoral fantasies at Versailles, where she went out to her "Petit

161

Trianon" palace to play with her friends at being a shepherd. But, of course, if the countryside in a pastoral is completely innocent and simple, you don't have a story. We would not have a book of Genesis if Adam and Eve had obeyed God and had gone on tending the Garden of Eden like the obedient children they were supposed to be. You only have a story when you have a serpent. You cannot have a novel unless you have complexity and evil. Some critics such as William Empson have sought to make the pastoral a way of "putting the complex into the simple." And in an important way, this is what Faulkner does here. He translates the complexities of modern life to Frenchman's Bend.

Faulkner does here what I have observed many times in the course of these lectures. He is the writer, the outsider to his society, a man not unlike V. K. Ratliff in that he is not at all like the people he observes except in his interest in telling their tales. The writer as observer in the South notices the dramatic changes that seem to overtake the South with more life-changing force than other parts of the country. In some sense Faulkner is watching change take place in a beloved character, the Hamlet itself, and he is watching the Snopes family take the land.

I want to conclude speaking about *The Hamlet* by making some observations. Faulkner returns in this novel to an omniscient, third-person narrator, the simpler, more traditional form of the novel. He shifts from person to person, from scene to scene with an almost casual artistry, and at the end all the disparate stories about this community come together in the triumph of Flem Snopes.

Flem is the single-minded self-promoter who has a remarkable similarity to Thomas Sutpen. They both want to rise in the world. Flem succeeds; Sutpen fails. Both of them are completely ruthless when other people are concerned. Sutpen casts off his "Spanish" wife when she turns out to be part African. But Flem Snopes very happily marries Eula Varner although Eula is pregnant by another man, and he happily claims her child by that union as his own simply because marrying Will Varner's daughter is a way for Flem Snopes to rise in the world. Flem Snopes rises out of not only a ruthlessness with others but with a ruthlessness with himself. He does not have Sutpen's warped sense of integrity. Sutpen so accepts the values of the South that he repudiates his first wife because she is 1/8th African, repudiates her because he knows she has African blood although it seems likely that no one else can tell that she is part African. But Flem Snopes marries Eula although it is public knowledge that the child Eula carries is not his but someone else's—Hoake McCarron's. This public knowledge troubles Flem Snopes not at all. He is impotent. He has been castrated by his desire for money, which is traditionally the sign of those who have been removed from nature by the artificiality that money induces.

Thomas Sutpen is not after money. He is after land, a hundred square miles of land, and a big house and a dynasty and a place in history stamped on the collective memory of this world. Like Flem Snopes, Sutpen is ignorant and not quite at home even at the apogee of his success with the biggest house around and a wife he has married to rise in the world and two children. Why does he fail? He fails because the grandeur of his vision is too much for him. He has created his own destruction.

But Flem Snopes has no grand design. He is, as his name suggests, phlegmatic, the stolid, enduring sort who creates nothing but whose patient tenacity allows him to advance one step at a time towards a vague goal that can be described as one simple word: "more." He does not invent. He does not create. He is the opportunist always ready to take advantage when advantage comes along. He is the opposite of those people in *Pylon* who live for the day, for the hour, for the moment when all they want is enough money to get to the next moment. Flem is relentlessly cumulative. Step by step he makes his way and never turns back, never retreats.

Flem settles into Frenchman's Bend—which later on will turn out to be the abandoned house taken over by Lee Goodwin and Popeye's crowd where Temple Drake is raped. To some extent the story of Flem's rise is framed by the legend at the beginning that the Frenchman had buried gold around the place and the tale at the end of how Flem salted the earth around with gold coins to fool Ratliff and the others into buying it from him. In the very last scene Armstid is madly digging in the ground, certain that gold is there, and Flem—now on his way to Jefferson and to a career in banking—looks at him without pity and says to his mules, "Come up." Flem is rising. Armstid has fallen in the dirt.

Why does Faulkner detest the Snopes clan so much? Because they have no vision. They move like rats into the world of people who have some sense of nature and natural feeling, and they prevail in a valueless, dead world where everything has a price.

Some things are fairly typical of Faulkner. Eula Varner Snopes is a sort of earth goddess figure, drawing men to her without any apparent desire to do so, fought over, and like some mountain sheep willingly accepting the male who is victorious, wounded though he may be. She is a mythological character, the woman who draws men to her and bears children and keeps the human race rolling along.

I have another thought about *The Hamlet* which I advance with some trepidation. That is that it is a homophone with Shakespeare's *Hamlet*, and I have wondered if we may find some connections in them. I suppose I might tentatively suggest that the brooding sense of the triumph of soulless evil in the form of the Snopes crowd is reminiscent of the comment of Marcellus in *Hamlet*, that there is something rotten in the state of Denmark. I believe that *Hamlet* is a play about fate, the working out of a destiny contrary to all the plans people make within a context of betrayal and distrust with only the loyal Horatio to play the role of observer and teller of the tale. It just may be that Ratliff is a Horatio-like character in *The Hamlet*, the loyal observer who sees the truth when others deny it, and who remains faithful to some sense of value that nearly everyone else in the play disdains.

And perhaps, too, we find in *The Hamlet* the same sense of predestination or fate that we find in *Hamlet*. Horatio tells Hamlet before the fencing match with Laertes at the end: "If your mind dislike anything, obey it. I will forestall their repair hither and say you are not fit" (V.ii.227–29). In short, don't do this if you don't feel good about it. But Hamlet will go forward:

> Not a whit. We defy augury. There is a special providence in the fall
> of a sparrow. If it be now, 'tis not to come; if it be not to come, it will
> be now; if it be not now, yet it will come; the readiness is all. Since
> no man of aught he leaves, knows aught, what is't to leave betimes.
> Let be. (V.ii.230–35)

Before the rise of Flem Snopes, Faulkner seems as resigned as Hamlet. And that may in part be what *The Hamlet* is all about. If Faulkner could see the mall and development culture spread across the South now, he would know that he was a prophet. Writers are prophets in that their job is to see and to tell. It is not for them to act.

FAULKNER AND THE MYTHOLOGICAL WORLD

Before we turn to the last novel of the course, *Go Down, Moses*, I want to touch on an issue that seems to me to be of extreme importance: Faulkner's relation to the mythology of the ancient world. Time and again I have called attention to the mythological symbolism in Faulkner's work that we have studied this term. Almost every week I have mentioned James George Frazer's great book, *The Golden Bough*, with its subtitle, *A Study in Magic and Religion*. Faulkner encountered the book apparently first in the home of Sherwood Anderson in New Orleans. The work was originally published in twelve volumes. Frazer himself kept studying and enlarging a work that he intended to produce in two, but in 1922 he brought out the one-volume abridgment, and that is what Faulkner apparently saw in Anderson's home.

Frazer's work is, in many ways, reminiscent of Mr. Casaubon in George Eliot's masterpiece, *Middlemarch*. Mr. Casaubon works throughout his life at a book he proposes to call the *Key to All Mythologies*, and if I am not mistaken, his aim is much like that of many Renaissance thinkers such as Pico della Mirandola, an effort to reconcile the major tenets in the various mythologies of the world to find a plausible and scientific unity in the quest for divine things. Pico tried to reconcile Judaism, Islam, and Christianity, much to the irritation of the pope of his day who condemned his efforts. Mr. Casaubon seems to represent a nineteenth-century mindset which saw faith in threat and sought to fend off the threat by a weighty exercise of scholarship. George Eliot never quite gives us Casabon's motives, but I believe that we can infer them.

Frazer's view seems to have been something else. He found in the various religions and mythologies of the world common patterns of superstition, and if I am not mistaken, his interest in these various superstitions served to rationalize their causes and to lead readers away from the supposition that divine revelation or divine intervention was responsible for any of them. One reads Frazer's work not as a guide to religion but rather as a guide to the anthropological study of those human societies that sought to explain the natural forces of the world—especially the ebb and flow of the seasons—on which humankind is always dependent.

Frazer wrote in a grand style with a prose that does not quite rise to Gibbon's magnificent cadences but that nevertheless provides a sense of drama and beauty and something of the sublime to the matters he discusses. Here is the beginning of his one-volume edition:

> Who does not know Turner's picture of the Golden Bough? The scene, suffused with the golden glow of imagination in which the divine mind of Turner steeped and transfigured even the fairest natural landscape, is a dream-like vision of the little woodland lake of Nemi—"Diana's Mirror," as it was called by the ancients. No one who has seen that calm water, lapped in a green hollow of the Alban hills, can ever forget it. The two characteristic Italian villages which slumber on its banks, and the equally Italian palace whose terraced gardens descend steeply to the lake, hardly break the stillness and even the solitariness of the scene. Diana herself might still linger by this lonely shore, still haunt these woodlands wild. (1)

It is the kind of poetic prose, restrained but still refulgent, that would have immediately attracted Faulkner. Its subject, carried on through page after page of Frazer's work, is the continual effort of human beings to make sense of their world in their primitive encounter with it, an encounter filled with moments of ecstasy, ritual, terror, and death. Part of making sense of the work, in Frazer's view, was the effort to control it by various forms of sympathetic magic. The marriage, either "real or mock" of human beings, according to Frazer, was supposed to stimulate the growth of crops and the fecundity of domestic animals. The earth goddess, represented by thousands of clay figurines recovered from manifold sites all over the world, is usually shown as a female form with distended breasts and pregnant belly, and it seems that to adore her, either in the figurine or in the form of a living female assigned to play her role in festivals, was to use sympathetic magic to encourage the growth of crops and the survival of the tribe. In like fashion the various tales of gods that die and rise again are closely linked to the ceaseless procession of the seasons, a summer of growing, an autumn of harvest, a winter of death, and a springtime of resurrection.

It is also important in Frazer that the superstitious rites attached to the veneration of these natural deities are not especially attached to morality. I am often bemused and sometimes amused by the confident assumption in the modern mind, especially the modern American mind, that God has to be moral, loving, and good according to human terms. We want the kind of God who delivers justice and mercy, the God who dons the white-and-black striped shirt of the football official on the field of life, racing up and down the field calling penalties for infractions of the rules. But in the world that James Frazer explored, the world of ancient superstitions of the human race, our kind of morality has almost nothing to do with the means and the ends of religious practice. Religion is a set of rituals, sometimes involving human sacrifice, intended to exercise at least some control over nature, and "righteousness" is the correct observance of those rituals so that they cause the desired effects. Frazer's view is that these rituals and rites go far into the human past, far before history, and that some of their parts linger on into our own society where they are mere festival, devoid of the deeper meaning that our ancestors found in them. The superstitions relate especially to fertility—fertility of the soil, fertility of animals, fertility of the tribe, fertility of individuals. And they involved practices that contradict the morality as it has been developed by a society intent not merely on fertility but on good order and on a rising economic expectation.

And that is the great conflict that rises in Faulkner throughout these novels. On the one hand, we have the fundamental drives and terrors of the human race evident in all stages of its development since we began to walk erect. We have a sexual drive. We have a drive to survive both as individuals and as a species, as families, communities, towns, nations. The sexual drive according to Sigmund Freud is the fundamental human motivation. Whether it is, as Freud says, THE fundamental drive lies in the airy room of speculation, a statement that can be neither proved nor disproved. But no one can doubt that sexuality is powerful, implacable, and necessary.

So we have throughout Faulkner references to these female figures who are earth goddesses, whose destiny is to procreate children, and who often do so in Faulkner in ways that come laden with mythological significance. Diana is the ancient goddess of groves; she was Ishtar in Mesopotamia, Diana to the Greeks. She presides over trees. She is a huntress. And she also blesses men and women with children (Frazer 3). So we have women in Faulkner who share these features—Caddy, who smells of trees in *The Sound and the Fury*; Addie Bundren, who is seduced (or who perhaps does the seducing) in a forest of trees in *As I Lay Dying*, Lena Grove, in *Light in August*, whose name calls up the kind of grove where Diana is supposed to preside. Laverne in *Pylon* has one child, a son at the beginning of the novel, and she is about to have another when the novel ends. And Eula Varner Snopes has the bovine indifference of a cow, completely indifferent to men until she herself seems to be aroused by the violent temperament of Hoake McCarron. When women have children in Faulkner's world, especially in the novels written after *Flags in the Dust*, they seem to settle into the act, become protectors of the children, become, in short, mothers rather than mother goddesses. But these are not women who are moved by conventional morality.

Sometimes, when women do not or cannot have children, they become Diana the Huntress rather than Diana the Goddess who blesses women with offspring. In this attribute we summon up another part of the mythology of Diana, that she hunted naked in the forest at night, a perpetual virgin, and that if any man were so unlucky as to look on her and see her nakedness her hunting dogs would tear him to pieces. Here we have Caddy in *The Sound and the Fury*, who seeks one man after another; yet never does she give a man her heart. Here we have Temple Drake in *Sanctuary*, who is raped but then who becomes herself the agent of death for several men, beginning perhaps with Tommy, who may try to protect her from Popeye and is shot to death for his trouble. Here we have Joanna Burden, the childless, middle-aged lover of Joe Christmas, who becomes fat and old and beyond the age of childbearing while they have their wild affair. She tries to kill him; he kills her instead, almost decapitating her with a straight razor, the stereotypical lethal weapon of the black man in the South. Rosa Coldfield in *Absalom, Absalom!* is a kind of huntress, resolved to blacken and damn the reputation of Thomas Sutpen. Charlotte Rittenmeyer in *The Wild Palms* aborts her child. It seems clear to me at least that Faulkner disapproves of the abortion. When she has the abortion, she herself dies, and she condemns to prison her lover, Harry Wilbourne, because abortion is considered a form of manslaughter.

Caroline Compson is hard to fit into this schema since she is a passive mother, passive aggressive as we would say in our modern psychological jargon. She may be the mythological mother who devours her own children as a sign that the order of the world is topsy turvy. Or she may not be mythological at all. She may be simply a spoiled southern woman, selfish, blind to her own flaws, in the habit of making people feel guilty because they do not pay her enough attention.

In all of these schemes, Faulkner is giving us a vision of human nature in its most primitive evolution. I believe it is demonstrable from the text that Faulkner was enormously influenced by the teaching of Charles Darwin, that human beings evolved from lower forms of life, and that the most important feature of any species is that it adapt itself sufficiently to its environment to survive. All of this is to find something within us that binds us to our bodily needs as surely as any animal or plant for that matter is constrained to the physical requirements of survival. In Faulkner's world, society may change, but human nature remains the same world without end.

But society does change, and what emerges from society is ultimately civilization. Civilization imposes on us rules of behavior so that we may have order, and the rules of behavior become morality. Especially is there a morality about sex. In many ways Faulkner follows Freud in teaching that civilization must repress sexual liberty if civilization is to exist. I'm not quite sure that Faulkner follows Freud in the next step of Freudian psychology, that when we repress sexuality, we sublimate, and therefore we produce the arts of living. I doubt that this part of Freud is true. If Pablo Picasso ever repressed his sexuality, I never heard of it, and the same can be said for a great many writers, painters, and even successful politicians. But certainly society has traditionally put tight restraints on the sexuality of individuals. And it is just this social restraint that becomes the source of tension in the novels we have studied thus far.

The restraint comes to us in two forms. One is religious. The religious taboos against incest are such that Quentin at least thinks about them when he surmises in a mad way that he and Caddy might end up in hell together. But that is a fantasy that to my mind does not carry much literal weight. The real restraint throughout Faulkner seems to be respectability. If you are to be allowed to hold your head up in decent society, to be respected and even honored, you have to obey the sexual rules. That is the attitude of Caroline Compson in *The Sound and the Fury.* The most precious possession of a girl is her virginity, and if a girl loses her virginity, the next most precious possession possible is the appearance of virginity and a convenient marriage to cover up the fall. Caroline Compson dresses herself in mourning when Caddy kisses a boy for the first time. But then when Caddy is pregnant, apparently by Dalton Ames, Mrs. Compson almost slobbers on Herbert Head when he comes courting Caddy, and Quentin sees through the hypocrisy and hates it. Narcissa Benbow Sartoris is so preoccupied with respectability that she happily double-crosses her brother's efforts to defend Lee Goodwin from the false charge of murder of which he will be convicted and then lynched. And as I have said, in the story "There Was a Queen," Narcissa goes so far as to sleep with a federal agent to get letters back that had originally been written anonymously to her by Byron Snopes. Why? Because her sense of respectability demands the appearances be kept up, regardless of the facts. And in *Absalom, Absalom!* the ultimate in respectability's power is manifest when Henry Sutpen kills Charles Bon not because Bon is about to commit incest with Henry's sister—and Bon's sister—Judith but because Bon has in him an invisible one-sixteenth of African ancestry, meaning that one of his great-great-grandparents was black. I wonder how many of you here can give me the name of any one of your great-great-grandparents.

The controlling metaphor remains the horse-drawn buggy that Luster tries to drive to the left of the monument of the Confederate soldier, causing the idiot Ben to set up a bellow or protest. The carriage must go to the right, and when Jason turns the carriage, and Luster drives it to the right, Ben the idiot settles down peacefully. Society is this idiot, demanding an arbitrary order that has no foundation in the order of things. Religion becomes in all of this only the preposterous cloak to convention and habit. Gail Hightower in *Light in August* is the most sympathetically portrayed minister in all of Faulkner unless we might credit the somewhat brief appearance of the Reverend Shegog in *The Sound and the Fury*. Why has Gail Hightower been forced to abandon his church, and why has he become an outcast in Jefferson? Because his wife died either falling or jumping from the window of a hotel room in Memphis.

> It was Sunday morning's paper which they saw, telling how she had jumped or fallen from a hotel window in Memphis Saturday night and was dead. There had been a man in the room with her. He was arrested. He was drunk. They were registered as man and wife, under a fictitious name. The police found her rightful name where she had written it herself on a piece of paper and then torn it up and thrown it into the waste basket. The papers printed it, with story: wife of the Reverend Gail Hightower, of Jefferson, Mississippi. And the story told how the paper telephoned to the husband at two A.M. and how the husband said that he had nothing to say. And when they reached the church that Sunday morning the yard was full of Memphis reporters taking pictures of the church and the parsonage. (*Light in August* 61–62)

Gail Hightower creates a scandal because he is married to a wife who dies a disreputable death. Is he at fault? No, perhaps the ministry itself is what kills her. How can she survive as a human being in the most demanding of all professions, the minister's wife! She must be respectability incarnate, and the tension between what society expects and what the body demands becomes most unbearable in the role of the minister's wife, looked upon by everyone as the model of perfection who must be as immaculate as a thin piece of Dresden China. And in all this Gail Hightower's name becomes the symbolic thump of irony. The name Gail is Hebrew, Gyeel, and it means boundless joy. And, of course, the high tower may be a phallic symbol as towers often are in those people who have become intoxicated with Freud. His name may indeed be a covert pun—the joy of erection, the joy of male sex. But Gail Hightower's profession as minister has unmanned him, and he seems to have no joy in sex, and he seems to give no joy in sex to his wife so that she must fly away to an adulterous lover and thence to her death either because she is drunk and falls out the window or because she is overcome by shame and leaps to her death as a suicide.

Whatever the story of Gail Hightower's wife, the conflict between what we are as human beings and what society demands of us when we are required to suppress our sexuality and channel it into monogamy and respectability is manifest throughout Faulkner. What we are as human beings he continually reasserts by returning to mythological symbols whose origins go back before history began, before writing signaled the emergence of organized civilizations and their panoplies of gods that buttressed an order established to keep some people in power and others safely ground under the feet of the powerful.

Yet throughout Faulkner some people care nothing for respectability, and they are the ones on whom his pen seems to settle with the most interest if not affection, even if he is sometimes tinctured with a fascination with the brutal and the macabre. Miss Emily Grierson seems respectable, but she sleeps, apparently happily, with a corpse for many decades. Ruby Lamar in *Sanctuary*, the pilot, the jumper, the mechanic, and Laverne in *Pylon*, and Anse Bundren in *As I Lay Dying*. Charlotte and Harry in *The Wild Palms*. They live *in extremis*. They are Faulkner's true existential heroes, the people who define themselves in the midst of time and consciousness and care nothing at all for anything beyond their own courageous self-definition. As true existentialists, the definition is more important than morality. Better that a man or a woman define himself or herself, have some mastery over life, than to be a dull, dead, passive instrument in the hands of social conformity. These are the people who at least try not to be the hollow men of T. S. Eliot's bleak and stricken world where all the symbols are dead and life is removed from its sources. They are amoral, people without any code of morality dictated to them by society, and by society's evaluation they can often seem evil. But their evil gives them a certain freedom. What gesture is more free than Popeye's seeming choice of death, a kind of suicide in *Sanctuary*, where his last words to the sheriff about to hang him offer no hint of remorse or anxiety or confession? No, none of these things that society demands we see in the hour of our death. Popeye says, "Fix my hair, Jack." It is a crudely heroic indifference to life or death which in the annals of romantic literature is the expected reaction of soldiers, martyrs, and saints. But it is Popeye, living beyond the boundaries of romantic literature.

But let me return to perhaps the most important point to be made about all these mythological references to that primitive old time, the Dionysiac Days that Faulkner evokes when he introduces Eula in *The Hamlet*. This mythology suggests that we are most human when we are closest to nature, when, so much as we possibly can, we allow ourselves to be faithful to the impulses within ourselves created by our long struggle to realize the human race from the rest of the animal world. The mystery, the awe, the terror, the joy, the wild release of emotions within the bright and dark and threatening world of the wilderness whence we sprang are part of us, and to forsake them is to sink into being something other than what we are in nature. We are most ourselves when we are part of the whole.

But now let's turn to another preoccupation throughout this term and throughout these novels. Let's ask about the classical resonances that we find again and again—a title such as *As I Lay Dying* that comes from *The Odyssey*, names like Jason Lycurgus Compson, Clytemnestra, Drusilla, Narcissa, Horace, Candace, and all the rest. I don't think we can make a point-by-point application of Faulkner's classical images to the stories where he uses them. I think he uses classical images to create a mood, and that mood is the spirit of tragedy.

Both the classical world and the world of the Hebrew Bible are filled with tragedy. The tragedy of Greece, reflected in the great tragic writers, is that after the stunning victories over Persia and the ransom from defeat and oblivion by unity and valor, Greeks fell to fighting Greeks and laid themselves open to conquest first from Macedonians and then from the Romans. The tragedy of Israel was that the chosen people lost Jerusalem, lost the temple, and ultimately lost their nation after so many great promises from God. Christians reply, of course, that, no, the history of Israel is not tragic because it led to Christ, and Christ came as the son of God, suffered death, conquered the tomb, and rose triumphantly on the third day. But Jews will have none of this story. They still lament the destruction of the temple, their dispersion throughout the world, and the loss of divine dreams. So Greeks and Jews remain the tragic people, the emblem of the human condition so that in reaching for glory the very reach brings destruction.

Faulkner will have none of this Christian redemption either. I have perhaps said enough of my own belief that, throughout Faulkner's work, he seems to be telling us that the Christian symbols are turned upside down and do not lead to redemption or to resurrection. T. S. Eliot can lament the fall of the Christian symbols and do what he can to make them live again by becoming himself a conservative and Antisemitic Christian. Faulkner notes the loss of the symbols and leaves the human condition sunk in tragedy. He never tries to turn his characters back to Christianity. He never suggests in the novels we have studied that Christianity can bring redemption. And even in the most symbolic Christian novel he ever wrote, *A Fable*, he does not allow his Christ figure to bring redemption. The soldier who leads a mutiny on the Western Front is killed. His body is resurrected—but by artillery fire that falls on the grave and blows the body to bits. Faulkner uses Christian symbols only to show us that we have lost the content of those symbols, that we can expect nothing beyond this life, and that we have lost also our connection with the wilderness, the primitive land that formed our being.

Only a few, it seems, can see what we have lost. They are the ones who perceive tragedy. Tragedy is the discovery that we can imagine a world where our life has meaning, but some chaotic force works in the human condition to bring our dreams crashing in pieces around our feet, and that is life. To experience tragedy is to know that we have pushed human beings to the extreme and known what it is to fail. Not to experience tragedy is to live the self-satisfied, comfortable life that never pushes anything to the extreme at all. It is the safe life of the tall convict in *The Wild Palms*. It is the life of unrealized calamities.

So here we have two elements in Faulkner's work touching each other. On the one hand is the basic stuff that we are beings that come out of a primitive society, that bear that faint, subconscious recollection of living close to the earth enwrapped in the seasons, filled with the awe and mystery of primitives before the forces of nature, and that as thinking animals we are attuned to that harsh and sublime world. Yet to live in society with one another in this constraint called civilization, we are robbed of our primitive heritage and plunged into a society of a million separate artificialities that all combine to dictate to us what we shall be and therefore to steal from us the choice of being whatever it is that we might have been. The tragedy lies in the inability we have of escaping this civilization. We must live with this double vision. On the one hand, we feel with every urge we have to primitive love, to sexual passion, to the fulfillment of our fantasies that throwback to our ancestral origins. And with every one of those urges and fantasies we also feel the iron grip of civilization telling us that we must conform or else life will become so uncomfortable for us that we will wish we had conformed. Perhaps if we do not conform, society will take our life away from us. Here is where we live. And here is where Faulkner makes his novels, showing people caught between these two poles, torn incessantly by these rival demands. And there's no escape from it except death. Real life is conflict between these desires. False life is the absence of conflict, the good moral life, the prosaic day-to-day monotony of respectable living, allowing ourselves and suffering in others the petty and sometimes grand hypocrisies that allow the appearances to be saved.

So now the question comes: Where is there room for morality in this scheme of things? To answer that question, we turn to the last of the novels under our consideration this term, *Go Down, Moses.* And in this novel, seemingly at times a collection of short stories, but truly a novel, I want to explore the themes of hypocrisy, mystery, liberty, and sympathy.

Go down, MOSES

AND OTHER STORIES

William Faulkner

A RANDOM HOUSE BOOK

GO DOWN, MOSES

Go Down, Moses is Faulkner's thirteenth novel, published on May 11, 1942, when the United States was suffering defeat after defeat in the war against Japan. Faulkner always considered it a novel. He likened it to *The Unvanquished* and *The Wild Palms*, books that he considered novels but that had the appearance of short stories. The title is from a spiritual sung by slaves before the Civil War and continuing to hold an important place in folk music. The song is one of those covert protest songs. Black slaves could sing about the slavery of Israel and how the Israelites were redeemed by God's almighty hand, and the song could promise to them a redemption for themselves. The "novel" that emerges from this collection may be united then under the general heading of freedom, but it is a complicated kind of freedom, expressed through both black and white characters in the story or the stories that are here told.

Throughout the book, we have a story about race. That is one reason we have to read *Go Down, Moses* as a novel. In the midst of the book is the great novella called "The Bear" that may be the single best known part of Faulkner's work. That is because Malcolm Cowley included a version of it in *The Portable Faulkner*, which did much to bring public literary attention back to Faulkner when his books were out of print and almost completely neglected just before he won the Nobel Prize in 1950. When Viking agreed in August 1945, as World War II was ending, to bring out *The Portable Faulkner*, every one of Faulkner's books except *Sanctuary* was out of print. Faulkner was back in Hollywood, miserable and depressed, and in September he went back to Mississippi. *The Portable Faulkner* did not appear until

March 1947—and I think it is one of the main reasons Faulkner won the Nobel Prize in 1950. "The Bear" is printed in the book, cut off from the rest of *Go Down, Moses*, and so for many people it is only a very long short story without the context that it requires, I think, to make full sense of it. From this version, "The Bear" has often been taught in high schools. But, as I say, it is incomplete.

Cleanth Brooks held that a good title for the book might simply have been *The McCaslins* since all the stories, with one exception, deal directly with the McCaslin family. The one exception is the story "Pantaloon in Black," but it is a reflection of the power of love in a black man's heart when he has lost his wife, a power that is strangely absent in the descriptions of the white McCaslins throughout the generations that we follow them here. I want to dwell just a moment on "Pantaloon in Black" because it seems to me to be an essential part of Faulkner's meditations on race, although it may not seem connected to the rest of the book.

Faulkner had in his library a book called *The Southern Plantation Overseer As Revealed in His Letters*, published by Smith College Press in 1925. Here is part of the introduction to that collection by John Spencer Bassett:

> We must not forget . . . that an important part of the problem [of overseeing a plantation] was the negro himself. A fundamental part of the slave problem was the negro problem. The African slaves were close to savagery. They were to learn much in the process of forced labor and they learned it very slowly. The finer feelings of advanced peoples were not for them. They had not developed such feelings in Africa—they could not be expected to acquire them in American slavery in one, two, or five generations. For them uplift was a thing that could only come gradually and painfully. The first generations died in order that those who came afterwards might make a slow and meager advance in culture. (in Kinney 63–65)

Now, in effect, what is argued here—in 1925—is that black slaves came from a culture where the finer human feeling of love did not exist, and there is the almost explicit notion that slavery helped instill these emotions in black people and so that it represents a step in the progress of their human consciousness. In "Pantaloon in Black" Faulkner takes on this demeaning concept with his story of Rider and his dead wife. Rider's love for his wife is expressed not in words exchanged between them but by the things they do together—improving the house that they rent from Carothers Edmonds, and how she settled his life down to a pattern of satisfied routine. Then she died, leaving imprinted on him her memory that appears to him sometimes as a ghost in the cabin that now seems unbearably empty.

In effect, Rider commits suicide from his grief. But it is a suicide with a bite in it. He enters a crap game. He catches in the act a white man named Birdsong who is playing with loaded dice, and Rider kills him with a straight razor. Then, of course, he is lynched by a white mob. A black man cannot kill a white man without dying for the offense. Rider has sought the death. But how do white men look on it? They do not understand. The deputy sheriff repeats almost exactly the sentiment that I have quoted above from John Spencer Bassett:

> "Them damn niggers," he said. "I swear to godfrey, it's a wonder we have as little trouble with them as we do. Because why? Because they aint human. They look like a man and they walk on their hind legs like a man, and they can talk and you can understand them and you think they are understanding you, at least now and then. But when it comes to the normal human feelings and sentiments of human beings, they might as well be a damn herd of wild buffaloes. Now you take that one today—" (154)

Well, that's when we find that Rider has killed Birdsong and then gone home to his cabin to wait to be arrested, and he has surrendered himself to the lynch mob to protect his old aunt who has come to the jail to spend the night with him in the belief that she can protect him. The deputy draws all the wrong conclusions. He doesn't understand anything. He and his wife stand as the unfeeling fools, for he has no compassion for a black man who has been lynched and no understanding of why Rider has done what he has done.

And here, I think, is where Faulkner makes a moral statement. Where do we get morals if all our codes are arbitrary and our union with nature broken and the Edenic world of human equality gone with the rise of civilization? We get morals from our ability to feel sympathy for others, the strange ability we have to suffer vicariously when we see the suffering of others. I believe Faulkner tells us that this is a natural human trait that, like other natural traits, can be destroyed or minimized in us under the sting of defeat and oppression and horrifyingly bad luck. A person like Popeye seems able to do without all human compassion for others. Yet Popeye has his reasons. We can understand his plight just as we can see why Shakespeare's villains are villains. They have motives that make sense even if we may reject both the motives and the acts that follow them. In giving us Rider, Faulkner does not lecture to us about blacks and our duties. He simply shows us a human being and leaves us in profound sympathy for him, and that sympathy is spontaneous and without command that we have it. We do not obey some command when we feel that sympathy; we respond only to the most fundamental human impulses of our hearts.

That gap in understanding is a major theme, perhaps the major theme in the book. In the opening section we meet Isaac McCaslin, "Uncle Ike," in a story called "Was," the title reflecting the fact that it all happened before Ike McCaslin was born. Isaac is named for the biblical character Isaac, the son born to Abraham in Abraham's old age, when Abraham's wife Sarah was thought to be too old to bear children. Isaac was the son whom God told Abraham to sacrifice as a test of Abraham's faith. It is a powerful story, one of the most difficult stories in the Bible for moderns to deal with when they want to find authority in the Bible, and one that has been the subject of much scrutiny by biblical scholars. In it God appears to Abraham apparently in a dream and says to him:

> Take now thy son, thine only son Isaac, whom thou lovest, and get thee into the land of Moriah; and offer him there for a burnt offering upon one of the mountains, which I will tell thee of. (Genesis 22:2)

So, the Bible says, Abraham got up early in the morning and took Isaac with him and some servants and traveled three days and came to a mountain that seemed to be the divinely designated mountain of human sacrifice. The Book of Genesis continues the story:

> And Abraham took the wood of the burnt offering, and laid it upon Isaac his son; and he took the fire in his hand and a knife; and they went both of them together. And Isaac spake unto Abraham his father, and said, My father: and he said, Here am I, my son. and he said, Behold the fire and the wood: but where is the lamb for a burnt offering? And Abraham said, My son, God will provide himself a lamb for a burnt offering: so they went both of them together. And they came to the place which God had told him of; and Abraham built an altar there, and laid the wood in order, and bound Isaac his son, and laid him on the altar upon the wood. And Abraham stretched forth his hand, and took the knife to slay his son. (Genesis 22:6–10)

The story supposedly ends happily. The Angel of Yahweh calls to Abraham from heaven at the very last moment and stops the hand holding the upraised knife over the bound and most probably terrified boy. Abraham had passed the test of faith. This was the faith that made him the patriarch of Israel, ultimately the Patriarch of the Jewish people—and, so the legend goes, the Arabs as well through his son Ishmael. All that history came about because he had faith enough to obey any command that God gave him.

Yet anyone who thinks about this story a little must wonder what Isaac thought of his father ever afterwards. How would you feel if you were bound up, laid upon an altar, saw the hand of your father holding the knife raised above you, and knew that your father was about to kill you to obey God? I have a feeling in looking at the text that Isaac himself never amounted to much after that moment. Yes, he continued the line and became the father of Jacob and Esau, and out of Jacob came Israel. But Isaac himself seems to have had a curiously passive life. The best that the Bible can say of him is that he digged again the wells of his father once the Philistines had stopped them up.

So it is certainly with Ike McCaslin. He lost faith in his own Patriarch, his grandfather, in his ancestry, Lucius Quintus Carothers McCaslin. Ike is the son of Theophilus McCaslin, known as "Uncle Buck" in the book, and Ike was born in 1867, two years after the Civil War. We meet him when he is close to eighty years old, and the time of the opening is about when Faulkner started writing the novel. On the first page of the novel we learn that he is childless, that he has been a widower for twenty years, that he had given up all claim to the land that the McCaslins had taken in patent from the Indians, and that, the narrator tells us:

> in all his life had owned but one object more than he could wear and carry in his pockets and his hands at one time, and this was the narrow iron cot and the stained lean mattress which he used camping in the woods for deer or bear or for fishing or simply because he loved the woods; who owned no property and never desired to since the earth was not man's but all men's, as light and air and weather were. (3)

Like the biblical Isaac, Isaac McCaslin was an "only child" in that he was the only male heir to his grandfather. His aunt Mary married Isaac Edmonds, who is known as "Zack" through these stories, and they have a son, also named Carothers, who becomes "Old Cass," seventeen years older than Ike. Ike is the lawful heir, but he gives up his claim to the land to his cousin, and he retires to a life of hunting and contemplation and solitude. In him the McCaslin clan seems to come to an end.

But we discover that there are other descendants of the Patriarch. Just as Abraham the Patriarch had many concubines and many children by them, so Lucius Quintus Carothers McCaslin had concubines, one of them a black woman named Eunice who died, as it happens, on Christmas Day, 1832. His grandchild is the Tomey's Turl, whom we meet after an abrupt transition from the ruminations about Ike McCaslin in this first story. Cleanth Brooks has worked out this complicated genealogy, and you will find it on page 448 of his book *William Faulkner: The Yoknapatawpha Country.*

So what we have in this opening sketch about Ike is a sort of introduction to the whole. We get a much larger picture than in the accounts that Ike peruses in "The Bear," the accounts that show trading of human beings and their genealogy, and those accounts show also the rape of the land. Ike McCaslin has to see first that his grandfather took the land from the Indians and that he had no real right to it except force and deceit, corrupting the Chickasaw or Choctaw Indian Ikkemotubbe to sell land he did not truly own.

Ike has to see then that Carothers McCaslin engendered a line of black slaves and that these slaves are part of his own, Ike's own, extended family. Yet he is free, and they are slaves. The opening story is all very comic. Before Ike is born, Uncle Buck, Ike's father, and Uncle Buddy are regularly engaged in running down a slave known as Tomey's Turl, who a couple of times a year breaks loose to go visit the woman he loves, Tennie, who is a slave on Mr. Hubert Beauchamp's plantation, where—wouldn't you know it—Hubert Beauchamp lives with his sister Miss Sophonsiba. Uncle Buck and Uncle Buddy have to track Turl down and bring him back. The story has some of the qualities of *Uncle Tom's Cabin*, except that Faulkner keeps it all comic. In the end he decides the issue with a poker game. It's all terribly confusing. In the end Uncle Buck loses the poker hand, and he has to buy Tennie from Hubert Beauchamp so she can marry Turl. In the end he marries Sophonsiba, too, and they become the parents of Ike McCaslin.

It's not only comic, but it's benign. These slaves are not mistreated. In the pre–Civil War world where slave families existed at the whim of the master and where husbands, wives, and children were often split up and sold to different owners in the slave markets, we find three white men who are doing their best to be humane and fair-minded in so far as they can be. At first it almost seems that Faulkner is trying to whitewash slavery. But then as we move along through the book, we realize that Uncle Buck, Uncle Buddy, and Tomey's Turl are all cousins. They are all in the same family. And in the midst of a slave society, they have to work out some way of being fair to one of their own—even if he is black, or almost black. This is a family working within a community where family is everything. There is responsibility here amid all the humor, and it is a responsibility based on guilt.

After this brief introductory story, we move to a story called "The Fire and the Hearth." And we move up to about 1941, and we meet Lucas Beauchamp, the son of Tomey's Turl and, therefore, the great-grandson of

Lucius Quintus Carothers McCaslin. The story involves another comic plot, a repeat of one of the episodes in *The Hamlet*, where people go after money supposedly hidden in the ground, this time with the use of some sort of metal detector that drives Lucas Beauchamp so crazy with desire that his wife threatens to divorce him. But this is a very complicated tale, a collection of many tales, and it rambles from one of them to the other. And yet it has order.

Early in the story, we learn of Lucas's marriage to Molly Worsham and how Molly went to live in the house of Zack Edmonds when the white man's wife gave birth to a child and died. Molly had a child of her own, but she stayed in the Edmonds's house to take care both of Edmonds and the white and motherless child. Lucas went to take her back, and we have a family confrontation made more intense by the racial divide. Lucas supposes that Molly has become Edmonds's concubine, and when he goes up to the white man's house after a year to demand that she return, he says to Zack Edmonds, "I reckon you thought I wouldn't take her back, didn't you?" The narrator continues:

> The white man was sitting down. In age he and Lucas could have been brothers, almost twins too. He leaned slowly back in the chair, looking at Lucas. "Well, by God," he said quietly. "So that's what you think. What kind of a man do you think I am? What kind of man do you call yourself?"
>
> "I'm a nigger," Lucas said. "But I'm a man too. I'm more than just a man. The same thing made my pappy that made your grandmaw. I'm going to take her back."
>
> "By God," Edmonds said, "I never thought to ever pass my oath to a nigger. But I will swear—" (47)

A lot goes on in this passage. Zack Edmonds wants to deny that he has fornicated with Lucas's wife. He wants to swear that he has not done so. But the moment that he sets out to swear, he recognizes that he is treating a black man as an equal. Yet he is willing to do it. It is acknowledgment and confession all at once, and it is this mood—acknowledgment and confession—that permeates the novel.

I agree heartily with Cleanth Brooks that it is unfortunate that the best-known part of this book is the novella, "The Bear," which occupies the largest number of pages. There are some other beautiful things in the book, beautiful and terrible at the same time. Yet it is "The Bear" that has the controlling metaphor in the book itself and to some degree the controlling metaphor of all of Faulkner. Like the controlling metaphor of *The Sound and the Fury*, it occurs at the end of "The Bear," and it begins with young Ike McCaslin hearing a sound.

> He couldn't tell when he first began to hear the sound because when he became aware of it, it seemed to him that he had been already hearing it for several seconds—a sound as though someone were hammering a gun-barrel against a piece of railroad iron, a sound loud and heavy and not rapid yet with something frenzied about it, as the hammerer were not only a strong man and earnest one but a little hysterical too. Yet it couldn't be on the log-line because, although the track lay in that direction, it was at least two miles from him and this sound was not three hundred yards away. But even as he thought that, he realized where the sound must be coming from: whoever the man was and whatever he was doing, he was somewhere near the edge of the clearing where the Gum Tree was and where he was to meet Boon. So far, he had been hunting as he advanced, moving slowly and quietly and watching the ground and the trees both. Now he went on, his gun unloaded and the barrel slanted up and back to facilitate its passage through brier and undergrowth, approaching as it grew louder and louder that steady savage somehow queerly hysterical beating of metal on metal, emerging from the woods, into the old clearing, with the solitary gum tree directly before him. At first glance the tree seemed to be alive with frantic squirrels. There appeared to be forty or fifty of them leaping and darting from branch to branch until the whole tree had become one green maelstrom of mad leaves, while from time to time, singly or in twos and threes, squirrels would dart down the trunk then whirl without stopping and rush back up again as though sucked violently back by the vacuum of their fellows' frenzied vortex. Then he saw Boon, sitting, his back against the trunk, his head bent, hammering furiously at something on his lap. What he hammered with was the barrel of his dismembered gun, what he hammered at was the breech of it. The rest of the gun lay scattered about him in a half-dozen pieces while he bent over the piece on his lap his scarlet and streaming walnut face, hammering the disjointed barrel against the gun-breech with the frantic abandon of a madman. He didn't even look up to see who it was. Still hammering, he merely shouted back at the boy in a hoarse strangled voice:
> "Get out of here! Dont touch them! Dont touch a one of them! They're mine!" (330–31)

Here again Faulkner uses one of his lesser characters, the somewhat idiotic Boon Hogganbeck. Remember that for the metaphor of the ride around the square in *The Sound and the Fury* Faulkner has used the mad protest of the idiot Benjy. In this text, Boon has claimed all the squirrels in the gum tree. He cannot shoot them. He's a lousy shot anyway. And he has broken his gun. The pieces of it lie about him, and he is hammering at the mechanism, the breech that allows the gun to be broken down so it can be loaded. Something about it—we are not told what—is not working, and Boon tries to repair it by beating on it. In his passionate fury he tries to claim all the squirrels. "Dont touch them! Dont touch a one of them! They're mine!"

Here is puny, idiotic man striving to claim the wilderness as symbolized by the moil of frenzied squirrels, and why? So he can kill them. That is the ultimate metaphor of this book, that men seek to claim the wilderness so they can destroy it. And throughout the novel, the most important subplot is that the wilderness is steadily receding, steadily being destroyed, the habitat of the wild things helpless under the implacable onslaught of humankind. In their effort they are idiotic. But they still succeed in destroying that which by natural law and right belongs to all people in common.

The story called "The Bear" embedded in this book embodies one of the most profound and enduring of the American myths—the lonely man confronting the vast and uncanny power of the wilderness in all its grandeur, mystery, and terror. When we walk with Ike McCaslin without compass or gun in the November forest where no direction is certain and a primitive spirit seems to brood mournfully over a vast land, we are in the world of James Fenimore Cooper and also of Daniel Boone. We are in the seaborne world of Ishmael and Captain Ahab and the great white whale. We are in the world of Lewis and Clark, the land of all the fairy tales ever told about dark forces lurking in the density of forest where nothing is certain, where reality is always glimpsed on the move and never quite still and face to face except as prophets may without warning come face to face with God at the risk of their lives.

What Ike McCaslin discovers in the forest is the primitive state of nature, the golden age of the wilderness where all things are held in common and where life is uncomplicated by anything more than the struggle for existence, survival. The search for Old Ben, the tracking of this huge beast with the trap-mangled foot, concentrates the mind on itself and shuts out for a time all the moral complications and perplexities of a "civilized" world. The hunt reduces life to a primitive simplicity, and Ike, at the moment when he lays aside compass and gun and goes it alone, represents a withdrawal into as complete a renunciation of civilization as he can manage.

As in *Absalom, Absalom!* and Sutpen's childhood in western Virginia, the forest of the Mississippi Delta and of the Tallahatchie bottom north of

Jefferson gives Faulkner a chance to create an Edenic world—or at least a world one step away from Eden. Since Faulkner's forest is a place for the hunt, it is also a place of death, and therefore it lacks the deathless serenity of Eden before the fall. Yet death comes to the human race in Eden, in consequence of violating the divine command that place Adam and Eve there in the first place, and Faulkner's world shares other qualities of Eden and one of the most important is a vision of equality—a vision not contradicted by the advent of death since death is equal to all of us.

It is striking to me that so many of the characters in the woods with Ike are people of mixed ancestry, Indian and African—Sam Fathers, Boon Hogganbeck, Tennie's Jim, and even the dog Lion—are mixtures of breeds, and when the others come, they too enter the worlds with an equality of purpose that is all absorbing. It is after the hunt that Ike McCaslin meditates on the prodigious and unjust inequality that brings with it the exploitation and the troubling issue of race that neither Faulkner nor his characters can resolve. Ike McCaslin tries to solve the problem for himself by withdrawal, renouncing his inheritance and living apart and alone. But he is like a vegetarian in a world of carnivores, unable completely to separate himself from the corruption he seeks to flee. One might say that even vegetarians wear leather shoes. Ike's encounter with the bear ends in his making an individual gesture that seems futile in stopping the march of this monstrous entity called "progress" through the wilderness and the clearing of the enduring land and the reduction of it all to the blandness and hollowness of this civilization.

So the bear is a wilderness story. But to me it is something else. It is the perfect metaphor of the writer seeking his prey, the words that will mark on paper and print the vague and turbulent vision that resides in the mysterious forest of his own brain. Ike does not shoot the bear; when Boon does kill Old Ben, something is not gained, but something is lost. Faulkner was asked in a class at the University of Virginia if he ever wished he had written his novels differently. He said, "I wish I had done them better [. . .]" (March 13, 1957, Session Eight in *The Sound and the Fury* 245). The writer struggles to embrace all the hopes and ambitions that swirl in that confused pool in the mind that lies behind the creative impulse. Yet the production of every book is a failure, for the product can never attain the reality. The unattained love is perhaps always the sweetest. In the long dialogue that Ike has with his cousin McCaslin, they ruminate over a line from the poem by Keats, "Ode on a Grecian Urn." Here is the whole verse:

Heard melodies are sweet, but those unheard
   Are sweeter; therefore, ye soft pipes, play on;
Not to the sensual ear, but, more endeared,
   Pipe to the spirit ditties of no tone:
Fair youth, beneath the trees, thou canst not leave
   Thy song, nor ever can those trees be bare;
    Bold Lover, never, never canst thou kiss,
Though winning near the goal—yet, do not grieve;
   She cannot fade, though thou hast not thy bliss,
    For ever wilt thou love, and she be fair!

The accomplished novel is never the bliss that the novel yet to come may be. The eternal hope is eternally unrealized. Yet it endures and drives the writer to the hunt for that great prey that looms always in the wilderness uncaptured and as elusive as dreams and ghosts.

Go Down, Moses is, in my view, the last of Faulkner's great novels. The rest do not match up. In 1942 he could look back on sixteen years of the most productive greatness in American literary history. In the forest during the long hunt for the bear Old Ben, Faulkner summons a great array of his characters from other stories and novels—General Compson, Colonel Sartoris, Major DeSpain, Sam Fathers, and the whole history of the South. It seems to me that Faulkner is saying to these characters: "Look at what I have created. It is not what I dreamed. But still I did well."

Bibliography

Primary Sources

Editions of the novels used in English 174F: William Faulkner from *Soldiers' Pay* to *Go Down, Moses*

Absalom, Absalom! The Corrected Text. New York: Vintage, 1990.

As I Lay Dying. The Corrected Text. New York: Vintage, 1990.

Flags in the Dust. New York: Vintage, 1974.

Go Down, Moses. New York: Modern Library, 1942. (In Marius's library is another marked copy of *Go Down, Moses* [New York: Library of America, 1994].)

The Hamlet: The Corrected Text. New York: Vintage, 1991.

Light in August. New York: Modern Library, 1959.

Mosquitoes. New York: Liveright, 1955.

Pylon. New York: Signet, 1968.

"A Rose for Emily." *Collected Short Stories of William Faulkner.* New York: Vintage, 1977. 119–30.

Sanctuary. The Corrected Text. New York: Vintage, 1993.

Selected Letters of William Faulkner. Ed. Joseph Blotner. New York: Random House, 1976.

Soldiers' Pay. New York: Liveright, 1954.

The Sound and the Fury. Norton Critical Edition. 1st ed. New York: Norton, 1994. (The second edition of the novel is also in Marius's library.)

"There Was a Queen." *Collected Short Stories of William Faulkner.* New York: Vintage, 1977. 727–44.

The Unvanquished: The Corrected Text. New York: Vintage, 1991.

The Wild Palms: William Faulkner Novels 1936–1940. New York: Library of America, 1990. 495–726.

Secondary Sources

Works cited in these lectures and related works on the shelves of Richard Marius's library

Ayers, Edward L. *The Promise of the New South: Life after Reconstruction.* Oxford: Oxford UP, 1992.

Barry, John. M. *The Great Mississippi Flood of 1927 and How It Changed America.* New York: Simon & Schuster, 1997.

Blotner, Joseph. *Faulkner: A Biography.* New York: Vintage, 1984.

Brooks, Cleanth. *William Faulkner: The Yoknapatawpha Country.* Baton Rouge: Louisiana State UP, 1990.

Budd, Louis J., and Edwin H. Cady. *On Faulkner: The Best from "American Literature."* Durham: Duke UP, 1989.

Butterworth, Nancy, and Keen Butterworth. *Annotations to William Faulkner's "A Fable."* Garland Faulkner Annotation Series. New York: Garland, 1989.

Cash, W. J. *The Mind of the South.* New York: Vintage, 1991.

Clarke, Deborah. *Robbing the Mother: Women in Faulkner.* Jackson: UP of Mississippi, 1994.

Empson, William. *Some Versions of the Pastoral.* London: Chatto & Windus, 1935.

Fadiman, Clifton. Review. *Absalom, Absalom!* by William Faulkner. *The New Yorker* 31 October 1936: 62–64.

Frazer, James George. *The Golden Bough: A Study in Magic and Religion.* New York: Touchstone, 1996.

Freely, John. *Blue Guide to Boston and Cambridge.* London: Ernest Bean, 1984.

Gray, Richard. *The Life of William Faulkner.* Cambridge, MA: Blackwell, 1994, 1996.

Gwynn, Frederick L., and Joseph L. Blotner. *Faulkner in the University: Class Conferences at the University of Virginia 1957–1958.* New York: Vintage/Knopf, 1965.

Hemingway, Ernest. *Death in the Afternoon.* New York: Penguin. 1976.

Holmes, Catherine D. *Annotations to William Faulkner's "The Hamlet."* Garland Faulkner Annotation Series. New York: Garland, 1996.

Honnighausen, Lothar. *Faulkner: Masks and Metaphors.* Jackson: UP of Mississippi, 1997.

Horton, Merrill. *Annotations to William Faulkner's "The Town."* Garland Faulkner Annotation Series. New York: Garland, 1996.

Howe, Irving. "The Wild Palms." *William Faulkner: Modern Critical Views.* Ed. Harold Bloom. New York: Chelsea House, 1986. 93–99.

Irwin, John T. *Doubling and Incest/Repetition and Revenge: A Speculative Reading of Faulkner.* Baltimore: Johns Hopkins UP, 1975.

Karl, Frederick R. *William Faulkner: American Writer: A Biography.* New York: Ballantine, 1990.

Kinney, Arthur F. *Critical Essays on William Faulkner: The McCaslin Family.* Boston: G. K. Hall, 1990.

Luce, Dianne C. *Annotations to William Faulkner's "As I Lay Dying."* Garland Faulkner Annotation Series. New York: Garland, 1990.

Lynn, Kenneth S. *Hemingway.* New York: Simon & Schuster, 1987.

McDaniel, Linda Elkins. *Annotations to William Faulkner's "Flags in the Dust."* Garland Faulkner Annotation Series. New York: Garland, 1991.

Meriwether, James B., and Michael Millgate. *Lion in the Garden: Interviews with William Faulkner 1926–1962.* Lincoln: U of Nebraska P, 1968.

Millgate, Michael. *The Achievement of William Faulkner.* Athens: U of Georgia P, 1989.

Minter, David. *William Faulkner: His Life and Work.* Baltimore: Johns Hopkins UP, 1980.

Mitchell, Margaret. *Gone With the Wind.* New York: Macmillan, 1936.

Morris, Wesley, with Barbara Alverson Morris. *Reading Faulkner.* Madison: U of Wisconsin P, 1989.

Otto, Rudolf. *The Idea of the Holy: An Inquiry into the Nonrational Factor in the Idea of the Divine and Its Relations to the Rational.* Trans. John W. Harvey. Rev. ed. New York: Oxford UP, 1936.

Sewall, Richard B. *The Vision of Tragedy.* New Haven: Yale UP, 1959.

Taylor, Nancy Dew. *Annotations to William Faulkner's "Go Down, Moses."* Garland Faulkner Annotation Series. New York: Garland, 1994.

Treitschke, Henri von. *Politics.* Trans. Arthur James Balfour. 2 vols. New York: Macmillan, 1916.

Vickery, Olga W. *The Novels of William Faulkner: A Critical Interpretation.* Rev. ed. Baton Rouge: Louisiana State UP, 1964.

Wasson, Ben. *Count No 'Count: Flashbacks to Faulkner.* Jackson: UP of Mississippi, 1983.

Weinstein, Phillip M., ed. *The Cambridge Companion to William Faulkner.* Cambridge: Cambridge UP, 1995.

Williamson, Joel. *William Faulkner and Southern History.* NY: Oxford UP, 1993.

Index

Reading Faulkner was designed and typeset on a Macintosh
OS X using QuarkXPress 6.5 software. The body text is set in
10/13 ITC Cushing and display type is set in Fenice. This
book was designed and typeset by Barbara Karwhite.